PLANNING FOR CHANGE

PLANNING FOR CHANGE

Industrial Policy and Japanese Economic Development, 1945–1990

JAMES E. VESTAL

CLARENDON PRESS · OXFORD

Oxford University Press, Walton Street, Oxford OX2 6DP

Oxford New York Toronto
Delhi Bombay Calcutta Madras Karachi
Kuala Lumpur Singapore Hong Kong Tokyo
Nairobi Dar es Salaam Cape Town
Melbourne Auckland Madrid
and associated companies in
Berlin Ibadan

Oxford is a trade mark of Oxford University Press

Published in the United States
by Oxford University Press Inc., New York

British Library Cataloguing in Publication Data
Data available

Library of Congress Cataloging in Publication Data
Vestal, James E.
Planning for change: industrial policy and Japanese economic
development, 1945–1990 / James E. Vestal.
p. cm.
Includes bibliographical references and index.
1. Industry and state—Japan—History—20th century.
2. Japan—Industries—History—20th century.
3. Japan—Economic policy—1945–ₚ I. Title
HD3616.J33V47 1993 338.952—dc20 93–13950
ISBN 0–19–828808–5

3 5 7 9 10 8 6 4 2

Printed in Great Britain
on acid-free paper by
Biddles Ltd.
Guildford & King's Lynn

ACKNOWLEDGEMENTS

This book owes a great deal to many people, in particular my colleagues at Keio University. Professors Kenichirō Obi, Iwao Ozaki, and Tsujimura Kōtarō have been unstinting in their support, and whatever originality this study may possess can be traced directly to discussions I have had with them. Patricia Kuwayama of both Morgan Guaranty in Tokyo and the Sangyō Kenkyūsho at Keio has provided not only encouragements but valuable comments on numerous drafts. Eleanor M. Hadley has also gone through the manuscript in detail, offering me the benefits of her lengthy experience with Japan. Useful suggestions and comments have also been given by Horii Akinari and Taguchi Hirō of the Bank of Japan as well as friends in business including Chris Calderwood, Jesus Duarte, Isabelle Hupperts, Ralph Grosby, Naoko Kuzu-Felder, and Cheryl Silverman. Had I been able to incorporate all of the suggestions I received, this book would undoubtedly be much better for it.

Regarding the romanization of Japanese, macrons denote long vowels. However, I have followed standard practice in not including macrons for place-names. While the extensive use of Japanese in the text may be tedious for some, it is necessary given the lack of standard translations not only for specific laws but also for organizations and institutions.

The usual caveats apply. Any remaining mistakes are my responsibility and the views held in this book are solely my own.

For
John and Patricia Vestal

CONTENTS

LIST OF FIGURES

LIST OF TABLES

1

Introduction

Few economic issues have sparked as lengthy a controversy amongst academics and government officials as the role of industrial policy in Japanese economic development. Japan's economic success is without peer: after losing one-third of its industrial base in World War II, Japan has seen its per capita GNP rise from 276 US dollars in 1950 to 23,463 dollars in 1989, making it the richest of the G-7 nations. Real growth has averaged 7 per cent in the last four decades, an unparalleled economic performance. In the latter half of the 1980s, Japan became the world's largest creditor nation, supplanting the US as global lender and economic leader. Determining the factors behind these phenomenal achievements is clearly crucial to improving the economic performance of other nations. Many assert that Japan's widespread use of industrial policy, measures designed specifically to influence resource allocation for selected industries,[1] holds the key. To others, however, the effects of industrial policy are negligible compared to the long list of other factors that have contributed to Japan's success. This study, by providing a detailed assessment of industrial policy, attempts to resolve this issue.

The debate about Japanese industrial policy arises not only because such policy was widely employed but also because it was consciously used for the express purpose of stimulating economic growth. Nevertheless, the unprecedented post-war expansion of the Japanese economy does not in itself constitute proof of the efficacy of such policy. First, it is extremely difficult to separate the impact of industrial policy from that of general macroeconomic policy. Secondly, the existence of a favourable external environment (the rapid growth of world trade, the availability of foreign technology, and payments by the US for Japanese defence) may also have played a greater part in Japanese economic development than did industrial policy. Finally, and most importantly, analysis of industrial policy is hampered by severe data limitations. Without knowledge as to how Japan would have developed in the absence of industrial policy, it is difficult to assess the contribution such policy made to growth. Claims that

---

[1] While general macroeconomic policy also affects resource allocation, industrial policy differs from macro policy by its narrower focus, its targeting of specified industries. Industrial policy has as its goal influence over the investment decisions of selected industries and explicitly attempts to affect the productivity of factor inputs. Macroeconomic policy will have an impact on investment decisions, but of industries in general rather than of select industries.

growth would have been as fast or faster without industrial policy cannot be directly refuted, nor can the impact of industrial policy on growth be directly quantified.

The debate about industrial policy has been intensified not only by these methodological problems but also by the ideological implications of the issue. Industrial policy involves a high degree of government intervention in the economy, and such intervention is anathema to many economists and politicians, particularly in the US. The emotional content of the debate has in many instances led to a lack of focus, particularly in regard to the issue of time. Industrial policy advocates and critics rarely differentiate between industrial policy in Japan's early stages of development and industrial policy after Japan had achieved advanced nation status. This is clearly incorrect, since changes in the functioning of markets and institutions that occur as development progresses will have an impact on how industrial policy can work. Equally important, this lack of differentiation fails to acknowledge the differing degrees of intervention that have characterized Japanese industrial policy over time.

Despite these methodological and ideological difficulties, few topics have more relevance than ascertaining the efficacy of industrial policy in promoting growth. This topic is arguably more important for developing countries. With over two-thirds of the world's population living in nations with per capita GNP of less than 1,800 US dollars and one-third subsisting on less than 300 dollars, the majority of people will greatly benefit from any means to accelerate the process of economic development. Should industrial policy prove to be a key factor behind Japan's economic success, then industrial policy could serve as a prescription for many of the world's economic woes. Developed countries too could benefit should Japan's recent experience with policy have contributed to economic out-performance.

At the same time, the dangers associated with industrial policy are equally profound. Even if industrial policy has contributed to success, the question remains as to how fair such policy measures are in an international context. Countries which deliberately attempt to affect the allocation of resources to select industries must also consider whether they may face retaliation for doing so. The dangers are obviously greater if industrial policy is ineffective, since its use would slow development and undermine growth. If this ineffectiveness is not perceived, then industrial policy holds a threat even to countries not explicitly practising industrial policy. In such countries, advocates of industrial policy may blame poor economic performance on the absence of policy. To the extent that such performance arises because of mistakes in macroeconomic management, these mistakes might not be addressed.

The importance of the topic, and related difficulties, have stimulated research on industrial policy across an unusually wide range of approaches. A large portion of the literature on industrial policy utilizes an institutional approach and offers valuable insight into the type of government organization necessary for effective formulation of industrial policy. Conditions commonly agreed upon as necessary for policy success include, first, a highly professional bureaucracy capable of formulating industrial policy. This condition clearly needs to be supplemented with power, the access to tools with which to implement policy. Third is the need for outside consensus on basic goals, lest conflicting interest groups derail policy formulation.[2]

These necessary conditions were all filled in post-war Japan, at least until the early 1970s. The professional capabilities of Japanese bureaucrats have been documented in detail,[3] as have the measures at their disposal. Perhaps less attention has been devoted to the process of consensus building, which is often presumed to have been facilitated by the homogeneous nature of Japanese society. In fact, the ability to forge consensus in Japan was greatly enhanced by the relatively equal distribution of income and wealth which Japan inherited from the US Occupation.[4] Without this equality, the willingness of any group to make sacrifices in the interests of the whole would have been limited if not non-existent.

The institutional approach also highlights one of the key functions of any sort of effective industrial policy, the gathering and dissemination of accurate information. No matter how capable and powerful the bureaucracy, policy measures based on incorrect information will not only fail to succeed in their intent but are likely to have a negative effect on growth. This is the greatest danger of any industrial policy. Even should a policy goal be correct, at least in some sense, the means to attain that goal will fail if information is inaccurate.

A second approach to evaluating industrial policy focuses on case studies of specific industries. This research often reveals valuable insight into the dynamics of industrial policy, providing specific knowledge of how policy has been formulated and implemented. However, while illuminating, it is extremely dangerous to form general conclusions about policy effectiveness based solely on the experience of a single industry. For example, if the average rate of return of a targeted industry over time is lower than the average return for all industries, it is tempting to conclude that industrial policy, at least for this industry, has not been successful. Such a conclusion could well be incorrect, since other industries could

---

[2] John Zysman, *Governments, Markets, and Growth* (Ithaca, NY, Cornell University Press, 1983).

[3] See, for example, George Eads and Kozo Yamamura, 'The Future of Industrial Policy', in Kozo Yamamura and Yasuba Yasukichi (eds.), *The Political Economy of Japan*, 1 (Stanford, Calif., Stanford University Press, 1987), 423–68.

[4] See pp. 15, 154–5.

have benefited from measures for the targeted industry. Important linkages could have been forged, both upstream and downstream, with the targeted industry spurring overall growth of the economy. By failing to consider all of the linkages that flow from one industry to another, the case study approach can lead to incorrect conclusions.

While the institutional and case study approaches have added much to our understanding of industrial policy, they do not help with the crucial question of the efficacy of such policy. Whether or not industrial policy stimulates growth requires detailed knowledge not only of each industry but also of how industries interact. In short, explicit knowledge as to the functioning of the entire economy is a prerequisite to evaluating industrial policy, and it is on this basis that traditional economic analysis can contribute. Economists have offered not only theoretical justification for industrial policy in a variety of circumstances, but have provided some empirical evidence of the effectiveness of such policy. The neoclassical economic paradigm, while making an irrefutable case for the efficiency of unimpeded competition in general, also makes a strong case for the necessity of government intervention so long as it is limited to the existence of market failures or externalities. Market failures typically include imperfect or underdeveloped capital markets; market externalities include instances where an industry learns over time or where knowledge obtained by one industry flows freely to others.

Standard neoclassical economic analysis thus provides a sound basis from which to judge the efficacy of industrial policy. The more industrial policy can be identified with market imperfections and failures, the greater is the ex post argument for policy success. In the case of Japan, many industrial policies fit nicely in such a framework. For instance, as is true for most developing nations, capital markets in Japan until at least the early 1970s were highly regulated and underdeveloped in several important aspects. Corporate access to equity financing was restricted, foreign capital inflows were constrained, markets for corporate bonds and paper effectively did not exist, and regulated interest rates shut many potential borrowers out of the lending market. Imperfections in capital markets provide some rationale for industrial policy.

A second important justification is provided by unequal bargaining positions in markets for technology exchange. One of the major characteristics of industrial policy in Japan was its control over the acquisition of foreign technology. The Japanese government negotiated on behalf of Japanese companies, limiting the prices paid for technologies and also the restrictions regarding use of acquired technologies. Given the monopolistic or oligopolistic bargaining positions of foreign firms selling technology, this role of the Japanese government helped to equalize the playing field for technology exchange. Furthermore, market imperfections concerning information in general can help to justify the government's participation in deciding what technology to purchase.

A third important rationale for industrial policy centres on the existence of linkages between industries. Should the profitability of investment in one industry depend on investment in other industries, government coordination of investment activities may be necessary. For example, if the profitability of investment in steel depends upon the potential output of electric power, government intervention may be necessary to ensure that optimal investment and output is achieved. Hence, to the extent that Japanese industrial policy targeted intermediate goods industries, the existence of dynamic investment complementarities could imply some efficacy of industrial policy.[5]

Of the three approaches used in evaluating industrial policy to date, the institutional approach, the case study approach, and the traditional economic approach, the analysis in this book will rely most heavily on the last. However, the traditional neoclassical paradigm usually fails to emphasize adequately the dynamics of economic development. When development is viewed as only a two-stage process, policy prescriptions generally concentrate on problems arising once a competitive market structure is broadly in place. This approach offers little insight into how a developed economic state can realistically be achieved because it rarely explicitly recognizes that development is not an instantaneous process.

In one sense, it is not surprising that many economists have not addressed the importance of dynamics in economic development. Knowing that perfectly competitive markets convey information best and result in the most efficient allocation of resources, economists often tend to assume that the most effective way to achieve growth is to perfect markets as quickly as possible for factors of production (labour and capital) as well as markets for goods and services. By such reasoning, there is no justification for intermediate stages of development between the initial position of a developing economy and the final goal of mature competitive market development. It is this type of reasoning that has led many economists to recommend the immediate introduction of market economies in Eastern Europe and the former Soviet Union.

However, such reasoning is fallacious since it fails to consider the costs associated with introducing a competitive market structure in a developing economy. Simply put, the cost of introducing such a structure can prove unbearable. The bankruptcy of traditional industries in a developing economy which suddenly faces global competition could raise unemployment to intolerable levels—levels so high that political and social

---

[5] Trade restrictions will widen this problem of investment complementarity. For further details, see Ch. 3.

instability results as a significant portion of the population faces the threat of starvation. In short, the cost of moving to a competitive market structure should often be spread over time, since the failure to do so can threaten the survival of some workers. Recognition of the dynamics of the development process and the costs associated with resource dislocation suggests another important role for industrial policy, that of minimizing dislocation costs while at the same time promoting growth.

Many neoclassical economists have dismissed the importance of industrial policy in the development process not only out of ignorance about the dislocation costs associated with development but also because effective industrial policy requires an enormous amount of information. Most economists seem to assume a sort of uncertainty principle for any form of economic planning: the collection of information necessary to implement effective industrial policy can consume the entire amount of resources a nation has at its disposal. From this perspective, planners can either choose to allocate resources using insufficient information or can spend all of the economy's resources in gathering sufficient data.

This argument, simplified at the expense of some economists and their contributions to the development literature, fails if one supposes that history has operative lessons for other nations—that the pattern of economic development has common characteristics, and that growth follows a certain set routine. In fact, nations do seem to follow a common path in the process of development, moving from light industries to heavy industries, then on to capital-intensive assembly industries before finally moving to knowledge-intensive industries. This common development pattern provides a blueprint for industrial policy for developing nations. In many cases, resources do not need to be spent to gather information since the next logical step in the development process is known. This information does not, of course, guarantee the success of industrial policy nor does it indicate that industrial policy is necessary.

In an attempt to analyse more realistically the role and efficacy of industrial policy, this study utilizes traditional economic methodology while explicitly recognizing the dynamic process of development. Arguably, a best solution for the development process exists, whereby the cost of resource dislocation (unemployment) is held at 'tolerable levels' but at the same time the speed at which the developing economy moves towards a competitive market structure is not 'intolerably slow'. It will often be probable that such a solution can only be defined politically, since unique determination is not a characteristic of any realistic intertemporal growth model. However, this study does not attempt to present a rigorous model of development; rather it does no more than offer an informed judgement of policy impact. This evaluation will highlight the trade-off between the efficiency of a competitive market structure and the cost of introducing competition, a trade-off apparent from types of policy actually adopted in Japan. Only one type was designed to stimulate growth; the other type of Japanese industrial policy was designed to block competition, rationalization, and growth in select industries. The widespread existence of such anti-growth policy indicates at least an implicit attempt to balance the growth process and control the cost of resource dislocation. This balancing is probably the single most important characteristic of post-war industrial policy in Japan.

The types of industrial policy utilized in Japan indicate that it is clearly inappropriate to assign a static neoclassical economic philosophy to Japanese policy-makers. Rather, they viewed market competition as a special case, one that occurs in the latter stage of economic development. In the development process, however, policy-makers emphasized the trade-off between growth and unemployment, and viewed policies which temporarily blocked competition as instrumental in making development succeed. At the same time, they believed that market competition should be introduced as quickly as was politically and economically possible. Their ability to expose successively sectors of the economy to competition and the inability of Japanese industries to resist the introduction of competition probably kept down the costs of protectionism, thus spurring development. Without the discipline of market competition, excessive minimization of resource dislocation would have caused economic stagnation.

In addition to keeping the process of economic development on track through maintaining acceptable levels of employment, what other success Japanese industrial policy has enjoyed may derive largely from the flexibility of policy-makers. Policies that did not accomplish their stated goal were abandoned; policies that appeared to work were pursued and also applied to other industries. The ability to learn from past mistakes, and the ability to change the type and degree of government intervention have played a key role in Japanese industrial policy. At the same time, this apparent flexibility owes a great deal to pluralism in the process of policy formulation. Not only did representation by diverse academic and business interests serve to limit the period that mistaken policies were pursued, but competition amongst bureaucratic groups also acted as a stimulus to disengage policy measures that were no longer needed or were not serving a useful purpose.

In retrospect, it appears that many of the policies to promote growth in select industries can be characterized by their market-correcting (and market-conforming) features. However, policy-makers themselves did not explicitly view the pro-growth side of industrial policy from this perspective. True, they did identify key industries which they thought would stimulate economic growth and then directed resources towards them.

8   *Introduction*

This behaviour can often be interpreted as an attempt to correct market failures and externalities, but such externalities and failures were not rigorously identified.

Policy-makers in Japan clearly did not place their faith solely in market competition. The neoclassical paradigm was not ideologically unassailable, and *laissez-faire* was not an unquestionable god-like state. Japanese policy-makers felt an explicit need to smooth the process of change accompanying economic growth. Growth was to be maximized and to this end competition was the single most important tool, but growth maximization was to occur under the constraint of maintaining social stability. This meant that disruption in factor markets was to be kept at some unspecified minimum acceptable level. In practice, this entailed blocking competition in select industries to ensure full employment. While such policies seem to represent an exact opposite to those designed to spur growth, this is really only true in a static framework. It is quite probable that they were a necessary counterpart to pro-growth policy measures, since the ability to direct resources to potential growth industries would have been undermined by social instability had the government not curtailed competitive forces in some high-employment industries.

Many of the supposedly unique characteristics of the Japanese economy also reinforce the appropriateness of a dynamic framework, whereby competition was an end state to be achieved but the costs of resource dislocation were to be helped down in the process of introducing fully competitive markets. Concepts such as excessive competition (*katō kyōsō*), dual structure (*nijū kōzō*), and the general emphasis on the industrial structure (*sangyō kōzō*) are inexplicable in a simple neoclassical paradigm but are consistent with a more dynamic development framework. The idea of excessive competition is foreign to a pure neoclassicist,[6] since competition leads to the lowest prices and the most efficient allocation of resources. However, control over the process of development can lead to excessive competition when competitive barriers are lowered: too many firms can attempt to enter a new industry if rewards are granted on the basis of market share.[7] This was often the case in Japan, and the empha-

[6] There is some limited discussion of damaging competition in the literature on industrial organization. Joseph Bain defined cut-throat competition as that which causes price to fall below average cost, chronically causing returns earned to fall short of the normal rate of return. Although this definition was applied to unconcentrated industries, it also assumed that labour and capital shifted only very slowly from industry to industry, thus violating one of the assumptions of pure competition. (Joseph Bain, *Industrial Organization* (New York, John Wiley & Sons, 1963).)

[7] Kozo Yamamura, 'Success that Soured: Administrative Guidance and Cartels in Japan', in *Policy and Trade Issues in the Japanese Economy* (Seattle, University of Seattle Press, 1982), 77–112.

sis on excessive competition signalled concern about the costs of resource dislocation generated by subsequent bankruptcies.[8]

The existence of the dual structure (*nijū kōzō*) in the Japanese economy, whereby smaller high-cost firms coexist with larger more efficient producers, is more consistent with a dynamic development framework than with a static neoclassical model.[9] Small enterprises in Japan, defined as those with less than thirty workers, have consistently employed approximately one-third of the non-agricultural work-force. The government initially supported small companies to minimize the cost of unemployment; this support also helps to account for the continued importance of small companies in the economy today.

Equally inexplicable to a neoclassicist is Japan's constant emphasis on the industrial structure (*sangyō kōzō*). In a neoclassical framework, the industrial structure is a consequence of competition, and the price structure of an economy contains all information relevant to it. The relative supply of output is not meaningful. However, when viewed from a dynamic perspective, the structure of output at various moments in time can be of importance, not only to evaluate linkages between industries but also because competitive markets have not necessarily been introduced across the board for all industries.

A dynamic perspective is also of use in explaining if not the success then at least the generally positive approach of Japanese policy-makers towards declining industries. Competition is viewed as a tool, probably the most important one, of industrial policy. It is a state to be achieved, but at the same time there is an implicit belief that the costs of competition are to be controlled. Hence, Japanese policy-makers find nothing unusual in using industrial policy for a declining industry. If an industry is in a structural downturn, they feel that they can and should minimize the costs of adjustment through appropriate measures such as trade protection or tax relief. Even so, whatever measures are implemented, the ultimate goal must be the same: to again expose the industry to the

[8] Similar cost concerns characterized the emphasis on excess competition which arose in the face of economies of scale, whereby the larger the firm, the lower are its costs of production and the greater is its ability to force competitors out of business. The drive to realize these scale economies will cause firms in an industry to over-invest and the subsequent over-capacity will force some companies out of business. Government measures to promote the development of an industry will also generate undesirable competition, since by stimulating investment, such measures will lead at least temporarily to excess capacity and the subsequent price volatility could potentially undermine the long-term growth of the industry. For more on this topic, see Chs. 2 and 5.

[9] Of course, a dual structure characterizes many developing economies, and the extensive debate about this supposedly unique feature of the Japanese economy sometimes falls wide of the mark by not recognizing this fact. However, the continuation of a dual structure, defined by the relative abundance of smaller firms to large firms, is somewhat unusual and probably is related to government support of smaller companies, support which may be difficult to justify outside a dynamic development framework.

discipline of competition. This contrasts sharply with policy towards
declining industries in the US. There is little justification in neoclassical
economics for exempting an industry from the forces of competition, and
if exemption is granted for political reasons, there is then no further justification for reintroducing competition at a later date. To a neoclassicist,
the mistake is in exempting the industry to begin with, and he can offer
no compelling rationale to restructure the industry before re-exposing it
to competition. Hence in the US, protection once introduced tends to
stay in force, whereas in Japan it is always viewed as only a temporary
expediency. Of course, this does not mean that Japanese industrial policy
towards declining industries has been a success, but on the whole it has
been better than policy in the US.

While certain types of industrial policy can be characterized as market
conforming or market correcting, other types of policy ran counter to
market forces. The sum total of industrial policy was an explicit attempt
to foster rapid growth in select industries and slow growth in others, a
skewed pattern inconsistent with perfectly competitive markets. That the
goal of industrial policy was not aimed at immediately creating perfectly
competitive markets is also revealed by the active promotion of disequilibria in the Japanese economy. Policy towards exchange rates and interest rates showed a conscious intent to prevent markets from clearing.
Support of disequilibria not only served to make industrial policy necessary, but it also indicates a fundamental distrust of the cost of market
forces in certain situations.

The analysis of Japanese industrial policy which follows does not
attempt to investigate whether such policy was optimal. Even were conditions for optimality obtained from a dynamic model of development,
without exact knowledge of the future, policy measures implemented
could not hope to fulfil these rigorous criteria. Nevertheless, it is still possible to offer an informed judgement as to whether Japan was better off
implementing industrial policy as it did. To the extent that some rigour is
feasible, this analysis does examine the relationship between production
externalities and industrial policy. The impact of policy on resource allocation at both the individual industry level and the overall macro level is
also investigated. Results strongly suggest that in the early post-war
period industrial policy led to a higher rate of growth than would otherwise have been achievable. Moreover, the single most important contribution of industrial policy to economic growth probably lies in the trade-off
between competition and the cost of resource dislocation. That Japanese
policy was at all successful must lie in the insistence by policy-makers
that competition eventually be introduced. The promotion of 'growth'
industries, while likely contributing to Japan's successful development,
possibly contains a less valuable lesson for developing nations.

Given its contribution to successful development in the early post-war period, Japan's experience with industrial policy probably does provide valuable insights for developing countries today. Managing the trade-off between competition and the cost of resource dislocation is particularly important if such costs generate social instability to such an extent that the viability of government and the development process is threatened. Put differently, the trade-off is crucial for countries with extremely low stocks of useful capital and for countries which are already facing upheaval. The difficulties facing Japan in the first decade following World War II are approximated by those facing countries in the former Communist bloc today. As such, Japan's experience with industrial policy can help to create a blueprint for development for many of the republics of the former Soviet Union and Eastern European nations. While the need to successfully manage dislocation costs may be greatest for these nations, other developing countries might also gain insights, particularly in regard to how Japanese policy managed to avoid the trap of stagnation by introducing competition as development progressed.

Japan's more recent experiences with industrial policy suggest that developed nations have little to learn from the Japanese case. Industrial policy has been disengaged substantially since the 1960s. Policy-makers, with an increasingly blurred role model to follow as development progressed, gradually became incapable of more efficiently allocating resources than markets, with the result that their influence declined. Another contributing factor was the deterioration in the government's ability to forge consensus about basic goals, the result of increasing consumer wealth as well as the growing independence of Japanese corporations which accompanied their increased competitive strength in the world economy. Because policy-makers did not adjust to these changes quickly enough, attempts to implement traditional policy measures probably worsened Japan's economic performance in the 1970s. However, by the 1980s, the scope of industrial policy had been substantially narrowed. It is now largely limited to functions that require government help, such as promoting technological development or the diversification of a structurally depressed industry, and its contribution to Japan's economic performance in the last decade has probably been modestly positive. The more narrow scope of policy today does, however, greatly limit the extent of that contribution.

This is an irony little appreciated by those in other developed nations advocating the adoption of a 'Japan-style' industrial policy. What positive effect industrial policy in Japan may currently have on growth is the result of its much more limited scope. This retreat of industrial policy from widespread intervention has proceeded to such an extent that Japanese industrial policy now differs little in intent from measures used in Europe and the US. In other words, Japan has 'adopted' a more Western type of industrial policy at a time when others are suggesting that Western countries increase their own use of industrial policy to more closely resemble Japan. This does not mean that there are no lessons to be learned from the types of policy measures currently used in Japan. It is possible that Japan has had more success with the measures it has used to promote technological development or to facilitate the adjustment of a declining industry. However, the goals of policy at present differ little from policy aims in other industrialized nations. Japan itself no longer implements a 'Japan-style' industrial policy.

This book is organized as follows. Chapter 2 presents a broad overview of Japanese economic growth from post-war destruction until the first oil crisis, focusing in particular on the role played by industrial policy. Chapter 3 discusses in detail the methodological issues involved in evaluating industrial policy in addition to the stated intentions of those who formulated industrial policy. Chapter 4 correlates industrial policy in the 1945–1973 period to market failures and externalities, examines the impact of these policies on resource allocation, and provides empirical evidence of the role played by industrial policy in Japanese economic development. Chapter 5 examines the formulation and implementation of industrial policy, using measures towards the steel industry as a focus. Chapter 6 summarizes Japan's experience with industrial policy from 1945 to 1973, highlighting insights derived from policy successes and failures for developing countries today which are tempted to imitate Japan.

The latter portion of this book first updates the Japanese experience with industrial policy, outlining in Chapter 7 measures over the last two decades when declining industries have been more the focus of policymakers than have expanding industries. This provides the basis for evaluating the efficacy of recent policy measures and the lessons Japan's experience may hold for developed nations, summarized in Chapter 8. In addition to the role that industrial policy can play in Japan's future, Chapter 9 contains concluding observations and qualifications about the importance of industrial policy for both developing and developed nations.

2

Economic Recovery, Rapid Growth, and Industrial Policy

In order to gain an understanding of the possible role played by industrial policy, this chapter presents an overview of the first three decades of
Japan's post-war development. Japan's remarkably rapid growth between
1945 and 1973 occurred simultaneously with the widespread use of industrial policy, and the changing focus and history of this policy serves to
divide Japanese growth into four distinct periods. The Occupation period,
from August 1945 to April 1952, witnessed the creation of many of the
tools of industrial policy and was characterized by the state's emphasis on
economic recovery. From 1952 to 1960, policy tools were perfected and
were used to promote the rationalization and modernization of select
industries in order to achieve economic autonomy. The 1960s was a
decade of trade and capital liberalization, and policy during this time
focused on strengthening the Japanese economy in order to successfully
meet these challenges. Economic growth also emerged as an explicit policy target for the first time. However, the tools of policy-makers were
reduced, forcing a reliance on more indirect pressure to implement policy.
While trade concerns remained a policy priority in the early 1970s, this
period was also characterized by a focus on an improved quality of life,
an emphasis that was interrupted by the first oil crisis. Moreover, as consensus about the goals of industrial policy grew increasingly fragmented,
so too did public support of industrial policy.

2.1 Post-War Recovery and the Occupation of Japan (1945–1952)

There will be no place for interference by management or labor with the *acceleration of production*, for the burden will be shared by every segment of Japanese
society. There will be no place for political conflict over the objectives to be
sought as these objectives are stated with crystal clarity. Nor will there be any
place for ideological opposition as the purpose to be served is common to all the
people.[1] (General Douglas MacArthur to Prime Minister Yoshida Shigeru, 19
Dec. 1948; italic added.)

[1] 'SCAP's Explanation of Stabilization Program to Japanese Government', 19 Dec. 1948,
Ōkurashō Zaisei Shi Shitsu, *Shōwa Zaisei Shi: Shūsen kara Kōwa made*, 20 (Tokyo, Tōyō
Keizai Shinpō Sha, 1982), 747–8.

Japan faced one basic challenge after World War II, that of survival. By
the end of the war, Japan had lost one-quarter of its national wealth
through damage to factories, equipment, commercial buildings, and
houses.[2] Industrial production was one-sixth of its 1934–6 average, 13.1
million individuals had lost their jobs in the military, in overseas colonies,
and in military-related production,[3] and the rice harvest in 1945 was two-
thirds that of normal.[4] Without aid from the Occupation forces, starvation on a wide scale would have been unavoidable.

Through 1946, Japan's economic prospects showed little improvement.
While unemployment did not emerge as a major problem, this was simply
because it was not a feasible alternative: unemployment at this time
equalled death. However, with the economy incapable of efficiently
absorbing a large number of new workers, many were underemployed, a
situation that would persist for more than a decade. Inflation soared: as
the Japanese government redeemed bonds it had issued to fund the war
and paid salary backlogs, currency in circulation doubled from August
1945 to February 1946.[5] Mining and manufacturing output did grow,
with output indices almost doubling from 11.2 in January to 20.4 by the
year end. Even so, the index average of 18 for the year was far lower
than the index average of 45 for 1945.[6]

Occupation policy initially acted as a general disincentive to economic
recovery, since the initial goal of the Allies was to limit Japan's economic
base, to below pre-war levels.[7] In particular, the Occupation undermined
corporate investment in plant and equipment. Viewing heavy industry as
the foundation of Japan's militarism, the Occupation aggressively blocked
investment in steel, shipbuilding, and machinery. A further rationale for
discouraging investment in such industries was provided by the classical
economic view that Japan's comparative advantage lay in light rather
than heavy industries. Reparations policy also acted as a general disincen-

---

[2] Ōkurashō Zaisei Shi Shitsu, *Shōwa Zaisei Shi: Shūsen kara Kōwa made*, 20 (Tokyo,
Tōyō Keizai Shinpō Sha, 1978), 14–15.

[3] 13.1 million individuals equalled 18% of the population in 1945 (ibid. 8). This 13.1 million consisted of 1.5 million repatriated from overseas colonies, 7.61 million troops released
from service, and 4 million who lost jobs in military-related production. (Nakamura
Takafusa, *The Postwar Japanese Economy: Its Development and Structure* (Tokyo,
University of Tokyo Press, 1981), 21.)

[4] Ibid. 21–5.

[5] Ōkurashō Zaisei Shi Shitsu, *Shōwa Zaisei Shi: Shūsen kara Kōwa made*, 19: 407.

[6] Ibid. 94–7.

[7] Japan was not only stripped of its sizeable overseas colonies, but initial reparations
plans suggested eliminating all production facilities for aluminium, magnesium, aircraft, ball
and roller bearings, half the production facilities for machine tools, a substantial portion of
the chemical industry, and more than three-quarters of Japan's steel capacity. In terms of
steel alone, this implied a retreat to production levels of 1930–1. (Edwin W. Pauley,
'Interim Reparations Policy—Pauley Report', 6 Dec. 1945, Ōkurashō Zaisei Shi Shitsu,
Shōwa Zaisei Shi: Shūsen kara Kōwa made, 20: 440–3.

tive to investment, since the Occupation did not clarify what equipment of what firms would be confiscated as part of reparation payments. The only major positive economic development in the early years of the Occupation was the recovery of the Japanese textile industry, which began in the first quarter of 1946 when the government received permission to import raw cotton into Japan.

Despite continued economic problems, the Occupation introduced several measures in its early years which were to shape the economic recovery that followed. Most importantly, land reform measures were implemented in two stages in December 1945 and September 1946, whereby land was transferred from absentee landlords or large landholders to tenant farmers. Fully 80.1 per cent of tenant farms were bought by the government for transfer; altogether 1.96 million hectares were purchased, or 37.5 per cent of total agricultural land in Japan.[8] This set the stage for the output increases of 4.3 per cent p.a. in the 1950s.[9] The breakup of Japan's industrial conglomerates, the *zaibatsu*, from November 1945 to 1947 also affected the later development process by raising the degree of competition in the economy overall. Of particular importance was the purging of many of the older industrialists, who were replaced by a less conservative younger group.[10] Finally, the promotion of organized labour by the Occupation at this time laid the foundation for collective bargaining, contributing to later wage increases which would fuel domestic demand.

While the importance of these three measures has been stressed innumerable times, their common characteristic has not. Land reform, labour rights, and the dissolution of the *zaibatsu* served to create a belief in economic equality. This belief that no single group should economically dominate others would find itself expressed later in government attempts to eliminate wage differentials between large and small companies as well as in agricultural support measures. Moreover, the commitment to and the realization of broad economic equality helped maintain consensus towards government measures to stimulate growth.

---

[8] Kōsai Yutaka, *Kōdo Seichō no Jidai* (Tokyo, Nihon Hyōron Sha, 1981), 21–3.

[9] Sōmu Chō Tōkei Kyoku, *Nihon Chōki Tōkei Sōran*, 2 (Tokyo, Nihon Tōkei Kyōkai, 1988), 100–1.

[10] Dissolution of family control over the ten *zaibatsu* groups affected 1,682 companies and involved the removal from office of 3,668 individuals. The economic purge by the Occupation also helped to introduce new blood into corporate management, as it affected approximately 400 companies where more than 1,500 individuals were purged. However, even more important to bringing in less conservative corporate management was the reorganization of companies under the Law for the Elimination of Excessive Concentrations of Economic Power as well as the self-motivated corporate reorganizations to escape bankruptcies threatened by the Special Indemnity War Tax, the loss of overseas assets, the freezing of bank accounts, and losses from old accounts. For details, see Eleanor M. Hadley, *Antitrust in Japan* (Princeton, NJ, Princeton University Press, 1970), 88–124.

Other Occupation measures in 1946 also had a profound impact on how industrial policy would be implemented in post-war Japan. First, the Occupation implicitly agreed on the need for government control over economic activity when anti-inflation measures proposed in February of that year failed to have their desired impact. The government was given broad powers to set prices and allocate production, acting to replace the market mechanism which was not operating effectively in this period of chaos. While Japan had already experienced a long history of government intervention and control in the economy, this stamp of approval from the Allied forces at least marginally reinforced the commitment to an active government role in economic management. The Occupation helped to centralize this control, supporting the creation of the Economic Stabilization Board (*Keizai Antei Honbu*) in mid-1946. This board, which survived until the end of the Occupation in July 1952, not only acted as the predecessor to the Economic Planning Agency (*Keizai Kikaku Chō*) in creating general long-term plans for the economy, but it also set precedents in how to build policy consensus. Directors of the Economic Stabilization Board came from varied backgrounds, including ex-bureaucrats, academics, and business leaders, and its policies were further shaped by equally diverse advisers. In addition, the Economic Stabilization Board acted to popularize policy with the public.

The Economic Stabilization Board also had control over basic trade policy. Trade itself was managed by the Board of Trade (*Bōeki Chō*), which bought imports and exports in turn through public corporations (*kōdan*) that were controlled by industry interests. Although actions by this multi-tiered structure were subject to Occupation approval, the ESB was nominally in charge of determining a budget for foreign exchange, and through this budget exercised a general control over foreign transactions. Until April 1949, exports were effectively subsidized, with exporters exchanging dollars for yen at a higher rate than importers.

1947 and 1948 witnessed both a profound shift in Occupation economic policy as well as the real start of modern industrial policy. The Occupation, which had initially concerned itself more with the social and political reform of a fascist Japan, began to stress the need for economic recovery.[11] This policy shift, which was facilitated by domestic political pressure in the US to reduce the cost of aid to Japan, was primarily motivated by the outbreak of the Cold War and the resulting argument for a strong Japanese economy. Naturally, this emerging focus on growth was accompanied by new ideas about the appropriate path for Japan's economic development. At first, the Allies had stressed the recovery of light

[11] See, for example, K. C. Royall, 'Royall's Speech on American Policy Towards Japan', 6 Jan. 1948, Ōkurashō Zaisei Shi Shitsu, *Shōwa Zaisei Shi: Shūsen kara Kōwa made*, 20: 183–6.

industry, not only as a means to achieve balanced trade but also as a means to eliminate Japan's ability to wage war.[12] This gradually gave way to a focus on heavy industry, in the belief that prospects were brighter for exports of machinery, metals, and chemicals.[13] Both schools of thought shared recognition of the need for Japan to export in order to grow, hardly surprising given Japan's extreme paucity of raw materials. However, as a strong Japanese economy became a priority, debate focused increasingly on which industries had the best growth prospects. Heavy industries came to replace light industries in the minds of Occupation officials as those most appropriate to drive economic recovery and expansion.

Japanese policy-makers themselves wasted little time in these years discussing what shape growth should take. Faced with sharply reduced output, debate about the pattern of development was a luxury Japan could ill afford. Rather, all initial policy efforts were devoted to achieving recovery, implicitly defined as increasing production in every industry to pre-war levels. To that end, Arisawa Hiromi, an economist at Tokyo University and adviser to Prime Minister Yoshida, proposed the priority production system (*keisha seisan hōshiki*), the first modern Japanese industrial policy. Arisawa identified supply bottlenecks which were limiting growth, stressing in particular how declines in coal output were negatively affecting steel production and in turn how the lack of steel was preventing expansion of coal output by limiting possible investment. Fertilizer was designated a third key industry, as this also utilized coal and, through increased agricultural output, would help to ease import demands. Arisawa's ideas about priority production were implemented by the Economic Stabilization Board in the first quarter of 1947 when Yoshida's Minister of Finance, Ishibashi Tanzan, became concurrent Director of the Economic Stabilization Board. Emergency imports of fuel, approved by the Occupation, were directed to the steel industry, and the increased output from this was in turn directed to the domestic coal industry.[14]

Allocations of imports and domestic output were not the only tools available to foster the priority production system. Government finance was also made available through the Reconstruction Finance Corporation

---

[12] Edwin W. Pauley, 'Reparations From Japan—Immediate Program', 18 Dec. 1945, Ōkurashō Zaisei Shi Shitsu, *Shōwa Zaisei Shi: Shūsen kara Kōwa made*, 20: 443–9.

[13] Economic and Scientific Section of SCAP, 'A Possible Program for a Balanced Japanese Economy', 27 Mar. 1947, Ōkurashō Zaisei Shi Shitsu, *Shōwa Zaisei Shi: Shūsen kara Kōwa made*, 20: 519–21.

[14] The Occupation at the end of 1946 approved emergency imports of 13,000 kl. of oil (with a promise of 67,000 kl. to follow) in order to get steel production going. Tsūshō Sangyō Shō Tsūshō Sangyō Seisaku Shi Hensan Iinkai, *Tsūshō Sangyō Shi*, 2 (Tokyo, Tsūshō Sangyō Chōsa Kai, 1991), 263–71.

(*Fukkō Kinyū Kinko*) which was established on 24 January 1947. This corporation, headed by the Minister of Finance, was initially capitalized with 4 billion yen of government funds, but raised additional monies through Bank of Japan discounting of special bills issued by the Reconstruction Finance Bank for the Reconstruction Finance Corporation. In 1947, outstanding loans by the RFC reached 59.5 billion yen, rising more than did all city bank loans. The coal industry accounted for fully 36.9 per cent of RFC loans outstanding at the end of 1947.[15]

The government also used price controls and subsidies to direct resources towards priority industries. At the time of the July 1947 price revisions, the price of coal for producers was set at 128 times the pre-war level. Although the consumer price was higher than the producer price, a special discounted price, lower than the producer price, applied to coal used in designated industries. Prices for steel in general were set below production costs, as were prices for fertilizer, non-ferrous metals, and soda. These below-cost prices necessitated large government subsidies, which in 1947 accounted for 11 per cent of general government expenditure, rising to 24 per cent in 1949. In 1947 alone, fully 61 per cent of government subsidies were given to the two priority industries of steel and coal.[16]

Just as there was no government debate at this time about what shape recovery was to take, so too was there no discussion about who was to pay for the cost of economic reconstruction. The Japanese worker was expected to bear this burden. The first post-war Economic White Paper of 1947, published under the auspices of the only socialist government ever to be elected, called for 'providing a comfortable life by increasing the fruits of labor through the sweat of workers'.[17] Even in these dark economic times, the Japanese consumer was expected to tighten his belt, a tenet that would remain unquestioned until the late 1960s and overwhelmingly accepted until the late 1980s.

By 1947, many of the tools and characteristics of post-war industrial policy were in place. The government selected those industries which it thought were key to increasing future economic growth and supported them through the allocation of imports, through the allocation of output,

---

[15] Data are for fiscal year 1947 (Apr. 1947–Mar. 1948). For more details see Ōkurashō Zaisei Shi Shitsu, *Shōwa Zaisei Shi: Shūsen kara Kōwa made*, 5 (Tokyo, Tōyō Keizai Shinpō Sha, 1982), 643–6.

[16] The data in this paragraph come from Kuroda Masahiro, 'Price and Goods Control in the Japanese Postwar Inflationary Period', in Teranishi Jurō and Kōsai Yutaka (eds.), *The Japanese Experience in Economic Reforms* (New York, Macmillan, forthcoming).

[17] Keizai Kikaku Chō, *Keizai Hakusho* (Tokyo, Ōkurashō Insatsu Kyoku, 1947), as quoted in Arisawa Hiromi (ed.), *Shōwa Keizai Shi: Fukkō kara Sekiyu Shokku made*, 2 (Tokyo, Nihon Keizai Shinbun Sha, 1980), 60.

through government loans, and through subsidies.[18] The Japanese worker was expected to pay policy costs. The tools of industrial policy would be refined as the Occupation progressed, and other new institutional factors would also arise, such as government influence over private banks. However, the biggest change would occur in how policy was formulated, as the government moved from state-determined intervention to policy set by a co-ordination of public and private sector goals.

In 1948, the Occupation became firmly committed to supporting economic growth and exports, goals not only very much welcomed by Japanese policy-makers themselves but goals that would persist for another twenty-five years. The shift towards emphasizing a strong Japanese economy which had begun the previous year became the official top policy priority in 1948, both because of rising Cold War tensions and also because the previous top policy priorities, Japan's demilitarization and democratization, had largely been realized.[19] Johnston's 26 April 'Report on the Economic Position and Prospects of Japan and Korea: Measures Required to Improve Them' is representative of this policy shift and highlighted the vicious circle in which the Japanese economy was then trapped: the shortage of raw materials constrained production, leading to export constraints and in turn limited imports of raw materials. To break this circle, the Johnston report recommended aid to raise imports and output, as well as export promotion measures.

Recommendations in the Johnston Report were formalized and augmented in proposals by the National Security Council (NSC 13/2) written in October 1948. This report states that 'the success of the recovery program will in large part depend on Japanese efforts to raise production and to maintain high export levels through hard work, a minimum of workstoppages, internal austerity measures, and the stern combatting of inflationary trends . . .'.[21] The die was cast, and Japan would shortly begin an unprecedented expansion of more than two decades duration.

First, however, the problem of inflation had to be addressed if these goals were to be achieved. Although mining and manufacturing output

[18] The ability to implement industrial policy was substantially enhanced by the establishment of industry groups (*gyōkai*) after the war. Representing firms in specific industries, these groups channelled information between government and business. For further details, see Ch. 4.

[19] That the Occupation felt that democratization had been achieved was apparent in its suppression of the general strike called for 1 Feb. 1947. This marked the end of the Occupation's unqualified support of labour interests against those of business.

[20] Committee Invited by the Secretary of the Army to Inquire Into Economic Problems of Japan and Korea (Percy H. Johnston, Chairman), 'Report on the Economic Position and Prospects of Japan and Korea: Measures Required to Improve Them', 26 Apr. 1948, Ōkurashō Zaisei Shi Shitsu, *Shōwa Zaisei Shi: Shūsen kara Kōwa made*, 20: 483–5.

[21] National Security Council, 'NSC Recommendations with Respect to US Policy Toward Japan (NSC 13/2)', 7 Oct. 1948, Ōkurashō Zaisei Shi Shitsu, *Shōwa Zaisei Shi: Shūsen kara Kōwa made*, 20: 192–5.

rose almost 50 per cent in 1948[22] and agricultural output gained 15 per cent,[23] inflation remained unchecked. After rising 3.7 times in 1947 (December to December), official statistics show that wholesale prices in 1948 increased 2.2 times.[24] In actual fact, increases were larger given the prevalence of black market transactions. This distortion makes particularly suspect consumer price movements, but even government statistics show rapid consumer price increases, with an 83 per cent rise in 1948 following the 115 per cent leap of the previous year.

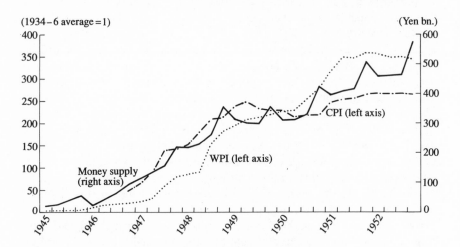

Fig. 2.1. Trends in Prices and the Money Supply, 1945–1951
Source: Ōkurashō, *Shōwa Zaisei Shi: Shūsen kara Kōwa made*, 19.

Government loans through the Reconstruction Finance Corporation and government subsidies through price controls were directly responsible for much of this inflation. These measures did have the desired effect of stimulating production: in terms of targets achieved, the priority production system was highly successful, with 97.7 per cent of the targeted increase in coal production achieved in 1947 as output grew to 29.3 million tons that year before advancing to 34.8 million in 1948.[26] At the same time, crude steel output rose from 0.6 million tons in 1946 to 1.7 million tons in 1948.[27]

Increases in output did help to alleviate one side of the inflation problem, identified as too much money chasing too few goods. However, the

[22] Output in Dec. 1947 was 46.6% higher than the previous year. (Ōkurashō Zaisei Shi Shitsu, *Shōwa Zaisei Shi: Shūsen kara Kōwa made*, 19: 103.)
[23] Ibid. 81.   [24] Ibid. 38.   [25] Ibid. 47.
[26] Nihon Kaihatsu Ginkō Jūnen Shi Hensan Iinkai, *Nihon Kaihatsu Ginkō Jūnen Shi* (Tokyo, Nihon Kaihatsu Ginkō, 1963), 221.
[27] Ibid. 237.

(1934–6 average=100)

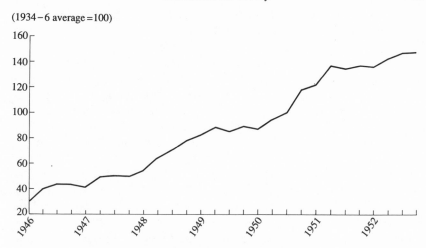

Fig. 2.2. Mining and Manufacturing Output, 1945–1951
Source: Ōkurashō, *Shōwa Zaisei Shi: Shūsen kara Kōwa made*, 19.

subsidies and government loans which helped to bring about these output increases worsened the other side of the inflation problem by raising the amount of money in circulation. RFC loans alone totalled 53.5 billion yen in 1947 and 72.5 billion yen in 1948;[28] special bills issued by the Reconstruction Finance Bank on behalf of the RFC reached 109.1 billion yen at the end of March 1948. Since the Bank of Japan held 79.7 billion yen of these bills, RFC activities accounted for 37.5 per cent of the tripling of the money supply from January 1947 to March 1949.[29] Government subsidies through price controls were also substantial, totalling 26.6 billion yen in 1947 and 70.5 billion yen in 1948.[30]

In order to solve the inflation problem and promote continued economic recovery, the US Joint Chiefs of Staff sent the Nine-part Interim Directive on Stabilization to Occupation authorities in December 1948. This directive, which was largely derived from the National Security Council's report (NSC 13/2), recommended the adoption of a balanced consolidated government budget, strengthened tax collection, credit limitation, strengthened price controls, improved operation of foreign trade controls, establishment of a programme to achieve wage stability, improved allocation and rationing of scarce materials, increased domestic production of raw materials and manufactured goods, and an improved food collection programme. Joseph Dodge was given the mandate to

---

[28] Figures represent the increase in total RFC loans outstanding on a fiscal year basis (Japan's fiscal year runs from Apr. to Mar.). See Ōkurashō Zaisei Shi Shitsu, *Shōwa Zaisei Shi: Shūsen kara Kōwa made*, 19: 646.
[29] Ibid. 407.   [30] Ibid. 168.

realize these nine points; he arrived in Japan in February 1949, quickly setting tough anti-inflation policies, which are now commonly called the Dodge Line.

First, Dodge insisted that the 1949 consolidated government budget show a surplus, with unspent revenues to be used to cover the redemption of bonds of the Reconstruction Finance Corporation. Not only were expenditure plans slashed, but taxes were also raised to achieve this aim. Secondly, Dodge eliminated the hidden subsidies in the price control system and in foreign trade accounts. In cases where prices were set below costs or where trade was promoted through the use of multiple exchange rates, Dodge forced the government to explicitly account for the subsidies involved, and wherever possible he limited the size of the subsidies. Thirdly, in order to constrain the expansion of credit, Dodge halted the issuance of new loans by the Reconstruction Finance Corporation. Dodge did establish the US Aid Counterpart Fund (*Mikaeri Shikin*) at this time, whose function was nominally to replace RFC lending as well as to promote trade. However, this fund in practice did little to offset the negative impact of Dodge's policies on economic growth.[31] Finally, Dodge called for a single exchange rate, which was implemented on 25 April with the yen set at 360 against the US dollar.

These policies were not just anti-inflationary; they were in fact deflationary and resulted in the darkest period of the Occupation. Unemployment soared, almost doubling from 260,000 in December 1948 to 430,000 in June of 1950.[32] With the curtailment of subsidies, bankruptcies and workstoppages became endemic: although only nine of the 356 large corporations halted operations in 1949, fully 42 per cent of small companies became insolvent or ceased production.[33] Social unrest rose, to the extent that insurrection was a real worry to the Japanese government. Although Dodge refused to amend his Draconian policies, the Japanese government did attempt to ease the deflation through monetary policy. The Bank of Japan introduced the Tight Money Neutralizing Measures (*Kane Zumari Kanwa Hōsaku*) in order to channel funds to corporations. Specifically, the Bank of Japan bought up bonds held by banks and also loaned large amounts to banks, thus giving private financial institutions the ability to bail out insolvent or almost insolvent companies.[34]

[31] Although the US Aid Counterpart Fund totalled 129 billion yen in fiscal year 1949, the fund was strictly administered and had as its primary goal the redemption of RFC bonds. Only 24.6 billion yen of the funds was made available to private companies; a further 27 billion yen was granted to government corporations in the form of a 15 billion yen loan to the national railway and a 12 billion yen loan to the communication industry. (Ōkurashō Zaisei Shi Shitsu, *Shōwa Zaisei Shi: Shūsen kara Kōwa made*, 19: 227.)

[32] Arisawa Hiromi (ed.), *Shōwa Keizai Shi: Fukkō kara Sekiyu Shokku made*, 2: 86.

[33] Ibid. 85.

[34] Nihon Ginkō Hyakunen Shi Hensan Iinkai, *Nihon Ginkō Hyakunen Shi*, 5 (Tokyo, Nihon Ginkō, 1986), 354–5.

Thus, policy by the Bank of Japan partially undermined Dodge's attempts to constrain government lending, with private banks, funded by government money, replacing some of the functions of the Reconstruction Finance Corporation. This marked the origin of the over-loan system, whereby loans granted by the city banks rose much faster than their deposit base, resulting in a high degree of dependency on central bank credit.[35] Although temporarily halted by the Occupation in 1950, BOJ lending to city banks would shortly re-emerge as an important complement to industrial policy, since the resulting dependency on the Bank of Japan would give the government some degree of control over the allocation of loans by private sector financial institutions. Moreover, the central bank's encouragement of aggressive lending by city banks also helped to re-forge partially the ties between companies that were broken by the Occupation dissolution of the *zaibatsu* groups. Not unnaturally, city bank loans tended to favour their oldest customers, at least in part because information about credit risk was greater in such cases. Because most city banks had been affiliated with a *zaibatsu*, loans were granted first to companies that had been a part of these groups, and these loans began to tie together companies that had been *zaibatsu* members with city banks at the centre.

1949 also witnessed the formalization of trade management. By adopting a single exchange rate, the government laid the foundation for the privatization of trade. The passage of the 'Law Concerning the Management of Foreign Exchange and Foreign Trade' (*Gaikoku Kawase Oyobi Gaikoku Bōeki Kanri Hō*) in December 1949 outlined the rules and conditions under which trade was to occur. This law required anyone who earned foreign exchange to hand it over to the Foreign Exchange Control Board, cementing the government's ability to control imports. As before, this control was concentrated in the Economic Stabilization Board, which was responsible for drawing up the foreign exchange budget, but the Occupation relinquished most supervisory functions over trade at this time.

The anti-inflationary policies promulgated by Joseph Dodge did achieve their primary goal. Consumer prices peaked in May 1949, and, with the adoption of a balanced budget for 1950, remained on a modest declining trend until July of that year. Wholesale prices, while continuing

---

[35] Commercial banks in Japan consist of two groups, regional banks whose business is concentrated in specific prefectures and city banks whose headquarters are in major urban areas and whose branches extend across the nation. Regional banks have a high share of stable deposits from individuals and concentrate lending to regional corporations; city banks lend to large corporations and are more dependent on more volatile corporate deposits. For further details of Japanese financial institutions, see Yoshio Suzuki, *The Japanese Financial System* (Oxford, Oxford University Press, 1987), 163–304.

to rise, increased much less rapidly: after more than doubling between April 1948 and April 1949, for the following year they increased by only 11 per cent.[36] This was clearly at the expense of manufacturing output, which grew 18.7 per cent in the year to April 1949 compared to 37.2 per cent growth during the previous twelve-month period.[37]

Dodge left a profound legacy for economic policy in Japan. His classical economic ideas, that neither a person nor a government should consume in excess of income and that savings are the key to growth, took firm root. Not only did the Japanese central government refrain from deficit financing until 1965, but it also actively encouraged corporate and household savings while acting as a net saver itself.[38] Less directly, Dodge's policies also began the process of rationalizing Japanese industries. Subsidy cuts forced firms to invest and improve efficiency in order to survive. Also, investments became concentrated in larger companies, since these represented the best credit risk for banks through which the Japanese government was indirectly extending credit. Dodge's policies were also indirectly responsible for the emergence of the over-loaned nature of city banks and their subsequent dependency on central bank credit. Finally, the Dodge Line also contributed to the failure of the stock market to emerge as a primary source of corporate funds, not only because the availability of bank loans was encouraged by the Japanese government in an attempt to offset the Dodge deflation, but also because that deflation caused a 50 per cent decline in share prices, making the equity market unpopular with investors.[39] In other words, the great dependency of Japanese corporations on indirect financing can be traced back to Joseph Dodge.

Not surprisingly, the Japanese government also attempted to use industrial policy to cope with the impact of the Dodge deflation. This role fell to the Ministry of International Trade and Industry, established on 25 May 1949 with most of the functions and personnel of the Ministry of Commerce and Industry (which was dissolved at the same time). MITI formulated the 'Policy Concerning Industrial Rationalization' (*Sangyō Gōrika ni Kansuru Ken*) which was adopted by the Japanese cabinet on 13 September 1949. This led in turn to the establishment of the Industrial Rationalization Council (*Sangyō Gōrika Shingikai*) in December, whose

---

[36] Ōkurashō Zaisei Shi Shitsu, *Shōwa Zaisei Shi: Shūsen kara Kōwa made*, 19: 38–9.

[37] Ibid. 94.

[38] The government itself was a net saver, spending less than it collected in taxes. It encouraged corporate savings through accelerated depreciation, and also encouraged household savings through tax-exempt savings accounts.

[39] The Tokyo stock exchange did not officially reopen until Mar. 1949, although shares had unofficially been traded since Japan's surrender. In the one year after its opening, share prices lost half their value because of the panic accompanying the Dodge deflation. (Arisawa Hiromi (ed.), *Shōwa Keizai Shi: Fukkō kara Sekiyu Shokku made*, 2: 93–6.)

function was to supervise and co-ordinate efforts by industries to cope with the Dodge deflation.

The halting of lending by the Reconstruction Finance Bank essentially stopped the priority production system. The little capital made available to private industry through US Aid Counterpart Funds was directed not to coal and steel but to export industries such as textiles. The Industrial Rationalization Council stepped into this gap, attempting to ease the pain associated with the termination of government loans and subsidies. This council was composed originally of 45 committees and 81 subcommittees covering every industry in the country; it brought together businessmen, academics, and bureaucrats to formulate rationalization plans for industries. Rationalization was thus to be a joint public sector–private sector effort, differing from the state-led guidance of the priority production system. Just as the halting of RFC lending led to the introduction of a market element in the government's distribution of capital as the role of city banks rose, so too did it result in more private sector input into the guidance of industry.

In addition to helping to formalize co-operation between the state and the private sector, MITI in 1950 made another substantial contribution to the future form of industrial policy. This contribution was to untie effectively technology imports from the importation of capital goods. MITI achieved this through the Foreign Capital Law (*Gaishi Hō*), enacted in May. This law established a Foreign Investment Committee under MITI's supervision, and required that foreign investors who wished to license technology, share patents, or acquire stock in a Japanese company first obtain the approval of the FIC. This law gave MITI power to bargain over the price of technology and conditions of sale, a tool that would be used frequently to reduce the total cost of imported technology.

At the same time that Joseph Dodge was restructuring government finance and limiting the intervention of the state in the economy, Occupation officials under Carl Shoup also restructured taxes. Many of Shoup's proposals, such as a value-added tax, would prove too controversial for acceptance. Furthermore, his plans to limit special tax measures, such as accelerated depreciation for select industries, would also be overruled after the Occupation ended. Nevertheless, his general plan for Japanese taxes, whereby revenues would be raised equally from the three sources of personal income taxes, corporate income taxes, and indirect taxes, would be followed assiduously for the next two decades. This principle helped keep Japanese growth on track, since it ensured that the progressive nature of personal income taxes in the subsequent rapid growth period did not get out of hand, stifling domestic consumption and hence economic growth.

The deflation following the introduction of the Dodge Line ended dramatically with the outbreak of the Korean War in June 1950, as did the achievement of price stability. The Korean War acted as a major stimulus to the Japanese economy: exports almost doubled between June 1950 and June 1951[40] while manufacturing output increased 44 per cent.[41] Special demand (*tokuju*) for Japanese goods and services arising because of the Korean War was 342 million dollars on a payment basis in 1951, approximately 25 per cent of total exports.[42] This special demand almost doubled Japanese foreign exchange reserves, which reached 914 million US dollars by year end.[43] Inflation, however, began to pick up, with wholesale prices increasing a sharp 49 per cent between June 1950 and June 1951 while consumer prices grew by 18 per cent.[44]

While the export boom from the Korean War would shape Japanese economic growth until its end in the summer of 1953, other notable developments in 1951 also had a significant impact on both growth and industrial policy. First was the establishment of the Japan Development Bank (*Nihon Kaihatsu Ginkō*) in April 1951 with operations beginning in May. The JDB nominally replaced the Reconstruction Finance Corporation. Like the RFC, the JDB was to provide equipment loans to industries 'to build up the firm groundwork of the Japan's self-supporting economy'.[45] Unlike the RFC, however, the Japan Development Bank was not initially allowed to issue bank debentures; with funds supplied by the government and dependent on the government's balance sheets, JDB loans were not inflationary.[46] Additionally, JDB loans were only used to fund long-term investment and were never used to cover operating expenses, thus clearly divorcing its function from that of city banks. Perhaps the most significant difference, however, was the stricter criteria used for granting loans. The JDB was only permitted to grant loans where it could expect repayment. The introduction of market principles in JDB lending practices was an attempt not only to improve the efficiency of loans but also to avoid some of the excesses and corruption that marked government control over the Reconstruction Finance Corporation.

Secondly, 1951 witnessed the beginning of policy autonomy for Japan. With the signing of the San Francisco Peace Treaty in September 1951 and its implementation in April of the following year, the Occupation came to an end. While Japan was at last ready to set its own economic course, the experiences of the Occupation would linger, shaping both

---

[40] Ōkurashō Zaisei Shi Shitsu, *Shōwa Zaisei Shi: Shūsen kara Kōwa made*, 19: 107.
[41] Ibid. 98.   [42] Ibid. 117.   [43] Ibid. 127.   [44] Ibid. 39–50.
[45] Ōkurashō Zaisei Shi Shitsu, *Shōwa Zaisei Shi: Shūsen kara Kōwa made*, 20: 823.
[46] The charter of the Japan Development Bank was revised in July 1952, allowing it to issue debentures as well as borrow funds overseas. However, approval of the Ministry of Finance was needed for these activities. (Nihon Kaihatsu Ginkō, *Nihon Kaihatsu Ginkō Jūnen Shi*, 3–5; Nihon Kaihatsu Ginkō, *Nihon Kaihatsu Ginkō Nijūgonen Shi* (Tokyo, Nihon Kaihatsu Ginkō 1976), Appendix, 73.)

policy choice and implementation. The Occupation reinforced the Japanese belief in government intervention in the economy. It did this by promulgating the most extensive controls over prices and the distribution of goods that Japan had ever experienced. At the same time, Occupation policies were instrumental in shaping how intervention would occur in later years. The Occupation's emphasis on the efficiency of competitive markets helped lead to the use of the market mechanism as a tool of industrial policy. For instance, market principles were introduced in the allocation of government loans through the Japan Development Bank, and the government also utilized market forces in allocating credit through city banks. Of course, Occupation measures which promoted the more efficient working of markets, including the dissolution of the *zaibatsu* and land reform, greatly increased the Japanese government's ability to utilize the market mechanism as a policy tool.

The Occupation also helped to shape the way in which policy would be formulated. The government was not to have sole responsibility for shaping policy response; rather this function was to be shared by both the private and public sectors. Policy came to be determined jointly both because of Japanese attempts to escape the Dodge deflation and also because of a widespread dissatisfaction with the efficacy of government-led policies. These had proved to be both inefficient, since they exacerbated inflation, and subject to corruption: allegations of bribery involved in granting RFC loans to Shōwa Denkō brought down the Ashida government in 1948.

More concretely, the Occupation witnessed the establishment of most of the institutions and financial relationships which would prove fundamental to later industrial policy. MITI was founded as was the Japan Development Bank, the over-loaned nature of Japanese city banks began, *zaibatsu* ties were re-formed through bank lending, the Foreign Capital Law and the Law Concerning the Management of Foreign Exchange and Foreign Trade were implemented, and the Industrial Rationalization Council was established.

Ironically, the Occupation also was responsible for directing policy to promote economic growth and exports, goals that would return to haunt the US in later years. The funds for growth were to come from savings, and workers were expected to pay the costs of development. At the same time, the ideal of income equality took firm root, implying not only that costs were to be spread evenly but also that wage differentials were to be eliminated and support provided for some sectors of the economy. The acceptance of the ideal of income equality led directly to management of the trade-off between promoting high-growth industries and protecting employment in others.

Naturally, the impact of Occupation policies was influenced by existing

Japanese beliefs. In some cases, such as the elimination of special tax breaks, the latter conflicted with the former and ultimately prevailed. Occupation ideas about economic concentration would also be overruled. In other instances where the two conflicted, Occupation ideas would temper Japanese beliefs, as occurred over the role of the government in providing industrial capital. Finally, in instances where Occupation policies reinforced Japanese beliefs, the two produced an unassailable consensus, notably in government commitment to fostering economic growth and the promotion of exports.

2.2   The Second Chance: Industry Rationalization, Modernization, and Growth (1952–1960)

The essence of economic policy in peace-time Japan is the speedy attainment of economic independence. To that end, hastening the rationalization of industry is vital. (Takahashi Ryūtarō, Minister of MITI, July 1952.)[47]

Japan in the early 1950s was in effect given the chance to rewrite its economic history. Japanese autonomy, regained with the ending of the Occupation, broadly coincided with the recovery in manufacturing output to pre-war levels of 1934–6. As if the decade of militarism, war, and destruction had not occurred, the Japanese economy in 1952 stood poised to redirect its economic development, not into another protracted period of militarization but on to a new path. This it did with such success that it surprised everyone, and probably no one more than the Japanese themselves.

Although the Korean War had acted as a catalyst to end the Dodge deflation, by 1952 there was considerable pessimism about the durability of the economic upturn. First, price inflation had returned with a vengeance: the WPI rose almost 40 per cent in 1951.[48] This was undermining the competitiveness of Japanese exports, which were benefiting only because of a geographical proximity to Korea. Declining export competitiveness and uncertainty about how long the Korean War would last cast a shadow over Japan's economic outlook. A second concern was highlighted by Professor Nakayama Ichirō of Hitotsubashi University, who noted that the 50 per cent increase in manufacturing output since the beginning of the Korean War had been accompanied by only a paltry 5 per cent increase in consumption. Claiming that this discrepancy was a

[47] Tsūsanshō Kigyō Kyoku, *Kigyō Gōrika no Shomondai* (Tokyo, Daini Dōkō Sha, 1952), Introduction.
[48] Ōkurashō Zaisei Shi Shitsu, *Shōwa Zaisei Shi: Shūsen kara Kōwa made*, 19: 40.

special characteristic of the Japanese economy, he cast doubt on the ability of consumption to promote further economic growth.[49]

Pessimism about Japan's economic prospects proved unfounded. In
1952, consumption surged 17 per cent, .nearly reaching pre-war levels.[50]
Sluggish consumption had been caused by low income levels rather than
deep-rooted structural factors, and high wage gains in 1952 and 1953
removed this constraint. Huge pent-up demand for consumer goods
emerged, fuelling economic growth in 1952 and 1953. Investment also
accelerated, helped in part by stronger domestic demand. Between 1951
and 1954, real growth averaged 7.4 per cent per annum.[51]

Of course, the continuation of the Korean War contributed greatly to
economic growth. Special demand (*tokuju*) for Japanese goods and services from UN forces in Korea reached 457 million US dollars in 1952,
up from 342 million in 1951, offsetting the sharp drop in US aid to
Japan. *Tokuju* in 1953 rose even further to 595 million US dollars.[52]
Tokuju allowed Japan to import needed raw materials and machinery far
beyond what would otherwise have been its abilities, yet even so,
Japanese holdings of foreign exchange doubled between 1950 and 1952,
reaching 1.1 billion US dollars before falling back slightly to 1 billion in

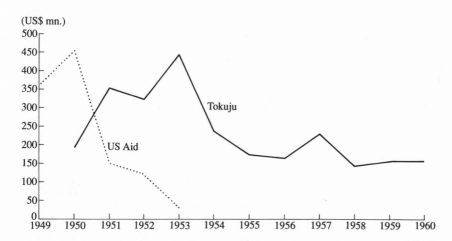

Fig. 2.3. US Aid and Special Procurement Demand (*Tokuju*)
Source: Ōkurashō, *Shōwa Zaisei Shi: Shūsen kara Kōwa made*, 19.

---

[49] Kōsai Yutaka, *Kōdo Seichō no Jidai*, 81–5.
[50] Measured in real terms based on average price levels for 1934–6. (Ōkurashō Zaisei Shi
Shitsu, *Shōwa Zaisei Shi: Shūsen kara Kōwa made*, 19: 28.)
[51] Real growth is measured in 1970 prices, and is the average of yearly growth for fiscal
years 1952–4 (the Japanese fiscal year runs from Apr. to Mar.). (Ibid. 29.)
[52] Ibid. 117.

1953.[53] Additionally, *tokuju* fuelled wage gains, and hence consumption and investment.

Japanese industrial policy shifted into top gear during this period. Japanese plant and equipment was obsolete, battered not only by damage in World War II, but also by the passage of time. Policy-makers quite rightly recognized that true economic autonomy could only be achieved by a modernization of Japan's industrial base. Windfall foreign exchange gains and high corporate profits under the economic boom of 1951–3 provided the ideal environment in which to promote industrial restructuring. Specifically, authorities attempted to continue the rationalization process that had begun under the Dodge deflation, promoting new investment to raise levels of technology and productivity. The goal of this rationalization was economic self-sufficiency, which meant both balanced trade and at least a recovery in living standards to pre-war levels.[54]

The term 'rationalization' (*gōrika*) has a long and specific history in Japan. It refers not only to a winnowing out process caused by economic recessions, whereby market forces pushed inefficient firms into liquidation and forced others to scrap obsolete plant, but also to attempts to raise productivity through the introduction of modern equipment, new technology, improved management, and product standardization. Moreover, rationalization was associated with firm size: the larger the firm, the more efficient it was expected to be. In part, this association was shaped by Japan's own economic history. The proliferation of small companies in the 1920s had been cited by government officials as one of the causes of economic stagnation. These small firms earned little foreign exchange, had difficulty covering their costs, and were squeezed by the giant trading companies, who bought their output for little but charged high prices on the materials they sold to smaller companies.[55]

Additionally, rationalization was associated with an explicit trade-off in

---

[53] Ōkurashō Zaisei Shi Shitsu, *Shōwa Zaisei Shi: Shūsen kara Kōwa made*, 19: 127.

[54] More specifically, economic self-sufficiency was defined as consisting of three components. First was a balanced current account, to be realized through export promotion and import substitution. This in itself was not enough, since balanced trade could be accompanied by an unbalanced economy, as was the case during the Korean War. Additionally, then, economic self-sufficiency required support of a rational level of employment and improved living standards. The former implied more or less full employment; the latter meant as a bare minimum recovery in per capita consumption and housing to pre-war levels. (Tsūsanshō Kigyō Kyoku, *Kigyō Gōrika no Shomondai*, 1–26.)

[55] Reports by Kishi Nobusuke, a Japanese bureaucrat with the Ministry of Commerce and Industry sent to Germany in 1930, reinforced this association. These reports stressed that the German experience with rationalization involved not only new technologies and machinery, but also the use of government cartels and trusts to promote rationalization. Japanese authorities then associated rationalization with both a lessening of competition and an increase in effective size through cartelization. Chalmers Johnson, *MITI and the Japanese Miracle: The Growth of Industrial Policy 1925–1975* (Stanford, Calif., Stanford University Press, 1982), 108–15.

unemployment. Rationalization measures in the 1920s and 1930s were criticized as causing unemployment, hardly surprising given the link between rationalization and firm size.[56] However, as a result of past criticism, rationalization policy in the 1950s would attempt to control the rise of unemployment, promoting modernization while at the same time ensuring that this did not lead to massive job losses.

Rationalization was applicable to three areas. It was to take place across industries, which entailed selecting and promoting industries deemed vital to economic autonomy, thereby resulting in a rational industrial structure (*gōriteki na sangyō kōzō*).[57] Rationalization was also to occur within industries (*sangyō gōrika*), which meant determining what should be the appropriate size and number of firms within an industry, and at times encouraging the merger of smaller companies to compete successfully with the larger ones. Finally, rationalization was to occur within firms (*kigyō gōrika*). Corporate rationalization had as its goals cost reduction and product improvement; these were to be achieved through new investment, through new technology, and through improved management.[58]

Amongst the conditions for economic self-sufficiency and the types of rationalization, policy initially emphasized rationalization within firms to promote exports and to encourage import substitution. Japan needed foreign exchange in order to pay for raw material imports, and policy-makers realized that the stimulation of exports by the Korean War could not last forever. Moreover, export industries needed to reduce costs while improving quality to offset the deterioration in competitiveness caused by domestic inflation. Finally, greater export strength was needed since import prices had risen. While generally beneficial to Japan, the Korean War did cut off the country from such traditional trading markets as China, necessitating a switch to costlier imports from the US. A similar argument held true for the marketing of Japanese exports: Japan was

[56] For an early criticism of rationalization policy in Japan see Nawa Shūichi, *Sangyō Gōrika ka Shitsugyō Gōrika* (Tokyo, Shunyōdō, 1930).

[57] This marks the real beginning of the Japanese emphasis on industrial structure (*sangyō kōzō*) as a focus of policy. MITI's comments in 1952 on this issue are enlightening. 'Various draft proposals for a rational economic structure have been formulated in the past through the Economic Stabilization Board. Even so, it is still difficult today to propose one which can conform to the widely fluctuating international environment. Despite these difficulties, a basic plan for a rational economic structure will be formulated from a national economic perspective, and it is vital and urgent that firms and the state work to realize it.' (Tsūsanshō Kigyō Kyoku, *Kigyō Gōrika no Shomondai*, 23.)

[58] These three categories are outlined in Tsūsanshō Kigyō Kyoku, *Kigyō Gōrika no Shomondai*. MITI later added a fourth, the rationalization of the infrastructure which would complement rationalization efforts by firms (Tsūsanshō Kigyō Kyoku, *Sangyō Gōrika Hakusho* (Tokyo, Nikkan Kōgyō Shinbun Sha, 1957), 3–5). However, this fourth category is not really distinct since it is related to the rationalization of the industrial structure.

forced to shift away from the less competitive Asian export markets towards globally competitive markets in the US and Europe.

By 1951, MITI already had many of the tools it needed to promote its version of rationalization. The Foreign Capital Law gave it control over technology imports, the Japan Development Bank was available to channel funds to designated industries, and the Industrial Rationalization Council was in place to co-ordinate investment activity. What else MITI felt it needed, it would shortly acquire. In March 1952, the Law to Promote the Rationalization of Firms (*Kigyō Gōrika Sokushin Hō*) was announced and implemented. In order to raise the technological level of designated industries, this law advocated tax breaks in the form of exemptions for special reserve accounts as well as accelerated depreciation for imported machinery and technology. With the abolition of the Economic Stabilization Board and the Foreign Exchange Control Board in August 1952, power over the foreign exchange budget was given directly to MITI. This gave it effective control over all imports, enabling it to channel imported goods as it wished. Cartelization was legalized, initially with the passage in 1952 of the Emergency Measures Law for the Stabilization of Specified Small and Medium Enterprises (*Tokutei Chūshō Kigyō Antei Rinji Sochi Hō*) which permitted small and medium enterprises to form cartels to compete with larger companies. This law was followed shortly by the Law of Export and Import Transactions (*Yushutsunyū Torihiki Hō*) which permitted exemptions from antitrust laws, allowing exporters and importers to cartelize trade. Opposition by the Japanese Fair Trade Commission to these laws resulted in a revision of the Anti-Monopoly Law in 1953 to quell disputes about the legality of cartels.[59] The revised Anti-Monopoly Law recognized both recession (*fukyō*) and rationalization (*gōrika*) cartels, relaxed restrictions on cross shareholdings, recognized the rights of manufacturers to set retail prices, and abolished provisions against industry associations.[60]

Cartelization, tax incentives, government funding, industry-based

[59] For details about revisions of the Anti-Monopoly Law, see Tsūshō Sangyō Shō Tsūshō Sangyō Seisaku Shi Hensan Iinkai, *Tsūshō Sangyō Seisaku Shi*, 5 (Tokyo, Tsūshō Sangyō Chōsa Kai, 1991), 243–347.

[60] At the time that MITI was completing the stockpiling of its armoury of tools for industrial policy, obsolete weapons were also being eliminated. Direct government control over the economy was lessened, making way for a more sophisticated co-ordination between the state and the private sector in shaping industrial policy. Price controls were gradually eliminated—these had fallen to controls over 531 goods in Apr. 1950 from 2,128 the previous year. By the end of 1952, controls remained on only 76 products, the majority of which were public service goods. More specifically, 45 were for such public services as utilities, rail charges, and mail, 14 were for food, 5 for food material, 1 for metal goods, 9 for chemicals, and 2 for rent. (Ōkurashō Zaisei Shi Shitsu, *Shōwa Zaisei Shi: Shūsen kara Kōwa made*, 10 (Tokyo, Tōyō Keizai Shinpō Sha, 1978), 558–77.) Similarly, controls over the distribution of goods gradually fell, and were virtually eliminated with the abolition of the Law Adjusting the Supply and Demand of Special Materials (*Rinji Busshi Jukyū Chōsei Hō*) in Apr. 1952.

investment plans, control over import allocation, and control over technology—all of these would be used extensively over the next two decades
to influence the pattern of capital accumulation and production. The list
of policy tools was almost, but not quite, complete; measures to promote
exports would shortly be added. These were in fact a necessity, given that
inflation during the Korean War had resulted in an overvalued yen.
Japanese authorities chose not to devalue their currency, but instead
directly blocked imports and supported exports in an attempt to balance
international payments. Through implementation of the Tax Exemptions
for Export Income (*Yushutsu Shotoku Haijo Seido*) in 1953, tax credits
were granted in proportion to export sales. This amounted to 50 per cent
of export sales or 3 per cent of total sales for manufacturers, whichever
was smaller.[61]

While there was no substantive debate about the active role the
Japanese government was to play in fostering development, the early
1950s did see a fierce debate about what type of development Japan
should effect.[62] This discussion could to some extent be reduced to a
debate about the merits of promoting light industry versus heavy industry, and thus partially mirrored earlier debates in the Occupation.
However, it was couched in slightly different terms. The eventual winners,
the international trade camp, argued that Japan, with its large population
and resource scarcity, could only hope to achieve high growth through
trade. After all, they reasoned, this was the means by which Great
Britain, another poor island nation, had achieved economic success. Their
arguments were countered by the domestic development school, who felt
that Japan should exert most of its energies to maximizing the use of
domestic resources, not only by extracting what coal and metal deposits it
possessed, but also by developing hydroelectric power through massive
investment in dams.

The domestic development school, led by Arisawa Hiromi, argued
against the international trade camp by noting that 'it is not that we dis-
card and ignore the gains from international trade. However, it is very
unstable to rely only on expanding world trade [to achieve economic
growth], and it must be realized that there are limits as to how much
trade can grow. In addition, . . . entrusting capital accumulation almost
entirely to capitalists will eventually not be forgiven [by the public]. The
socialization of the economy must proceed through the introduction of
revolutionary technologies arising from national capital accumulation and
through the start of large-scale, comprehensive development of national

---

[61] Tsūshō Sangyō Shō Tsūshō Sangyō Seisaku Shi Hensan Iinkai, *Tsūshō Sangyō Seisaku Shi*, 6 (Tokyo, Tsūshō Sangyō Chōsa Kai, 1990), 332–3.
[62] In actual fact, this debate began in 1949 but intensified in the early 1950s.

resources.'[63] The international traders eventually won this debate, and the export drive phenomenon that characterized Japanese growth in later decades can be traced, if not with perfect precision, back to these discussions. Ironically, Arisawa's criticisms would prove correct, but not for another thirty years.

Despite the victory of the international trade school concerning the process of economic development, this victory did not unambiguously emerge in policy until later in the decade. Industries initially selected for rationalization in 1952 under the Law to Promote the Rationalization of Firms included not only steel, but also coal and fertilizer, all sectors that had been promoted in the priority production system of 1947–9. Textiles and electric power[64] were also designated, sectors that had benefited from Occupation and Japanese government support. In essence, the list consisted of most areas previously targeted and included industries selected by both proponents of domestic development and international trade.[65] This example, as much as anything, shows clearly that industrial policy was not driven by one comprehensive world-view. It was and would continue to be an amalgamation of past policies and experiences, concerned more with practicality than with a single *raison d'être*.

Steel was one of the first industries to be the focus of guided rationalization. At the urging of MITI and in conjunction with the Industrial Rationalization Council, the steel industry drew up its own rationalization plan in 1950 and submitted it to the government. Covering the three fiscal years from 1951 to 1953, the plan called for a tenfold increase in capital expenditure. This investment was supported by a variety of special tax measures.[66] The government also aided in obtaining land to establish

[63] Arisawa Hiromi, *Saigunbi no Keizaigaku* (Tokyo, Tokyo University Press, 1953), as quoted in Tsuruta Toshimasa, *Sengo Nihon no Sangyō Seisaku* (Tokyo, Nihon Keizai Shinbun Sha, 1982), 25.

[64] Equipment to generate electric power and the cable industry was designated under the Law to Promote the Rationalization of Firms. The electric power industry itself was designated separately in the Law to Promote the Development of Electric Power (*Dengen Kaihatsu Sokushin Hō*) passed in July 1952.

[65] The Law to Promote the Rationalization of Firms (*Kigyō Gōrika Sokushin Hō*), which survives to this day, initially listed 32 industries as targets for rationalization. These were: silk reeling; dyeing; fibreboard; chemical fertilizers; soda; carbide; tar products; dyeing material inputs; animal and vegetable oils and fats; intermediate products for synthetic drugs; fireproof bricks; iron, steel, and rolled steel; steel casting; steel forging; non-ferrous metal manufacturing; non-ferrous metal rolling; turbines and boilers for electric power; machine tools; bearings; electric generators; cables and electric wire; electrical communication equipment; cars; shipbuilding and repair; rolling stock; whaling; metal mining; coal mining; mining of sulphur and sulphur ore; civil engineering and construction for the electric power industry; and marine transport. (Tsūsanshō Kigyō Kyoku, *Kigyō Gōrika no Shomondai*, 454.)

[66] These tax breaks included an import tax exemption for special equipment (Apr. 1951), special depreciation for important equipment (Aug. 1951), establishing reserve accounts to counter price fluctuations (Oct. 1951), establishing reserve accounts for loans (Feb. 1952),

new factories, provided the necessary infrastructure, and granted low-interest government loans to the industry. MITI ensured that foreign exchange for necessary material and equipment imports was made available, and supervised the introduction of foreign technology.

In addition to steel, a five-year rationalization period for the coal industry began in 1951, and rationalization of the shipbuilding industry began in 1950. The first five-year plan for the electric power industry appeared in 1953, as did a rationalization plan for the fertilizer industry.[67] For most of these industries, the government provided low-interest loans, tax breaks, guidance over the introduction of foreign technology, and foreign currency to purchase technology, imported machinery, and necessary material inputs. It also attempted to ensure that the plans were consistent with one another—that industries were not planning investment that was too large given the general direction of the economy.

Treatment of agricultural, distribution, and small and medium enterprises in the first half of the 1950s provides further proof of the practicality of industrial policy. Agricultural policy emphasized improved productivity. The government encouraged the diffusion of improved techniques by employing technical personnel to distribute information in person to villages. These technical personnel also promoted the use of new crop strains, a greater use of chemicals, and mechanization. The government also provided funds for irrigation projects and land development. Coincidental or not, agricultural output rose an average of 6.4 per cent between 1950 and 1955; excluding the disastrous harvest of 1953, annual growth averaged 11.2 per cent.[68]

Policy towards small and medium enterprises had as its primary goal maintaining employment. To that end, the government provided low-interest loans, initially through the Japan Development Bank but from 1953 through the newly established Smaller Business Finance Corporation (*Chūshō Kigyō Kinyū Kōko*). Funds were used to modernize equipment, and the government also attempted to improve the competitiveness of smaller companies against large firms by promoting cartelization. However, these attempts to raise productivity took second place to the social concerns associated with the large number of workers employed in small and medium-sized companies.

Policy towards distribution also emphasized the employment issue, in this case with essentially no focus on productivity in the sector. The government simply blocked competition in distribution, thereby ensuring that jobs were maintained. Included in the 1953 revision of the

and granting a 50% write-off in the first year for equipment to promote rationalization (Mar. 1953). See Ch. 5 for further details.

[67] For details, see Nihon Kaihatsu Ginkō, *Nihon Kaihatsu Ginkō Jūnen Shi*, 165–277.

[68] Sōmu Chō Tōkei Kyoku, *Nihon Chōki Tōkei Sōran*, 2: 100.

Anti-Monopoly Law was the right for manufacturers to set retail prices. This not only stifled competition and directly transferred to the Japanese consumer the costs of maintaining employment in the sector, but this right also helped to guarantee profits for manufacturers, thereby assisting in providing funds for rationalization.

The economic boom from 1951 to 1953, which had generated profits and foreign exchange for rationalization, gradually came to a halt with the cessation of hostilities in Korea in July 1953. Japan found itself faced with a looming balance of payments crisis, as export growth slowed sharply. An extremely poor harvest in 1953 compounded the problem by necessitating higher imports, leading to a drastic tightening of both fiscal and monetary policy. The 1954 government budget was revised down, calling for a 9 per cent decline in general expenditure from outlays of the previous year, and the Fiscal Investment and Loan Programme, which allocated low-interest government loans to industries and to infrastructure projects, was slashed by 20 per cent.[69] The Bank of Japan also tightened monetary policy in September of 1954 by limiting increases in loans by city banks, making use of the high dependence of city banks on central bank credit to influence their behaviour.

Although these measures quickly halted the expansion, the downturn in 1954 was shorter than had been anticipated, lasting only eleven months. Rising agricultural output contributed to the economic recovery, as output grew 10 per cent in 1954 and 20 per cent in 1955.[70] Of more significance was the global economic recovery during those years. This not only supported Japanese exports, but the lag between Japanese export growth and the recovery in domestic demand helped result in stable prices. Obviously, strong investment in plant and equipment in the early 1950s also promoted price stability through improved productivity, and tighter monetary policy provided the third key to stable prices.

While the surge in exports together with the easing of monetary policy started an economic boom in 1955, the recovery quickly spread to domestic consumption. On one side, wage gains and tax cuts contributed, but so too did demand for relatively new products such as transistor radios, televisions, washing machines, and synthetic textiles.[71] During this year,

[69] (Arisawa Hiromi (ed.), *Shōwa Keizai Shi: Fukkō kara Sekiyu Shokku made*, 2: 148–9.) In the Fiscal Investment and Loan Programme, the government allocates funds deposited in postal savings accounts under the jurisdiction of the Ministry of Posts and Telecommunications to other government financial institutions such as the Japan Development Bank, the Housing Loan Corporation, the Smaller Business Finance Corporation, and the Export–Import Bank of Japan. These government financial institutions then make loans to the private sector, often at below-market interest rates.

[70] Sōmu Chō Tōkei Kyoku, *Nihon Chōki Tōkei Sōran*, 2: 100.

[71] By 1960, the diffusion rate for transistor radios was 24.9%, for televisions 54.5%, for washing machines 45.4%, and for refrigerators 15.7%. Diffusion rates soared further in 1960–5, during which time televisions, washing machines, and refrigerators were commonly

the consumer at last achieved levels comparable to those enjoyed prior to World War II. Moreover, with export gains and a record rice harvest, the current account registered a surplus. Stable prices, real economic growth in excess of 10 per cent, rising living standards, and balanced trade— Japan could at last feel confident of achieving economic autonomy.[72]

However, policy-makers did not rest on their laurels. Further growth would require greater imports, in turn necessitating export expansion and by implication further rationalization. Within industries, the latter half of the 1950s witnessed the formulation and implementation of second-stage plans for rationalization. Shipbuilding began its second round of rationalization in 1955, as did the coal industry.[73] The second plan for rationalizing the steel industry appeared in 1956, and the next major five-year development plan for the electric power industry also appeared that year.[74] Policy efforts broadened during this period to include the rationalization of other industries as well as the fostering of industries entirely new to Japan. The first example of the latter was the synthetic textile industry, which was targeted in April 1953 with the announcement of the Five-Year Plan to Foster Synthetic Textiles (*Gōsei Seni Ikusei Gokanen Keikaku*), and in July 1955, MITI proposed to develop the petrochemical industry in Japan, specifically targeting synthetic rubber in 1957.[75] Rationalization efforts also spread with the 1956 Law Concerning Temporary Measures for the Promotion of Machinery Industries (*Kikai Kōgyō Shinkō Rinji Sochi Hō*) and the 1957 Law Concerning Temporary Measures for the Promotion of the Electronics Industry (*Denshi Kōgyō Shinkō Rinji Sochi Hō*).

Rationalization policies during this time also began to address more directly the trade-off between modernization and employment. The second rationalization plan for the coal industry was concerned most with closing inefficient mines and reducing costs, thereby cutting total employment in the industry. Policy towards the general and electric machinery industries also reflected the trade-off between employment and improved efficiency. These industries were characterized by an extremely large number of small companies; rationalization efforts that aimed at raising

called the 'three sacred treasures' (*sanshu no jingi*). (Arisawa Hiromi (ed.), *Shōwa Keizai Shi: Fukkō kara Sekiyu Shokku made*, 2: 191.)

[72] This confidence is apparent from the slogan used in the 1956 Economic White Paper, 'Recovery from the war is complete' (*Mohaya 'sengo' de wa nai*).

[73] The rationalization plan for the coal industry was one of the few to be passed as a law (Law Concerning Temporary Measures to Rationalize the Coal Industry (*Sekitan Kōgyō Gōrika Rinji Sochi Hō*), 1955).

[74] The 5-year plan for the electric power industry announced in 1952 was revised in both 1953 and 1954, but 1956 marked the first major extension of the planning period, signalling the second stage of electric power development.

[75] The Law Concerning Special Measures for the Manufacturing of Synthetic Rubber (*Gōsei Gomu Seizōgyō Tokubetsu Sochi Hō*) was passed in June 1957.

productivity and increasing technological know-how entailed an increase in firm size and some decrease in the number of firms operating. In the textile industry as well, policy did not favour a structure characterized by numerous small firms. In all of these cases, however, rationalization and the probable decline in the number of firms operating was not to proceed so rapidly as to cause a surge in unemployment.

Rapid global advances in technological innovation lay behind this promotion of new industries, and industrial policy in the latter half of the 1950s differed from that in the first half by its emphasis on new technology. Technological innovation was causing a revolution in the materials industries, as breakthroughs for synthetic fibres, synthetic resins, synthetic rubber, plastic, and aluminium created new materials, reduced costs, and improved quality. In turn, these changes affected demand for final goods, as wider use of these improved materials in cars, houses, consumer white goods, and consumer electronics essentially created new products.[76] Against this background, the role of industrial policy was expanded to ensure not only that new industries were successfully introduced but also that the industrial structure shifted in a suitable fashion to meet changing demands.[77]

Industrial policy in the second half of the decade also added a new tool to its arsenal in the form of the first medium-term economic plan. Titled 'A Five-Year Plan for Economic Autonomy' (*Keizai Jiritsu Gokanen Keikaku*), it was adopted in December 1955 and called for promoting trade, promoting technology, strengthening industry, and increasing employment.[78] Rather than detailing targets and measures to achieve them, this first economic plan and others which succeeded it simply identified economic objectives. Formulation of the plans was entrusted to the Economic Planning Agency, which canvassed opinions from business, other government ministries, and academia, and helped forge consensus amongst diverse groups about the broad aim of policy. This first and later economic plans were not operative in the sense that they determined specific levels of investment and growth; rather they broadly indicated the direction that economic development was to take. Their value thus lay in the generation of consensus about development as well as the dissemina-

[76] Arisawa Hiromi (ed.), *Shōwa Keizai Shi: Fukkō kara Sekiyu Shokku made*, 2: 188–9.

[77] Tsūshō Sangyō Shō Kōgyō Gijutsuin, *Gijutsu Kakushin to Nihon no Kōgyō* (Tokyo, Nikkan Kōgyō Shinbun Sha, 1964), 38–87.

[78] This economic plan made more explicit the goals and intentions of policy-makers who had had a basic framework in mind when they formulated policy. MITI, under Minister Okano Kiyohide, first attempted to draw up a national economic plan in 1953, but the Prime Minister at the time, Yoshida Shigeru, was not an ardent supporter of widespread government intervention in the economy and refused to sanction publication. Nevertheless, many of the ideas in this failed plan—the promotion of exports, the support of import substitution and the rationalization of industry—reappeared in the '5-Year Plan for Economic Autonomy' in 1955. (Chalmers Johnson, *MITI and the Japanese Miracle*, 227–30.)

tion of this information to the public. In this fashion, they may have added an element of consistency to investment decisions by industries in addition to helping ensure consistency amongst policy measures for individual industries.

The economic upturn which began at the end of 1954 was to last another two years, with strong gains in both consumption and investment. Despite high aggregate wage gains, however, the economy at this time had a dual structure (*nijū kōzō*), with large wage differentials between big and small companies. This dual structure was impeding the realization of economic equality, to which the Japanese government was strongly committed. The causes of these wage differentials were variously identified as surplus labour, higher productivity of large companies, and labour immobility, but policy-makers agreed that innovation would help equalize wages amongst companies, providing a further incentive to promote technological change.[79]

Investment in the latter half of the 1950s was stimulated not just by the materials revolution and investment in materials industries. Rather, it was

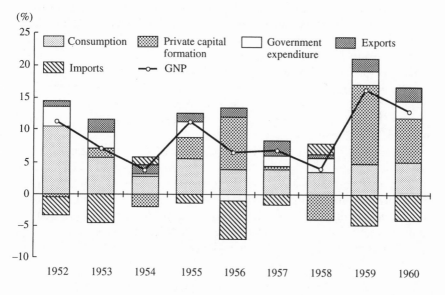

Fig. 2.4. Real GNP Growth and its Breakdown by Principal Component, 1952–1960

Source: Ōkurashō, *Shōwa Zaisei Shi: Shūsen kara Kōwa made*, 19. Data used in constructing this figure were in constant 1934–6 prices.

[79] Nakamura Takafusa, *The Postwar Japanese Economy*, 151–206.

also driven by investment in industries using these materials since demand for products made from them soared. Hence, greater demand for refrigerators increased applications for thin sheet, high-quality steel, generating increased investment in the steel industry. Furthermore, as household demand for cars appeared in the late 1950s, increased investment in that industry generated investment in the steel and machine tool industries. This marked the origins of the phrase 'investment generates investment' (*toshi ga toshi o yobu*):[80] between 1955 and 1960, corporate investment rose at an annual average rate of 26.5 per cent, far outstripping annual real GNP growth of 9.2 per cent.[81]

While the introduction of new technologies and the synergy between investments in different industries accounted for most of the rapid growth in capital expenditure, a third factor may also have contributed. Bank lending in the 1950s loosely re-forged the links between the *zaibatsu* companies; these business links were formalized through cross shareholdings, creating webs of corporations called *keiretsu* groups with city banks at their centres.[82] However, city banks were not content to leave unchallenged the virtual monopolies that individual *zaibatsu* had had in certain industries: they encouraged their *keiretsu* companies to expand into new areas as well as to compete fiercely in existing industries. Essentially, bank lending promoted a phenomenon called one set-ism, whereby each *keiretsu* group had at least one affiliated company in every industry. This behaviour probably did stimulate corporate investment, but the power of city banks to determine investment by affiliated companies was far from absolute. Hence, one set-ism was not as motivating a factor behind high growth in capital expenditure as was technological change or the synergy between investments amongst industries.

The economy turned down in the summer of 1957 as deterioration in the trade account necessitated tightening of monetary policy. This deterioration was partially caused by the surge in oil prices arising from the Suez incident in late 1956. However, import growth was also fuelled by an overheated domestic economy, stimulated by tax reductions of 100 billion yen in 1957 as well as by an increase in public works spending of the same amount. Tight fiscal policy had been maintained for the previous

[80] This phrase first officially appeared in the 1960 Economic White Paper. However, it is applicable to investment patterns in the latter half of the 1950s.

[81] Figures are measured in real terms based on 1980 prices and are for the fiscal year (Apr.–Mar.). (Keizai Kikaku Chō, *Kokumin Keizai Kessan Hōkoku: Shōwa 30 Nen – Shōwa 44 Nen* (Tokyo, Ōkurashō Insatsu Kyoku, 1988).)

[82] Because equity and bond markets were underdeveloped, Japanese companies were highly dependent on bank financing, and this dependency gave the banks influence over loan recipients. At the same time, banks themselves were highly dependent on central bank credit, since their loans expanded much faster than their deposit bases. (Kōsai Yutaka, 159–62.)

three years, with the government budget kept unchanged at 1 trillion yen. Nevertheless, strong economic growth had raised government revenues beyond expected levels, and the government in 1957 attempted to pass on the fruits of growth through tax cuts that were aimed primarily at the individual. Over the next fifteen years, fiscal policy would be character- ized by its intent to pass on the benefits of growth, but the timing of the 1957 tax reduction was unfortunate, and public works spending was put on hold in June of that year, several months after monetary policy was tightened.

Although the economic downturn was relatively brief (the economy began expanding again from the following summer), most economists and policy-makers anticipated a lengthier recession. With corporate invest- ment having almost doubled between 1955 and 1957, adjustment of cap- ital stock was expected to cause a severe downturn.[83] In actual fact, the dynamic synergy between corporate investment in diverse industries, strong consumption, and a surge in exports caused the downturn to be brief.[84] While policy-makers consistently underestimated growth from 1951 to 1972, what is even more striking is their over-pessimism about the duration of downturns. It is this which truly reflects Japan's lack of confidence about the durability of growth, and shows more clearly than anything else how surprised the Japanese must have been by their eco- nomic miracle.

With the economic recovery in 1958 came more concrete criteria for determining a rational industrial structure. Industries were no longer to be selected in the belief that they were somehow important in promoting economic autonomy, through their contribution to trade, employment, or improved living standards. Rather, industries were to be selected on the basis of income sensitivity and potential advances in productivity.[85] Industries which grew faster as incomes rose were to be promoted, as were industries where large productivity gains could be expected. Thus, industrial policy moved a step closer to explicitly promoting economic growth, since by attempting to influence resource allocation in such a way as to increase the weight of high-growth industries in the entire economy,

[83] The name given to this downturn was '*nabezoko fukeiki*', literally 'bottom of the pan recession'. The economic growth pattern was expected to show the shape of a pan—a sharp downturn followed by a lengthy period of almost no growth before an eventual upturn.

[84] The rise in exports as domestic demand slowed was a notable feature of Japanese development not only in the 1950s but in the following decades as well. This is commonly called the 'export drive' phenomenon.

[85] Recommendations from the Council for Adjusting the Industrial Structure (*Sangyō Kōzō Chōsa Kai*) of MITI in Nov. 1958. Although this may be the first instance where the government explicitly recognized the value of promoting those exports with a high income elasticity, the idea itself was reflected in MITI's 1953 attempt to produce a long-term eco- nomic plan. (Chalmers Johnson, *MITI and the Japanese Miracle*, 224.)

policy could conceivably increase the rate of growth of the economy over-all.

At the same time, for the purpose of supporting full employment, industrial policy also continued to target select income-insensitive industries. Policy supported agriculture through price supports, and a variety of new measures were introduced to block further competition in the distribution sector. The Department Store Law (*Hyakkaten Hō*) enacted in June 1956 set restrictions on store expansion, new store openings, and sales methods in order to protect small retailers. In July 1959, the Law on Special Measures to Adjust Retail Trade (*Kouri Shōgyō Chōsei Tokubetsu Sochi Hō*) restricted the activities of co-operatives and retail markets to ease competitive pressures. Small and medium enterprise policy in general also continued to emphasize protection rather than modernization.

The economic recovery which began in July 1958 would last forty-two months, the longest since the war. Growth would be more balanced, with strong advances in consumption, exports, and investment. Nevertheless, investment would exhibit a dynamism of its own, as capital outlays in one industry would stimulate capital expenditure in others. GNP growth for the decade would average slightly more than 8 per cent[86] and the strengthening of Japan's industrial base with its subsequent increased ability to export resulted in the achievement of economic independence. The problem of the dual structure eased greatly in the late 1950s under high economic growth, and would essentially disappear as a labour shortage emerged in the following decade.

Industrial policy in the 1950s, through rationalization and the promotion of new industries, had as its goals balanced trade, full employment, and improved living standards. The government deliberately attempted to affect resource allocation, promoting investment in potential export industries and in industries which might act as import substitutes. While many of the measures adopted, including tariffs and subsidies, seemed to run counter to market forces, one common characteristic to most measures was a commitment to competition in the long term. Even when MITI was promoting an industry, it fostered competition amongst firms in that industry by ensuring that foreign exchange allocations were granted to many firms rather than only to a few. Similarly, MITI stimulated the diffusion of technology amongst firms in an industry to prevent any one company from gaining a permanent advantage. Measures to support industries were also designed to be temporary: tariff rates and subsidies were reduced as industries became competitive.[87]

[86] Average annual growth in 1970 prices for fiscal years 1952–9. (Ōkurashō Zaisei Shi Shitsu, *Shōwa Zaisei Shi: Shūsen kara Kōwa made*, 19: 29.)

[87] For reductions in government loans, see Tables 4.1 and 4.2. The Japanese government reduced few trade barriers in the 1950s, but aggressively reduced tariffs in the 1960s.

While rationalization measures appeared most concerned with increasing the competitiveness of designated industries, they also controlled the economic costs associated with modernization. Specifically, rationalization policy attempted to supervise the trade-off between maintaining employment and promoting modernization, as can be seen in rationalization policy towards machinery, electric machinery, and coal. Concern over employment is also apparent from policy measures towards agriculture, small and medium enterprises, and distribution. For these latter two, employment considerations in the 1950s probably outweighed short-run arguments for economic efficiency, and industrial policy blocked competition rather than using it as a tool to shape development.

Policy formulation and implementation was by no means exclusive to MITI. While MITI's input in determining the allocation of low-interest loans through the Japan Development Bank was undoubtedly large, the Ministry of Finance nominally supervised JDB activities. The over-loaned nature of Japanese city banks[88] also gave the government some control over the allocation of bank loans, but again it was not MITI but the Bank of Japan which exercised this power. The Ministry of Finance had final say over tax breaks, the Economic Planning Agency, with input from politicians, industries, and all bureaucracies, determined the final shape of the mid-term economic plans, and the Ministry of Finance also set tariff rates. The Ministry of Agriculture controlled policy towards farming, the Ministry of Transport had power over ocean shipping and thus influenced shipbuilding, and the Ministry of Construction helped to decide infrastructure investment. MITI's direct powers were substantial, particularly since it controlled the allocation of all imports, but it was not alone in shaping industrial policy.

2.3 Trade Liberalization in a Maturing Economy (1961–1970)

In other words, through liberalization, inefficiencies and irrationalities that accompanied previous administrative controls will be eliminated. It will become much easier to freely procure inexpensive foreign materials, production costs will fall, and firms will be required to try to rationalize to an international standard. Liberalization will make possible much more efficient use of economic resources, facilitating an improved economic system and contributing to broad improvements

---

[88] The over-loaned nature of city banks rose from 1949 to 1951 and then eased slightly until 1954. It essentially disappeared in 1955, with the large trade surplus, but thereafter the over-loaned position of city banks increased with high demand for loans arising from the investment boom of the latter half of the 1950s. (Kōsai Yutaka, *Kōdo Seichō no Jidai*, 99–101; 112–13.)

in national living standards, thereby promoting gains for the entire national economy. (Plan to Liberalize Trade and Foreign Investment, 1960.)[89]

Japan in the 1950s had moved from economic recovery to independence and expansion. The 1960s would witness equally dramatic change, as Japan recorded unprecedented growth while removing controls on trade and foreign capital inflows. Many of the concerns that plagued Japan in the 1950s, surplus labour, a dual economic structure, and trade deficits, would disappear as the economy grew 10.7 per cent per annum, up from the average growth of 9 per cent in the latter half of the previous decade. Phrases such as the 'consumer revolution', 'doubling national income', and 'investment generates investment' would characterize much of the 1960s. Even so, the decade would end on a sour note as concerns over social welfare produced the 1970 slogan 'Down with GNP' (*Kutabare GNP*).

The major challenge facing the economy in the early 1960s was the liberalization of foreign trade. Japan, who had joined the IMF in 1952 and GATT in 1955, had lagged far behind European nations in freeing imports.[90] Additionally, the US share of world exports had declined sharply, dropping from 29.4 per cent in 1953 to 18.7 per cent in 1959 while Japan's share rose from 2.8 to 4.9 per cent.[91] International pressures had caused Japan to voluntarily limit exports of textiles and other light manufactures in the 1950s, but mounting criticism of Japan by 1960 necessitated more drastic measures. As a result, the Japanese government pledged in 1960 to liberalize fully 90 per cent of its imports by 1963.

Plans to liberalize trade were included in the National Income Doubling Plan (*Kokumin Shotoku Baizō Keikaku*), the third mid-term economic outline proposed by the Japanese government since World War II. Like its two predecessors, this plan called for raising living standards and maintaining employment. It differed, however, by covering a ten-year rather than a five-year period. More importantly, this plan also explicitly recognized growth as a policy goal for the first time, targeting an average annual increase in economic output of 7.2 per cent between 1961 and 1970.[92]

[89] Keizai Kikaku Chō Chōsei Kyoku, 'Bōeki Kawase Jiyūka Keikaku Taikō', *Bōeki Kawase Jiyūka Keikaku* (Tokyo, Keizai Kikaku Chō Chōsei Kyoku, 1960), 80–7.

[90] In 1960, only 40% of Japanese imports were liberalized while on average 90% of European imports had been freed. Tsuruta Toshimasa, *Sengo Nihon no Sangyō Seisaku*, 83–5.

[91] William Branson, Herbert Giersch, and Peter Peterson, 'Trends in the United States International Trade and Investment', in Martin Feldstein (ed.), *The American Economy in Transition* (Chicago, National Bureau of Economic Research, 1990), 196.

[92] The National Income Doubling Plan did not provide any detailed quantitative analysis as to how growth was to be achieved. Rather, it called for government investment in social capital to rise, and advocated growth which is effected through self-determined corporate activities. Hence, it was market-orientated, as can also be inferred from the plan's assertions

Following the publication of the National Income Doubling Plan in December 1960, the economic upturn was to last another year. In line with stated intentions, government spending accelerated sharply through 1962. While this supported the expansion, the driving force behind growth was again capital expenditure. The synergy between investments in different industries continued, with investment in a single industry stimulating investment across all industries. To this autonomous cycle was added increased demand for investment to cope with trade liberalization, with the result that corporate outlays on plant and equipment almost doubled in the two years 1960 and 1961.

Consumer outlays in 1960 and 1961 also rose more than 10 per cent for the first time in post-war Japan, marking the start of a consumer revolution.[93] Demand for new products increased, as can be seen by the rising diffusion rates for vacuum cleaners, stereos, and transistor radios in addition to the 'three sacred treasures', televisions, washing machines, and refrigerators. Wage gains were instrumental to this growth, rising almost twice as fast for the first five years of the 1960s as they had in the latter half of the previous decade.[94] Falling production costs and prices also contributed, by increasing the purchasing power of the consumer.

A worsening balance of payments position necessitated monetary tightening in July 1961 and again in September, causing the economic expansion to falter from year end. Once more, the downturn was expected to be prolonged, since a lengthy adjustment in capital stock was anticipated following the enormous increase in investment. This pessimism again proved false: as Japan's trade position improved in 1963, monetary policy was eased, sparking another upturn which would last until the final quarter of 1964.[95]

Against this background of trade liberalization and the explicit promotion of growth raged a debate about how industrial policy should be used to effect the smooth transition to a free economy. On one side was the bureaucracy, who advocated that the state should actively promote a new industrial order to cope with foreign competition. According to this theory of a new industrial order (*shin sangyō taisei ron*), the government

that any strengthening of regulations should be avoided as should policies which are difficult to administer. The plan was also market-based in that it called for freeing foreign trade and replacing direct controls on rice with indirect controls. See Keizai Kikaku Chō Keizai Shingi Kai, *Kokumin Shotoku Baizō Keikaku* (Tokyo, Ōkurashō Insatsu Kyoku, 1960), 3–66.

[93] This phrase appears for the first time in the 1960 Economic White Paper.

[94] After rising 5.6% between 1955 and 1960, wage gains average 10.4% for the 1960–5 period.

[95] The Tokyo Olympics also contributed substantially to economic growth in the early 1960s. Infrastructure investment related to the Olympics totalled 970 billion yen, while Olympic-related outlays by the private sector constituted fully 0.9% of GNP from 1961 to 1964. (Kōsai Yutaka, *Kōdo Seichō no Jidai*, 169–70.) In particular, the Tokyo Olympics acted as a catalyst to sales of colour televisions.

should establish councils on troubled industries, with representatives from business, academia, and the government deciding appropriate measures to facilitate the adjustment of such industries. This concept was a direct extension of past efforts to help industries rationalize or adjust to a cyclical downturn, but it was broader since it applied to any industry facing strong competition from foreign imports. The bureaucracy also suggested that it should have an active role in debating mergers, adjusting investment, promoting specialization, and promoting diversification in order to strengthen Japanese industries to meet foreign competition.[96] To achieve these goals, MITI drew up the Law Concerning Temporary Measures to Promote Designated Industries (*Tokutei Sangyō Shinkō Rinji Sochi Hōan*); after receiving cabinet approval, the government submitted it to the Diet in March 1963.

On the other side of the debate were those who advocated a theory of autonomous adjustment (*jishu chōsei ron*). Proponents shared many ideas in common with supporters of a new industrial order: both sides believed in increasing firm size, in the dangers of excessive competition, in the need for mergers, and in the desirability of relaxing the Anti-Monopoly Law. However, advocates of autonomous adjustment, mainly businessmen, saw little need for state input in responding to trade liberalization. By exerting pressure on politicians, this group managed to ensure that MITI's new legislation never came to a vote.

Trade liberalization itself eliminated two major tools of industrial policy. First, the government's ability to control directly the allocation of imports was reduced, thereby breaking one of the sticks the state had wielded to guide corporate investment.[97] Secondly, the government's ability to offer industries protection from trade as an inducement to domestic investment was also weakened. The failure to pass the Law Concerning Temporary Measures to Promote Designated Industries meant that these tools were not replaced. Even so, the actual implementation of industrial policy suffered little in the early 1960s. The government still promoted investment through tax breaks and subsidized loans and continued to support industries that were income sensitive and were likely to be subject to productivity advances. Thus, industrial policy continued to target

---

[96] The government did not feel that it should determine mergers on its own, but rather should do so in co-operation with business (*kanmin kyōchō hōshiki*). (Tsuruta Toshimasa, *Sengo Nihon no Sangyō Seisaku*, 90–6.)

[97] The government did not entirely lose its ability to use trade controls as a stick to influence corporate behaviour. For example, in 1965, MITI threatened to cut off Sumitomo Metal's access to imported coking coal under the Import Control Ordinance (*Yunyū Bōeki Kanri Rei*), a cabinet order of 1949, unless the company agreed to limit production (Chalmers Johnson, *MITI and the Japanese Miracle*, 268–71). However, trade liberalization ended the government's power to regulate imports in all but the most exceptional circumstances.

industries such as steel and shipbuilding and at the same time policy emphasized new industries such as computers and anti-pollution equipment. Moreover, the private sector and the state broadly agreed on actions needed to increase Japanese competitiveness to meet foreign competition. This meant that the government could, through its various councils with industry representation, lead business to accept specific policies since both groups agreed on general policy outline. As a result, the government was able to smoothly promote mergers. Industrial policy thus continued to target growth industries, utilizing many of the measures it had used in the past. Control over the import of foreign technology gave the government power to promote new industries and to shape the pattern of development of existing industries. Low-interest loans and tax breaks offered further incentives, although their relative magnitude declined. As a percentage of new industry loans, those offered by the Japan Development Bank fell from 11 per cent in 1955 to 3.5 per cent by 1960, tax breaks declined in importance, and export subsidies were also reduced.[98] Nevertheless, these loans and tax breaks affected investment decisions at least at the margin. Moreover, by acting as a signal of reduced risk to private banks, government support for select industries positively influenced the flow of private sector capital to those industries.[99] Even so, industrial policy in the early 1960s differed in that the government's unilateral ability to determine policy response was reduced. Private sector agreement on policy direction was crucial, since the government's control over import allocation was dissipating.

Although pro-growth industrial policy was largely unchanged, the disappearance of surplus labour in the Japanese economy in the early 1960s had a substantial impact on policy to support employment. Industrial policy towards small and medium enterprises and towards the distribution sector became much more positive, promoting rather than blocking competition and modernization. The Basic Law for Small and Medium Enterprises (*Chūshō Kigyō Kihon Hō*), implemented in July 1963, called for the modernization of plant, improved technology and mergers to raise the competitiveness of smaller enterprises, increased exports, and protection (where possible) from imports. The law also advocated utilizing tax breaks, government funds, and government guidance to raise the productivity of smaller enterprises.[100] In short, rather than passively supporting

---

[98] Nihon Ginkō Chōsa Tōkei Kyoku, *Honpō Keizai Nenpō* (Tokyo, Nihon Ginkō, various years).

[99] For more on the signalling function of government loans, see Jenny Corbett, 'International Perspectives on Financing: Evidence from Japan', *Oxford Review of Economic Policy*, 4 (1990), 1–23.

[100] *Roppō Zensho*, 2 (Tokyo, Yūhikaku, 1990), 3172–3. This law followed the implementation of the Law to Promote the Modernization of Small and Medium Enterprises (*Chūshō Kigyō Kindaika Sokushin Hō*) in Apr. 1963, and is in many aspects an extension of it.

smaller enterprises to ensure employment, policy began to move towards promoting the rationalization and modernization of smaller enterprises just as it had other industries in the past.

That the government adopted a more positive approach towards smaller enterprises can also be inferred from the opening of the Tokyo Second Section stock exchange in 1961. This move facilitated trading in the equity of medium-sized companies and thus increased the ability of smaller companies to raise capital. Capital was also provided by the government through the Smaller Business Finance Corporation, whose loans rose 1.8 times in the 1960–5 period. However, despite these efforts to promote modernization, competition amongst smaller enterprises was not meant to be cut-throat; it was to be gradual to ensure few bankruptcies and hence continued employment of workers.[101] This attempt to control competitive forces can also be seen in policy towards the distribution sector. Despite permitting the establishment and expansion of supermarkets in Japan, distribution policies continued to block expansion of department stores.

The concept of controlling unemployment by regulating competitive forces undoubtedly lay behind the emphasis on the problem of 'excessive competition' (*katō kyōsō*) that appeared during this time. This term in its simplest sense was used to describe an industry characterized by numerous producers, too small to be competitive internationally, but unable to increase size because low profits limited their ability to invest. This simple definition does not necessarily have any economic validity;[102] it merely reflects the widely held belief that larger firms would be more productive. However, the term 'excessive competition' also implied concern over the dislocation of capital and labour that would arise as unregulated market forces caused bankruptcies.[103] The government, in using this term, implicitly suggested that policy should curtail dislocation costs by helping select industries to restructure.

Usage of the term 'excessive competition' did not stop here. It had a third and even more misunderstood meaning, signifying the capacity

---

[101] The Law Concerning the Organization of Small and Medium Enterprise Groups (*Chūshō Kigyō Dantai no Sōshiki ni Kansuru Hōritsu*; implemented in Apr. 1958, and revised numerous times since) called for forming smaller enterprises into groups to ensure that they received a fair chance to participate in economic activity. As such, this law limited competitive forces facing smaller companies.

[102] Only if economies of scale are present will large firms have an advantage over smaller ones.

[103] The perceived need to regulate competition may have arisen in part because of the Chinese characters that the Japanese adopted to define the word 'competition' when it was first introduced from the West in the 19th cent. The two characters used literally mean 'to fight for power' and 'to war with'; with competition associated with battle, it is not surprising that regulating competition came to be of concern. Conversations with Tsujimura Kōtarō, Professor (ret.), Keio University.

excesses generated by investment competition amongst large firms in an industry. Such excess capacity can arise in a fully competitive industry which is subject to unanticipated increases in demand, and government measures to promote investment in an industry can also contribute to the emergence of excess capacity.[104] In this sense, the term 'excessive competition' became synonymous with excess capacity, and policy attempted to minimize the economic costs associated with overly large investment.

Industrial policy was also used in the early 1960s to control competitive forces in industries which had previously received government support to stimulate growth. Japan's first experience with this sort of policy reversal occurred in the coal industry in the previous decade. Originally expected to expand, the coal industry had received the usual tax breaks, low-interest loans, and trade protection to stimulate increased investment. However, as oil became relatively cheaper and easily available,[105] the Japanese coal industry was dealt a blow from which it could not recover, and industrial policy towards coal from 1956 was aimed at fostering an orderly decline. The marine transport industry, the expansion of which the government had targeted at least partially in an attempt to support the domestic shipbuilding industry, fell into a five-year recession from 1958. To cope with the downturn, policy initially emphasized reducing costs and limiting damaging price competition. Efforts culminated with the Law on Special Measures to Reorganize the Marine Transport Industry (*Kaiungyō no Saiken Seibi ni Kansuru Rinji Sochi Hō*; July 1963) which fostered mergers in order to adjust industry capacity.

If policy towards smaller enterprises and towards distribution began to emphasize productivity increases, policy towards agriculture became the reverse, focusing on supporting employment and agricultural income at the expense of productivity. By 1960, rapid gains from introducing new cultivation techniques and the widespread use of chemical fertilizers had been exhausted. Further major increases in productivity were constrained by farm size, and policy in the 1960s did not address this issue. At the same time, price supports for agriculture were increased, guaranteeing a livelihood for those remaining in agriculture.[106]

The expansion came to an end in October 1964 as tighter monetary policy and falling corporate earnings caused another downturn. During

[104] For further details, see Ch. 5, pp. 130–2, 141–3. It is also possible that government concern reflected a fear that bankruptcies would occur in industries which suffered occasionally from excess capacity and that as a result such industries would become more tightly oligopolistic as time passed. In other words, the term 'excessive competition' may be related to the belief that competition in certain industries is unstable over time—that it may ultimately produce tight oligopolies.

[105] Oil imports were liberalized in July 1962.

[106] With a tighter labour market, the number of workers in agriculture and forestry declined from 16 million in 1955 to 11.5 million in 1965. (Ōkurashō Zaisei Shi Shitsu, *Shōwa Zaisei Shi: Shūsen kara Kōwa made*, 19: 31.)

the first half of the 1960s the Japanese economy had undergone a remarkable transformation. Economic growth became entrenched as an explicit policy target in the National Income Doubling Plan; actual performance exceeded those targets to the extent that national income had doubled by 1965 rather than by 1970.[107] With high growth, the problem of surplus labour disappeared: worker income had been more than three times agricultural income in 1955 but this had shrunk to approximately twice by the early 1970s.[108] At the same time, trade was largely liberalized. Japan had liberalized 89 per cent of imports by 1963,[109] and promised the following year to liberalize foreign investment into Japan. Even so, the Japanese current account showed only a small deficit in 1964 and would show a chronic surplus thereafter.

Despite this incredibly smooth transition to freer trade, Japan again dramatically overestimated the severity of the economic downturn. In part, this pessimism was caused by a rash of corporate bankruptcies, the result of the over-expansion of corporate credit in the first half of the decade.[110] Total liabilities of bankruptcies in 1964 and 1965 exceeded those of the previous twelve years, reaching 1 billion yen.[111] Any initial hopes of an economic recovery when the Bank of Japan eased in January 1965 were dashed as large firms went under. Sanyō Special Steel declared bankruptcy in March 1965; it, together with the bankruptcies of Sun Wave and Japan Special Steel, were amongst the largest in a decade. In June 1965, Yamaichi Securities, the second largest broker in Japan, was saved from insolvency only by large government-secured loans. In 1965 alone, 5,690 firms declared bankruptcy, a record total since the end of the Occupation. These insolvencies, together with a tight labour market and disappointed expectations of stable growth, underpinned a belief that the 1964–5 recession was structural in nature and would consequently be protracted.[112]

This pessimism would once more prove unfounded as economic activity picked up from October 1965. This upturn would last almost five years and real GNP would grow at its fastest rate ever, expanding on average over 11 per cent per annum.[113] Government spending would act as the initial catalyst to accelerating growth. In July 1965 the government

[107] In current prices, GNP doubled between fiscal years 1960 and 1965. In constant 1980 prices, GNP had doubled by fiscal year 1968.

[108] Nakamura Takafusa, *The Postwar Japanese Economy*, 159.

[109] Kōsai Yutaka, *Kōdo Seichō no Jidai*, 148–9.

[110] Corporate accounts payable rose to 17 trillion yen in 1965, up from 8 trillion in 1960; corporate current assets more than doubled during this time, reaching 36.1 trillion yen in 1965 from 16.7 trillion yen in 1960. (Sōmu Chō Tōkei Kyoku, *Nihon Chōki Tōkei Sōran*, 4 (Tokyo, Nihon Tōkei Kyōkai, 1988), 196–7.)

[111] Ibid. 215.   [112] Kōsai Yutaka, *Kōdo Seichō no Jidai*, 171–5.

[113] Growth rates are in real terms using 1980 prices. (Keizai Kikaku Chō, *Kokumin Keizai Kessan Hōkoku: Shōwa 30 Nen – Shōwa 44 Nen*.)

announced plans to issue deficit bonds[114] for the first time since 1949; these were included in the 1966 budget, which called for tax cuts of 310 billion yen in addition to deficit bonds of 730 billion yen.[115] As a result, government spending surged more than 19 per cent in 1966.[116] Consumption also contributed, as tax cuts resulted in a 10 per cent rise in outlays. Consumption was again characterized by expenditure on new products: the 'three sacred treasures' gave way to the 'three Cs', cars, air conditioners, and colour televisions, and diffusion rates for these products soared in the latter half of the 1960s. However, even more than consumption, corporate investment was the driving force behind the economic expansion. The 1965–70 period saw corporate investment rise 2.7 times, as firms actively increased plant size. Investment in one industry continued to fuel investment in others; partly as a result of this investment synergy, plant and equipment investment accounted for over one quarter of

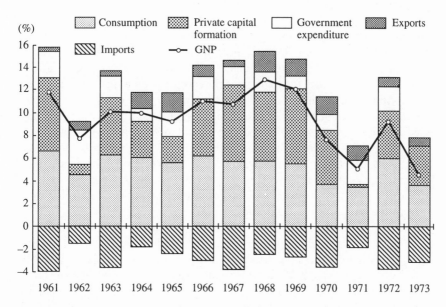

Fig. 2.5. Real GNP Growth and its Breakdown by Principal Component, 1961–1973
Source: Ōkurashō, *Shōwa Zaisei Shi: Shūsen kara Kōwa made*, 19.

[114] Japan has a rather curious and misleading classification system for government bond issues. These are divided into two types, construction bonds and deficit bonds. The only difference between the two is that revenues raised from construction bonds must be used for public works, but both are issued to cover deficits in government revenues. According to the Japanese classification, the bonds issued in 1966 were construction bonds.
[115] Kōsai Yutaka, *Kōdo Seichō no Jidai*, 174.
[116] Keizai Kikaku Chō, *Kokumin Keizai Kessan Hōkoku: Shōwa 30 Nen – Shōwa 44 Nen*.

GNP growth. More importantly, investment was driven by the liberalization of foreign direct investment. In order to meet the perceived threat that foreign capital flowing into Japan might pose, Japanese companies undertook massive investment in newer and larger plants.

When Japan in the early 1960s agreed to meet international guidelines on trade and capital restrictions for developed countries, it implicitly promised to liberalize foreign direct investment. Nevertheless, Japan dragged its feet until 1967, after which the liberalization of inflows of foreign capital proceeded in five steps until 1973.[117] Just as industrial policy had concentrated on strengthening the economy to cope with trade liberalization in the early 1960s, its goal in the latter half of the decade was to help promote adjustment to capital liberalization. In practice, industrial policy would target industry and firm size, attempting to increase effective size through adjusting investment, forming cartels, promoting mergers, strengthening vertical ties across industry groups, and strengthening corporate balance sheets.

Although the Law Concerning Temporary Measures to Promote Designated Enterprises failed to pass the Diet, the government had sufficient tools at its disposal to influence corporate activities. Cartelization, tax incentives, government loans, and government guidance were all used to shape investment decisions. Not surprisingly, many of those industries which had first been targeted as crucial to economic autonomy, then targeted as subject to strong income effects and productivity increases, and finally targeted as needing help in responding to trade liberalization were once again the focus of industrial policy. Hence, steel, chemicals, and shipbuilding continued to receive government support albeit at reduced rates while policy also fostered electronics, nuclear power, computer software, and anti-pollution technology.

While the government had promoted mergers between large companies in the early 1960s, such as that between Mitsubishi Japan Heavy Industry and New Mitsubishi Heavy Industry in 1964, the pace of large mergers picked up in the latter half of the decade. Prince and Nissan Motors were merged in 1965, Nisshō and Iwai merged in 1968, Yawata Steel and Fuji Steel were merged into New Japan Steel in 1970, and Daiichi Bank and Nippon Kangyō Bank were combined in 1971. This emphasis on increas-

---

[117] The first step towards liberalizing foreign capital was taken in July 1967. The second round of liberalization occurred in Mar. 1969, the third in Sep. 1970, the fourth in Aug. 1971, and the fifth in May 1973. After the third round of capital liberalization, foreign investment in Japanese companies was permitted up to 50% ownership; this was raised to 100% as liberalization proceeded. In actuality, restrictions on investment in Japan were initially strengthened in the mid-1960s. From 1956 to 1963, yen-denominated foreign investment had been allowed for US firms as long as they agreed not to repatriate income, and UK firms were permitted such yen-based investment from 1962. However, yen-denominated foreign investment was outlawed from 1964, and until 1967 almost all foreign investment was blocked. For details see Tsuruta Toshimasa, *Sengo Nihon no Sangyō Seisaku*, 116–20.

ing firm size has its roots in Japanese ideas about excessive competition
and an implicit belief in economies of scale in production. However, the
merger frenzy was stimulated most by a fear that Japanese companies
would be overwhelmed by US capital. MITI compared capital liberalization to foreign demands in 1853 that Japan open up to the rest of the
world.[118] Those demands had brought down the Tokugawa government,
and MITI worried that capital liberalization could have a similar cata-
clysmic effect as Japan lost control of its industrial base. Such worries
also lay behind revisions of Japan's Commerce Law (*Shōgyō Hō*) in the
mid-1960s, permitting corporate boards to issue new shares and place
them directly with other corporations, all without shareholder approval.
The cross placement of shares increased sharply in the latter half of the
decade, not only providing protection from foreign take-overs but also
strengthening existing *keiretsu* ties.[119]

Industrial policy that had been shaped by employment concerns in the
1950s continued, in the latter half of the 1960s, more to promote competition than to block it. The government supported modernization of
smaller companies: the gradual disappearance of surplus labour motivated smaller companies to invest heavily in new plant and equipment,
and government funds for smaller companies were increased 2.5 times
between 1965 and 1969, as loans from the Smaller Business Finance
Corporation reached 308 billion yen.[120] Policy towards distribution continued to permit the expansion of supermarkets, thus promoting some
rationalization in the sector even though controls over expanding department stores remained in force.[121] Only in the case of agricultural policy
was there little genuine attempt to stimulate modernization. The government provided price supports and protection from foreign imports, guaranteeing agricultural income but giving little or no incentive to improve
productivity. If anything, government agricultural policy became more
concerned with maintaining the status quo in the industry. Subsidies to
farmers rose with the adoption in 1960 of an income compensation formula for determining the price at which the government bought rice, and
sizeable subsidy increases became a trend as the decade progressed.[122]

[118] Capital liberalization was called 'the second coming of the black ships' (ibid. 120), a
reference to the three US ships under Admiral Perry which sailed into Yokohama Harbour
in 1853 and demanded that Japan, closed for centuries to foreigners, sell them supplies. By
caving in to these demands, the Tokugawa government revealed its weakness, and this acted
as a catalyst to its subsequent fall and the success of the Meiji Restoration in 1868.

[119] Itō Takatoshi, *The Japanese Economy* (Cambridge, Mass., MIT Press, 1992), 190–2.

[120] Chūshō Kigyō Kinyū Kōko, *Chūshō Kigyō Kinyū Kōko Sanjūnen Shi* (Tokyo, Chūshō
Kigyō Kinyū Kōko, 1984), 684–5.

[121] The expansion of supermarkets was regulated from 1974 with the passage of the
Large-Scale Retail Law (*Daikibo Kouri Tenpo ni Okeru Kourigyō no Jigyō Katsudō no
Chōsei ni Kansuru Hōritsu*).

[122] From 1952 to 1960, the government used an income parity formula to determine rice

Industrial policy in the 1960s underwent several important changes. True, policy for some industries continued to promote growth, while policy for others emphasized controlling the costs of competition. This duality between types of industrial policy had existed for the entire post-war period, and would continue to characterize industrial policy up to the present. However, the 1960s saw a lessening of the government's role in the economy. Trade and capital liberalization effectively removed important tools that the government had used to influence corporate activity, including control over the import of materials and technologies as well as the ability to grant trade protection. Additionally, by blocking the passage of MITI's Law Concerning Temporary Measures to Promote Designated Industries, Japanese business won the debate for limiting active government participation in formulating corporate investment strategy.

Even more important to changing industrial policy was growing public discontent in the late 1960s. Although the government and business agreed on the need to pursue mergers and larger firm size, this agreement was accompanied by a heated public debate about the economic impact of bigger companies. The press generally sided with economists, emphasizing the efficiency losses arising from oligopolistic or monopolistic industries.[123] Public dissatisfaction hit a new high with the merger of Yawata Steel and Fuji Steel in 1970 and this contributed to the strengthening of the Anti-Monopoly Law in 1977.[124]

Not only was there growing public mistrust of industrial policy in regard to its emphasis on firm size, but so too was there a public reassessment of the basic purpose of industrial policy. Such policy had had as its primary goal high economic growth, and to that end it had promoted corporate investment. There had been little focus on social welfare, and the problems of pollution, overcrowding, and a low quality of life became of increasing concern in the latter half of the 1960s. These problems helped start another re-evaluation of industrial policy by the government. Noting in 1968 that 'industrial policy which enriches industry while pauperizing individuals clearly is theoretically incorrect',[125] Amaya Naohiro of MITI stressed the need to redefine industrial policy. Nevertheless, the

prices. This formula essentially maintained real agricultural incomes since rice prices moved with changes in the prices of goods purchased by farmers. In 1960 this formula was replaced with a production cost, income compensation scheme which assigned the average industrial wage to evaluate agricultural labour inputs, thus assuring that agricultural income rose with urban wages. (Nakamura Takafusa, *The Postwar Japanese Economy*, 195–6.)

[123] Tsuruta Toshimasa, *Sengo Nihon no Sangyō Seisaku*, 145–54.

[124] This was one factor, but more important were revelations of price collusion amongst Japanese corporations at the time of the first oil crisis.

[125] Amaya Naohiro, 'Sangyō Seisaku no Hanshō to Tenkai no Tame ni', *Tsūsan Jaanaru*, 2.5 (1969) (Tokyo, Tsūshō Sangyō Shō), 22–34.

government was slow to act,[126] and as new pollution scandals rocked the nation,[127] public disgust with policy mounted.

Tighter monetary policy brought an end to the fifty-seven-month expansion in July 1970, but whereas monetary policy had been tightened in the past to avoid a balance of payments crisis, tightening in 1970 occurred because of an acceleration of inflation. Achieving real growth of 10.7 per cent per annum in the 1960s, the Japanese economy in 1967 surpassed West Germany's in size, becoming the second largest non-

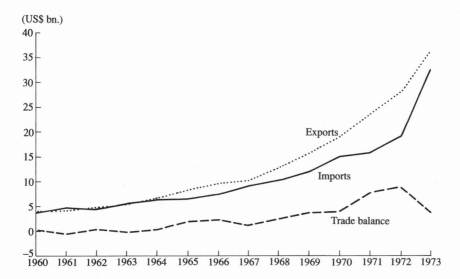

Fig. 2.6. Trends in Exports, Imports, and the Trade Balance, 1960–1973
Source: Nihon Ginkō, *Keizai Tōkei Nenpō*.

[126] Not until the early 1970s did the government acknowledge the need to focus industrial policy on solving the problems of overcrowding, pollution, inflation, and the shortage of affordable quality housing. See Sangyō Kōzō Shingikai, '70 Nendai no Tsūshō Sangyō Seisaku', *Tsūsan Jaanaru*, 4.3 (1971) (Tokyo, Tsūshō Sangyō Shō), 1–67. This report also stressed that industrial policy should contribute to international aid, promote new technologies, and foster new industries.

[127] Pollution scandals were not new to post-war Japan, including as they did the 1953 outbreak of mercury poisoning (the Minamata disease) in Kyushu, the 1959 outbreak of Yokkaichi asthma caused by sulfuric acid fumes, and the outbreak of cadmium poisoning (itai-itai disease) in Toyama Prefecture. However, the 1970 pollution scandals helped convince the public that pollution was not limited to isolated instances but in fact threatened the whole of Japan. These 1970 scandals included a report by the National Medical Students Union on lead poisoning in Tokyo, the discovery of more cadmium-poisoned rice in Toyama, and photochemical smog poisoning cases in Tokyo. See Uchino Tatsurō, *Japan's Postwar Economy: An Insider's View of its History and its Future* (Tokyo, Kodansha International, 1983), 165–9.

communist economy in the world.[128] Despite substantial trade and capital
liberalization, the Japanese current account showed a cumulative surplus
of 5.2 billion US dollars between 1965 and 1969.[129] This phenomenal
growth was not without problems. Japanese exporters invested as if there
was no limit to the possible increase in exports, and as exports surged,
friction with trading partners deepened. Public dissatisfaction with government policy steadily increased, and widespread use of the slogan
'Down with GNP' (*Kutabare GNP*) in 1970 reflected perceptions that
government policy favoured corporate interests while ignoring the problems of pollution and a poor quality of life.

2.4   Fragmenting National Consensus and External Shocks (1970–1973)

Public distrust of industrial policy deepened further in the early 1970s.
Broad agreement that the goal of policy was economic growth had
already been battered by concerns over social welfare, but unanticipated
external events would call into question the basic ability of policy-makers
to direct economic growth in the appropriate direction. Macro-policy
mistakes would compound this declining public faith in the omniscience
of state management. Overly expansive fiscal and monetary policy, a
response both to the demands for improved social capital as well as to
the 1970–1 downturn, would cause inflation to soar even before the first
oil shock. As a result, when OPEC more than quadrupled oil prices, the
Japanese economy would actually contract, falling 0.8 per cent in real
terms in 1974.[130]

Richard Nixon's presidency has left an indelible mark on Japanese history, but not because of Watergate or its similarity to Japan's own political débâcle, the Lockheed Scandal which brought down the
government.[131] Rather, his name lives on in the Japanese language in the
phrase 'Nixon shock' (*Nikkuson Shokku*), a reference to his decisions to
recognize China and to suspend convertibility of the US dollar. Both of
these events caught the Japanese completely off-guard and undermined
confidence in the bureaucracy's ability to shape policy.

[128] Keizai Kikaku Chō, *Kokumin Keizai Kessan Hōkoku: Shōwa 30 Nen – Shōwa 44 Nen*.
[129] Sōmu Chō Tōkei Kyoku, *Nihon Chōki Tōkei Sōran*, 3 (Tokyo, Nihon Tōkei Kyōkai, 1988), 100.
[130] Measured in 1985 prices on a calendar year basis. (Keizai Kikaku Chō, *Kokumin Keizai Kessan Nenpō* (Tokyo, Ōkurashō Insatsu Kyoku, 1991).)
[131] The Lockheed Scandal broke in Feb. 1976 and eventually led to the arrest of former Prime Minister Tanaka Kakuei on charges of accepting bribes from Lockheed Corporation. The LDP lost the Upper House election late in 1976 forcing Miki Takeo, then Prime Minister, to resign.

The economic downturn which began in mid-1970 lasted seventeen months, almost half as long again as the previous recession. For once, however, there was not much pessimism about the severity of the downturn. Following as it did a record expansion of almost five years in length, an adjustment period was viewed as natural. Ironically, however, this downturn marked the end of double digit growth in real GNP. Growth in 1971 was only 4.3 per cent, and during the 1972–3 expansion, average real GNP growth was 8 per cent.[132] This expansion was sparked by both an easing of monetary policy, as well as rising government outlays which helped to promote first consumption and then corporate and residential investment.

Industrial policy in the early 1970s attempted to respond to public demands for improved social welfare in an effort to provide a rationale for its continued existence. This is apparent from the 1971 report 'Industrial and Trade Policies in the 1970s' (*70 Nendai no Tsūshō Sangyō Seisaku*) issued by MITI's Industrial Structure Council (*Sangyō Kōzō Shingikai*).[133] This report emphasized the management of economic growth, rather than the simple pursuit of growth as a policy goal. To that end, the report recommended several new criteria in selecting industries appropriate to Japan's industrial structure. Not only were industries to be selected on the basis of high income elasticity of demand, rising productivity, and ability to absorb employment, but also important were considerations of pollution, improving working conditions, and easing urban overcrowding. The report also recommended that policy help to solve trade friction by directing investment towards the infrastructure and away from exporters.

At the same time, industrial policy was to continue to foster new industries and promote adjustment of declining industries. New industries thought to fulfil many of the above criteria were largely knowledge-intensive industries, those that involved intensive R&D including electronic machinery, industrial robots, ICs, nuclear power, computers, and fine chemicals. Industries with a high degree of processing were targeted, including telecommunications equipment, office automation equipment, pollution equipment, and machine tools, while knowledge industries themselves, such as information management, software, and system engineering, were also selected. The report also identified the fashion industry as knowledge-intensive on the grounds of its high content of skilled and creative labour. In regard to declining industries, the report called for government guidance to promote adjustment in labour-intensive industries and low value-added industries.

---

[132] Keizai Kikaku Chō, *Kokumin Keizai Kessan Nenpō*, 1991.
[133] '70 Nendai no Tsūshō Sangyō Seisaku', *Tsūshō Jaanaru*, 4.3 (1971), 1–67.

External developments would limit the influence of this plan in shaping industrial policy; they would also serve to undermine confidence in industrial policy itself. First, recognition of China by the US in 1971 caught Japanese foreign policy unawares. Not only did the infallible image of Japanese bureaucrats receive a shattering blow, but this event forced the resignation of the government. Second was Nixon's suspension of US dollar convertibility in August 1971 and the immediate imposition of a 10 per cent surcharge on imports into the US. This second Nixon shock also included a demand that foreign countries appreciate their currencies against the US, unilaterally suspending the fixed exchange rate regime that had lasted in letter if not fully in practice from 1944.

Rising trade friction lay behind this sudden announcement by the US. The US current account had deteriorated dramatically from 1967, registering a deficit of 2.8 billion dollars in 1971. On the other hand, the Japanese current account showed a cumulative surplus of 5.1 billion US dollars in the three years from 1968 to 1970 as exports rose almost 50 per cent.[134] Trade conflicts between the two countries centred on textiles. Japanese producers resisted the extension of voluntary export restraints during the protracted negotiations from 1968 to 1971 but were finally forced into an agreement that set the stage for the 1974 world Multi-Fibre Agreement. Negotiations over steel trade were less fractious, since the Japanese voluntarily limited exports from 1966 and strengthened export restraints in 1969.[135] The government supplemented this industry specific approach to alleviating trade friction with more general measures. In June 1971 it announced an eight-point plan to help reduce its trade surplus in order to decrease demands for an appreciation of the yen. Measures included tariff reductions, favourable tariffs for imports from developing nations, further capital liberalization, eliminating non-tariff trade barriers, and the abolition of tax incentives for exports.

These measures proved insufficient, and the US exerted further pressure on Japan and its other trading partners with Nixon's 15 August announcement. Public confidence in industrial policy collapsed, both because of its failure to anticipate US actions as well as because of its failure to alleviate trade friction. Most damaging, however, was the perceived incorrectness of past policy decisions. Japanese policy had targeted exports as a means to achieve growth: consequently it was held responsible both for Japan's heightened vulnerability to any dampening of trade and trade friction itself.

In the light of the collapse of confidence in industrial policy, it is ironic that macro-policy decisions exacerbated economic difficulties. Instead of

[134] Sōmu Chō Tōkei Kyoku, *Nihon Chōki Tōkei Sōran*, 3: 100.
[135] Komiya Ryūtarō, *The Japanese Economy: Trade, Industry, and Government* (Tokyo, University of Tokyo Press, 1990), 23–9.

temporarily halting central bank foreign exchange transactions after the 15 August announcement, the Bank of Japan defended the yen at 360 against the dollar until 26 August. This contributed to a surge in growth in the money supply, as did periodic defence of the yen until the signing of the Smithsonian Agreement[136] on 18 December and overly easy monetary policy. These central bank mistakes set the stage for hyper-inflation from the autumn of 1972.

Japan's reluctance to appreciate the yen continued through 1972: the government's announcement of further measures to defend the yen that year showed a preference for direct controls over market pricing. That is, the government restricted exports, lowered import tariffs, increased public spending, and eased terms for import financing while tightening terms for financing exports, trying itself to balance trade rather than encouraging trade flows to adjust through the market mechanism of the exchange rate. The government also eased monetary policy in 1972, after tightening briefly in 1971, in an attempt to stimulate domestic demand and raise imports.

Expansionary government policies in 1972 were not just an attempt to circumvent yen appreciation. They may have been of some use in that regard, since they directed investment towards social capital rather than towards export industries. More importantly, however, increased government expenditure was the agreed policy response to answer the criticism that social welfare in Japan lagged far behind economic growth. Tanaka Kakuei, who replaced Satō Eisaku as Prime Minister in July 1972, emphasized public spending as a means to spread the fruits of development. In his 'Plan for the Restructuring of the Japanese Archipelago' (*Nihon Rettō Kaizō Ron*), Tanaka called for a massive increase in the transportation network, the development of new urban sites, and the deconcentration of industrial areas. Tanaka also advocated increased outlays on social security and national health.

Unfortunately, this attempt to respond to public criticism of past policies would prove counter-productive. Government outlays rose more than 20 per cent in nominal terms between 1970 and 1973; together with overly easy monetary policy and the increase in world inflation that accompanied the Vietnam War, this sparked a surge in domestic prices from the autumn of 1972. For the first time in more than a decade, wholesale price rises led consumer price increases. Shortages of goods appeared, including steel, cement, and chemicals, as manufacturers, faced with a labour shortage, plant accidents, and complaints over pollution, found it difficult to increase output. A rise in speculative demand also

---

[136] In the Smithsonian Agreement, Japan agreed to a new yen/dollar rate of 308, a 16.88% appreciation.

contributed to these shortages, as manufacturers and consumers, anticipating price rises or delivery interruptions, stockpiled goods.[137]

Similarly, efforts to prevent further appreciation of the yen also ended in failure. Not only had these efforts sparked inflationary pressures, but they probably contributed to both the new high set by the Japanese current account surplus in 1972 and the collapse of the Smithsonian Agreement. Japan was unable to justify not participating in the general float that ensued after February 1973. Even so, limited defence of the dollar thereafter kept money supply growth high, with Japan essentially choosing to adjust its trade surplus through domestic price increases rather than through further strengthening of the yen.

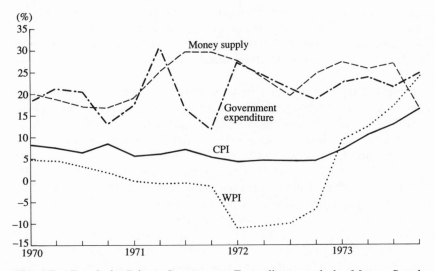

Fig. 2.7. Trends in Prices, Government Expenditure, and the Money Supply, 1970–1973

Source: Keizai Kikaku Chō, *Kokumin Keizai Kessan Nenpō;* Nihon Ginkō, *Keizai Tōkei Nenpō.*

Against this background of already high inflation, the first oil crisis struck in October 1973, causing real GNP to decline for the first time in post-war history. The omniscience of industrial policy was dealt its final blow, since policy had promoted an energy-intensive industrial structure for the previous three decades. Not surprisingly, industrial policy would still play a role in aiding adjustment to the oil shock, and the first half of the 1970s would actually witness an increase in direct government control, both in the management of trade flows and in price and output

---

[137] Nakamura Takafusa, *The Postwar Japanese Economy*, 227–34.

guidance. However, the scope of industrial policy became more limited as evidence of policy failures mounted. Rather than helping to determine the pattern of development, the response of industrial policy to external events became increasingly passive. Never again would it be viewed as dominating the shape of economic activity.

The first oil shock marked the end of a phenomenal economic performance. Between 1955 and 1973, real GNP grew at an average annual rate of 9.5 per cent while capital expenditure showed an average annual increase of 17.4 per cent.[138] This growth was unparalleled in history, and Japan became the world's second largest non-communist economy by 1967.[139] All the more surprising is the fact that the fastest growth occurred during the period of trade and capital liberalization.

During this period the government actively influenced corporate investment through industrial policy, utilizing government loans, tax incentives, trade barriers, control over the allocation of imports, control over foreign technology, and cartels in an attempt to create an industrial structure which was consistent with its own goals. Industrial policy promoted growth in industries selected for their ability to export, for their productivity increases, for their sensitivity to rising incomes, and finally for their ability to improve the quality of life. At the same time, industrial policy also supported industries on the basis of their capability to absorb employment. In this way, the government attempted to control the costs associated with competition, the dislocation of labour. This concern over controlling costs was also apparent in attempts to smooth the decline of certain industries, a characteristic which would become even more pronounced later in the 1970s and in the 1980s.

The post-war period until 1973 also saw a gradual decline in the power of industrial policy. Power was arguably at its peak during the Occupation, when the government directly controlled much of the economy. State control then gave way to state–private sector co-operation later in the 1950s and 1960s. As liberalization reduced the government's influence in the 1960s, the private sector's role in shaping policy rose. This was accompanied by diverging consensus about the goals of economic management from late in the decade, which in turn weakened industrial policy. Finally, the failure of industrial policy to anticipate external shocks in the early 1970s, as well as the perceived blame that it bore for increasing economic vulnerability, further decreased its stature, permanently reducing the role that industrial policy would assume in the future.

---

[138] Measured in constant 1980 prices. (Keizai Kikaku Chō, *Kokumin Keizai Kessan Hōkoku: Shōwa 30 Nen – Shōwa 44 Nen*; Keizai Kikaku Chō, *Kokumin Keizai Kessan Nenpō* (Tokyo, Ōkurashō Insatsu Kyoku, 1989).)
[139] Keizai Kikaku Chō, *Kokumin Keizai Kessan Hōkoku: Shōwa 30 Nen – Shōwa 44 Nen*.

3

Methodological Issues in Evaluating Japanese Industrial Policy

The simultaneous occurrence of Japan's highly successful development with a widespread use of industrial policy does not in itself imply a causality between the two: growth might have been the result of favourable macroeconomic policy or expanding world trade, and industrial policy might have contributed little or nothing to Japan's development. Nevertheless, this apparent correlation is striking and worthy of investigation. To that end, this chapter outlines economic criteria which are useful in assessing the possible impact of industrial policy on Japan's post-war growth. These criteria fall short of providing an empirically verifiable model, impossible given data limitations. Even so, they act as a basis from which to make an informed judgement about policy efficacy.

3.1 A Simple Dynamic Framework

Industrial policy, which includes all measures designed specifically to influence resource allocation for selected industries, can be divided into two distinct and seemingly contradictory types in Japan's first two decades of post-war autonomy. One set of measures was designed specifically to foster growth in select industries in order to further industrialization. Industries were chosen on the basis of their perceived growth potential and their expected future competitiveness. Whatever protection or subsidies were applied, the final goal of this set of policies was to create industries capable of surviving and expanding in free domestic and international markets. In short, this type of pro-growth industrial policy was viewed as a temporary support, to be eliminated once an industry was capable of withstanding the discipline of the market.

On the other hand, a second group of measures directly undermined the market mechanism. Industries which were not thought to possess favourable future growth prospects were nevertheless protected because of their ability to provide employment. Competition was blocked, yet there was often no expectation that productivity could be raised to levels which would ensure survival in a free international market. Little thought was given to the eventual removal of support measures. Such measures can be broadly categorized as anti-growth industrial policy.

In order to forge a single framework in which to assess the efficacy of these two conflicting types of industrial policy, consider first the economic rationale for an industrial policy which explicitly fosters the expansion of industries thought to possess future competitiveness. The need for pro-growth policy is commonly accepted in classical and neoclassical econom-ics; it is outlined in the literature on infant industries. These infant industry arguments advocate government intervention under certain con-ditions. Conceptually, the term 'infant industry' describes an industry in a developing economy which is not initially competitive in the world mar-ket but which would become so with time. John Stuart Mill, the first well-known proponent of the infant industry argument, defined such an industry as arising because 'the superiority of one country over another in a branch of production often arises only from having begun it sooner. There may be no inherent advantage on one part, or disadvantage on the other, but only a present superiority of acquired skill and experience.' Because 'it cannot be expected that individuals should, at their own risk, or rather to their certain loss, introduce a new manufacture, and bear the burden of carrying it on until the producers have been educated up to the level of those with whom the processes are traditional',[1] Mill advocates the temporary imposition of a protective tariff to subsidize the future growth industry.

Infant industry arguments can generally be divided into two categories, those based on dynamic internal economies and those based on dynamic external economies.[2] In the case of dynamic internal economies, factors within a firm or industry cause gains in efficiency over time. In other words, the average cost of a firm or an industry falls the longer its output has continued. The industry learns from experience. In such a case, sub-optimal investment in the industry will occur if the industry does not cor-rectly anticipate this cost reduction or if capital markets are imperfect so that financing at an appropriate rate cannot be obtained for the infant industry.

Capital market imperfections deserve further comment since such imperfections can be particularly widespread in a developing economy. One problem in capital markets is that the rate of interest for all long-term investment may be too high. Private enterprises and private lenders may demand a higher return in the short run, creating a bias against investments which will only exhibit a good return after a period of several years. A second problem is the large amount of funding that may be nec-essary to support an infant industry. Capital markets may be unwilling to

---

[1] John Stuart Mill, *Principles of Political Economy*, 5.10, *Collected Works of John Stuart Mill*, 3 (Toronto, University of Toronto Press, 1965), 918–19; as quoted in W. M. Corden, *Trade Policy and Economic Welfare* (Oxford, Clarendon Press, 1974), 248.

[2] W. M. Corden, *Trade Policy and Economic Welfare*, 250–68.

bear the risk of lending such sizeable amounts to an industry which may be loss-making for a long period of time. Finally, there may be a bias in capital markets against investment in new industries, with lending going almost entirely to existing firms and industries. All of these factors can undermine the ability of infant industries to secure funds for growth.

The second type of infant industry argument centres on the possible existence of dynamic external economies. If over time, an industry creates an asset which is used free of charge by other industries, dynamic external economies exist. For instance, a dynamic external economy would arise if production in an industry improves not only the training of its own workers but also the quality of other workers. Dynamic external economies may also occur in the case of knowledge formation, which may be paid for by one firm but which may spread without cost to others. A more general dynamic external economy will exist when an atmosphere is created by one or several industries which fosters automation, organized economic activity, or the development of mechanical or scientific interests across the entire manufacturing sector.

These traditional infant industry arguments provide the basic framework for analysing Japan's pro-growth industrial policy, creating a rationale for government intervention in industries which will become more competitive over time. However, other factors may also have contributed to the rationale for pro-growth Japanese industrial policy. The first is the possible existence of static economies of scale, whereby average production costs fall simply as output increases. In some instances, static scale economies do not necessitate subsidies, since the country would be better off starting production at a later date once domestic demand has grown sufficiently to achieve these scale economies. However, if static scale economies are inseparable from learning by doing effects, then capital market imperfections reinforce the case for government support. More importantly, even if production costs fall only because of increased output, a subsidy can still be needed if brand loyalties are present. It will not necessarily be optimal for a developing country to wait to establish an industry if in the meantime loyalty to a foreign product is formed.

Scale economy concerns have also motivated many recent advances in the theoretical trade literature. The focus of this 'new' trade theory lies in analysing trade policy under imperfect competition.[3] In industries where scale economies have resulted in monopolistic or oligopolistic behaviour, imperfect competition drives a wedge between prices and marginal cost, thus implying the need for government intervention. In an extreme case where economies of scale are so large that only a small number of firms

---

[3] See, for example, Elhanan Helpman and Paul Krugman, *Trade Policy and Market Structure* (Cambridge, Mass., MIT Press, 1989).

can survive in the world market, then government policy which guarantees the domestic firm total control of the domestic market can not only reduce its costs but also help to increase the domestic firm's share of the world market.

In addition to static scale economies, a second important factor behind Japan's pro-growth industrial policy is the possible existence of dynamic investment complementarities. In the case of industries which complement one another, the more expansion there is in one industry, the more profitable it may be to expand in the other. In the car and steel industries, for example, it may only be profitable to expand car production if steel production increases, and the profitable expansion of the steel industry may depend upon increased production in the car industry. This type of dynamic external economy will be of importance the greater the minimum size of investment necessary to increase production. That is, if only a small amount of investment is necessary to raise production in either steel or cars, investment may occur despite the complementarity between the two industries. If investment is not divisible in that raising output in either industry requires a large amount of capital, then dynamic investment complementarities require some form of government intervention to ensure that investment occurs.[4]

The third, and possibly most important factor, concerns the introduction of foreign technology. Markets for technology are not perfectly competitive; suppliers are generally either monopolists or oligopolists in regards to technology. This provides another economic rationale for government intervention, not unrelated to the 'new' trade theory. In order to even the playing field, the government arguably should control the process by which technology is imported in order to ensure that foreign companies cannot extract monopoly rents on the technology that they sell.

These arguments indicate a positive role for industrial policy in promoting economic development. However, all of the cases considered are applicable only to industries which will eventually become competitive in world markets. The reasoning is not consistent with the second type of industrial policy in Japan, the support of industries characterized by low productivity and bleak survival prospects. A more explicit consideration of the dynamics of the development process is needed to provide a rationale for this second type of anti-growth policy, which will also suggest a

---

[4] The existence of dynamic complementarities will generally arise only in a closed economy. If trade is possible, then the profitability of investment in one industry will not be affected by the domestic production level of another industry since the investing industry would have access to the foreign output of the complementary industry. The presence of static scale economies naturally strengthens the case for investment complementarities in a protected economy, and in the case of non-tradable goods such as electric power, investment complementarities will arise even if the economy is open.

66 *Methodological Issues*

unified framework that can be used to analyse both pro-growth and anti-growth industrial policy.

Suppose that an economy begins its development process with a large population but with a very limited stock of capital. The principal concern of such an economy must initially be the survival of its population. If a country's population is so large that full employment cannot be achieved at a subsistence wage, reliance on only the market mechanism will result in starvation for some portion of the population. This is clearly the situation that Japan faced immediately after World War II. As much as one-third of its industrial equipment had been destroyed in the war,[5] and at the same time, the economy had to absorb over 13 million individuals released from military-related jobs, a substantial number representing almost 20 per cent of the population. In such a situation, the government must intervene to prevent massive starvation, and targeting labour-intensive industries which are low in productivity and have poor future growth prospects will probably be necessary.[6]

Anti-growth industrial policy can be economically rational in the face of a large surplus population. Even if infant industries also exist in such developing countries, it may not be possible to absorb all of the surplus population through support measures to infant industries. This is because they are generally capital intensive, and resource constraints limit the total amount of subsidies a government can provide. Hence, in the case of a developing economy with a large population and with infant industries, the government should direct as much as possible of the resources it has at its disposal to such industries since these have the best future growth prospects. However, because it is unlikely that the government can thereby ensure employment for all of its citizens, it may also at the same time have to spend some of its resources in supporting low-productivity, labour-intensive industries to guarantee worker survival. In other words, the simultaneous implementation of pro-growth and anti-growth policy is often appropriate.

Moreover, the time during which these two policy types overlap depends on assumptions about the costs of moving labour and capital between industries. If these costs are zero, an assumption often made in economic literature, the period during which different policy types should overlap will be limited. If resources can be moved freely from one industry to another, the rationale for anti-growth policy disappears once a subsistence wage level has been achieved. This would suggest a fairly clear

---

[5] Ōkurashō Zaisei Shi Shitsu, *Shōwa Zaisei Shi: Shūsen kara Kōwa made*, 19: 14–15.

[6] Tsujimura *et al.* have rigorously analysed a surplus labour economy in the context of a generalized Edgeworth bartering process, outlining the need for policy intervention. For details see Tsujimura Kōtarō, Kuroda Masahiro, and Shimada Haruo, *Economic Policy and General Interdependence* (Tokyo, Kogakusha, 1981).

ranking of policy types over time. In the early stages of development, most resources might be devoted to supporting low-growth, labour-intensive industries, but after wages rise to a subsistence level, all government resources should be devoted to promoting growth industries.

On the other hand, if there are costs involved in transferring resources between industries, this ranking over time between anti-growth and pro-growth industrial policy becomes much more blurred. Such costs exist: labour cannot move from the agricultural sector to the manufacturing sector without paying relocation expenses including the costs of transferring belongings and establishing a new household. In addition to these private costs, there are social costs as well. The social infrastructure (roads, sewers, and schools) must be increased in urban areas to provide a foundation from which to absorb migrating workers. The existence of such social and private costs involved in relocating labour can imply the need to continue to support industries with low productivity even after a general subsistence wage level has been achieved for the economy overall. To see this more clearly, assume a government is supporting agriculture and at the same time is directing its remaining resources to promoting capital accumulation in urban manufacturing. This urban manufacturing industry is assumed to fit the criteria of an infant industry in that it will eventually emerge as a world competitive industry.[7] In such a case, it makes economic sense to continue to support agriculture if the cost of relocating workers exceeds the amount paid in support to agriculture. In order to maximize future growth, the government needs to direct as many resources as it can to the infant industry at each moment in time while simultaneously guaranteeing full employment. If the support to agriculture costs less than relocating agricultural workers, the government should continue to subsidize agriculture.

Even if the private and social relocation costs are less than the subsidy to agriculture, the continuation of an anti-growth policy can still be justified. Assume that as a result of the subsidy, there is limited technological progress in agriculture. Further assume that the government wishes to maximize total growth of the economy subject to the survival of the population. Economic growth can now arise from two sources, the urban manufacturing industry and to a smaller degree the agricultural industry. Hence, the government will not only promote the urban manufacturing industry once the survival of the population is assured, but it will continue to subsidize agriculture so long as the subsidy paid to agriculture is less than the relocation costs plus the increased production arising from technological progress in the agricultural industry.

[7] In order for an infant industry to warrant protection, it is not sufficient that the industry merely catch up to its international competitors. Rather, the long-term benefits accrued from fostering the industry should offset the short-term costs of protecting it.

In short, simultaneous pro-growth and anti-growth policies are rational in a dynamic development framework. Anti-growth policy is necessary not only when a portion of the population faces starvation because labour supply exceeds labour demand at subsistence wage but also when relocation costs and the possibility of minimal technical progress exist in industries with low productivity. The latter case implies an extended period during which anti-growth policy should occur together with pro-growth policy.[8]

This framework also implies an explicit trade-off between the two policy types. Anti-growth policy minimizes the problem of worker survival, while pro-growth policy maximizes economic expansion. With limited resources at its disposal, the government will attempt to direct as much as possible to high-growth industries, while at the same time ensuring worker survival and extracting any potential technological gains that might be possible in low-productivity, low-growth industries. This trade-off between maximizing growth and minimizing social disruption is not only the key to this dynamic development framework, but also is the single most important characteristic of post-war industrial policy in Japan.

3.2   Policy Optimality, Policy Feasibility, and Policy Effectiveness

The simple dynamic framework outlined thus far provides a basis from which to evaluate Japanese industrial policy. It can be economically rational for a country to pursue simultaneously both pro-growth and anti-growth policies. The former is needed in the case of infant industries, investment complementarities, and technology transfer, while anti-growth policy can be necessary to ensure the employment and survival of a large population. Moreover, minimum technological progress in labour-intensive industries with poor future growth prospects together with positive costs involved in transferring labour and capital from one industry to another can prolong the period during which support should be provided to such labour-intensive industries, allowing for a substantial overlap between pro-growth and anti-growth policies.

[8] Literature on economic development does outline some instances where it is rational to subsidize both traditional and modern industries. (See, for instance, John R. Harris and Michael P. Todaro, 'Migration, Unemployment, and Development: A Two-Sector Analysis', *American Economic Review*, 60 (Mar. 1970), 126–42.) When wage differentials between urban and rural industries exist, and migration to urban areas in the hopes of finding higher paid work leads to unemployment, a first-best solution may be to subsidize both industries, thus eliminating the wage differential between the two. Promoting only the modern industry to solve the unemployment problem could well result in the productivity of an additional worker in the modern industry being lower than that in agriculture. (This is complicated by costs in collecting and disbursing subsidies (Corden, *Trade Policy and Economic Welfare*, 153).)

In such a world, what are the optimal policy responses? Anti-growth measures should clearly be formed so that they encourage what minimal technological progress may be achievable. In this regard, wage subsidies are arguably the worst type of policy response. Such direct support of labour provides no incentive for increased output. On the other hand, price supports for products produced by such labour-intensive industries do not suffer from this defect. Not only will price supports guarantee some minimum level of income, but they also give incentives for raising output, thus promoting technological change.

The issue of optimal policy response in the case of pro-growth industrial policy is more complicated. As a rule, the best response is the one that directly addresses the cause behind the need for intervention. The logic behind this is simple: intervention obviously affects the allocation of resources, and any unintended or unwanted impact of intervention is minimized the more specific is the policy design. Thus, in the case of an infant industry which will improve productivity by learning over time, policy should directly stimulate investment in that industry through a subsidy to capital. If a less direct policy is chosen, perhaps one that raises the price of the product produced in the infant industry, then investment in that industry will almost certainly increase. However, the increased price will also have an impact on users of the product. If it is a consumption good, consumers bear the burden of higher prices; if it is a product used in producing other goods, then producers bear the burden. In the latter case, investment in the industries using the intermediate input could decline as the price of that input rises.

Optimal policy response is complicated by the existence of costs involved in the disbursement of a subsidy as well as by costs related to the collection of taxes to finance a subsidy. Clearly, these costs should be minimized, and in the case of a subsidy disbursement, this involves getting funds to an industry as directly as possible. Where feasible, corporate tax breaks can provide the ideal solution, since the subsidized firm then merely retains funds it would have paid to the government. Government loans may provide a second-best alternative, since the administrative costs involved may be low, especially if the government itself does not have to actively search for loan recipients. Collection costs for taxes to pay for subsidies will probably depend upon the stage of a country's economic development. In the very early stages of development, a tariff may be the cheapest way to raise funds despite the effects tariffs may have on income distribution (the user of the imported good bears the entire burden of the tax). As development progresses, the costs of collecting income taxes and production taxes fall, implying that cost minimization could well entail a combination of tariffs and income taxes, especially since the income distribution effects of the latter can be more easily controlled. The existence of collection and distribution costs also affects the optimal size of the subsidy to be granted. Simply put, there is a trade-off between the subsidy and these costs. The ideal size of the subsidy will be somewhat less than it would be were collection and disbursement costs zero since the benefits arising from the subsidy must to some extent be traded off against the cost of implementing it.

If problems in the capital market necessitate intervention, then interest rates or the allocation of capital should be the target of intervention. Similarly, in the case of dynamic investment complementarities, better co-ordination of planning is the optimal response. If this does not suffice, then production subsidies will be a second-best policy. If the problem is a spill-over in training labour from one industry to others, the most direct way to deal with the problem is through subsidizing the training of labour, and a similar solution obtains when knowledge is transferred costlessly from one industry to another.

Trade policy is theoretically the first-best solution in four cases, but only if there is no retaliation by trading partners. First, in instances where a country can affect its terms of trade, changing the international price of traded commodities, then it can improve its position by restricting demand through tariffs (or limit supply through export taxes). This is the best known argument for tariffs, and arises when a country has market power over some goods. In such a case, however, tariffs are optimal only if trading partners do not retaliate against the country introducing tariffs, limiting that country's exports. The likelihood of retaliation in this case is probably high, since the sole reason for the country to introduce tariffs is to improve its terms of trade at the expense of its trading partners.

The 'new' international trade literature greatly expands these terms of trade argument, investigating the need for trade policy in industries that are characterized globally by oligopolistic or monopolistic production.[9] In cases where firms compete in third markets, export subsidies can help a domestic firm increase its total market share.[10] In cases where economies

[9] Baldwin shows concisely how the 'new' trade literature is largely an extension of traditional trade arguments regarding monopoly power in trade and domestic distortions. (R. Baldwin, 'Are Economists' Traditional Trade Policy Views Still Valid?', *Journal of Economic Literature*, 30 (June 1992) (Nashville, Tenn., American Economic Association), 804–29.)

[10] If oligopolists follow a Cournot game whereby they make production decisions assuming that the quantity exported by competitors stays constant, then an export subsidy would convince these oligopolists that the subsidized firm (or firms) would raise output, inducing them to reduce output. Whether or not the subsidizing country benefits, however, depends crucially on the possibility of free entry. If the subsidy induces more domestic firms to enter, average industry costs will rise because of higher entry costs, thus absorbing the benefits of profits shifted from overseas competitors. Additionally, the conclusion is dependent on the type of oligopolistic behaviour: for instance, if firms take competitor prices as given rather than competitor output levels, then an export subsidy will worsen that country's welfare while an export tax could improve it.

of scale are substantial and only a few firms survive to compete in all markets, then tariffs can allow the domestic firm to increase output by capturing the domestic market. Increased output would reduce costs, potentially leading to increased exports.[11] These represent just a few of the cases outlined in the 'new' trade theory, but policy recommendations from this 'new' theory are not robust. Not only are they predicated on the assumption of no retaliation, but they are extremely sensitive to the type of oligopoly in existence, data about which a government is unlikely to have.

Related to insights from the 'new' trade theory but stronger in policy implications is the case where a small country faces a world with monopoly power over technology. If the world can freely export to this small country, then it can capture the full value of its technology through its export of products which embody the technology. If trade is blocked, however, incentives to sell the technology rise. Furthermore, trade and capital controls will strengthen the bargaining position of the small country, helping it to reduce the prices it pays for technology. Of course, a general tariff for a small country in this instance will only prove optimal if the rest of the world does not retaliate against it. Retaliation would adversely affect the small country's exports, possibly leaving it in a worse situation than at the beginning.

Finally, the existence of dynamic external economies provides a fourth argument for active trade policy. It is conceivable that the entire manufacturing sector of an economy benefits indirectly from production increases in any other manufacturing industry. For instance, manufacturing industries could create a synergy amongst themselves, whereby familiarity with automation in one industry can lead to its rapid acceptance elsewhere. Synergy could also result when the training of workers in one manufacturing industry leads to an improved work ethic in other industries or when training workers in one industry improves the abilities of all workers in the manufacturing sector. In such cases, trade protection for the entire manufacturing sector may be an optimal solution.[12]

One important instance where a generalized tariff is not a first-best solution involves a country with a balance of payments deficit. Clearly, a tax on imports and a subsidy to exports may achieve a balance of payments equilibrium. However, it is preferable to devalue the currency to achieve this result. Devaluation involves less intervention and is more likely to avoid government mistakes in calculating the appropriate size of

---

[11] Helpman and Krugman, *Trade Policy and Market Structure*, 117–31.

[12] This argument must be limited to one sector or sectors of an economy rather than the entire economy itself. Trade protection involves favouring one domestic group at the expense of another, and if all domestic sectors are subject to dynamic external economies to the same degree, a general tariff is clearly an incorrect policy response.

export subsidies. Even if export industries are subject to dynamic internal economies to various degrees, a differing rate of export subsidies is not as preferable as a uniform depreciation coupled with varying production subsidies.

Cases for active trade policy are especially important because such policy often reinforces the need for other types of intervention. In particular, trade protection increases the likelihood of dynamic investment complementarities occurring. Investment in each of two industries may only be profitable if the other invests first, implying the need to subsidize investment in these industries. However, such dependency can only occur if each industry does not have access to a global market for the other industry's product. If the domestic steel industry has access to the global car market, investment in the domestic steel industry will be little influenced by investment decisions in the domestic car industry. Similarly, the domestic car industry, if it has access to imported steel, will not be constrained by the development of the domestic steel industry. Even in a free trade environment, however, important investment complementarities involving non-traded goods will still arise. Thus, the profitability of investment in both cars and steel will be influenced by investment in the electric power industry.

The issue of policy optimality is in practice far more complex than the discussion thus far indicates. Not only are there costs associated with implementing policy, such as the disbursement of a subsidy which must be traded off against the benefits of the subsidy, but there are also costs involved in formulating an industrial policy, namely collecting sufficient information. These costs in turn depend largely upon institutional factors, such as a bureaucracy sufficiently trained to absorb what lessons can be learned from the development process in other countries. Even greater costs are associated with the detailed knowledge about each industry that a government must have in order to formulate policy. In the case of Japan, these costs were probably held down by the formation of industry associations in the post-war period which acted as a buffer between individual firms and the bureaucracy. Industry associations not only gave the government detailed statistics about production and investment of individual firms, but also gave firms information about government policy, helped to co-ordinate the introduction of policy, and helped to explain members' opposition to a possible policy decision before its implementation.

The existing institutions of a political economy (and its ability to create new institutions) complicate the issue of policy optimality, but so too does the identification of true market failures. It is not possible to verify, for example, that pro-growth policy in Japan in fact targeted real infant industries, since targeted industries might have developed in the absence of government intervention at a cheaper cost to the economy overall. Moreover, asymmetric risk in the case of infant industries would bias policy against optimality. That is, even if a targeted industry did need government support to begin, support would almost certainly continue past the point where survival could occur in its absence. Should the government discontinue support too early, it would risk the success of the targeted industry and waste the entire subsidy spent thus far; however, should the government continue support too long, then the only extra cost is that unnecessary portion of the subsidy.

Optimal policy depends not only on institutional factors and the ability to identify real market distortions, but also on the government's ability to forecast change. Technological advances can either reinforce the government's targeting of a particular infant industry or undermine it, but without exact knowledge about what those developments will be beforehand, it is not possible to implement policy to exactly the right degree. A similar argument holds for changes in consumer preferences and changes in raw material prices. In other words, looking back at an industrial policy, it will always be possible to improve upon it given information about what was then the future.

This argument against the feasibility of optimal policy response is not, however, an argument against the efficacy of industrial policy. It is still possible that industrial policy may have contributed positively to Japan's development, even if that contribution was not as great as it might theoretically have been. It is this issue that this book hopes to address. To that end, targeted industries will be matched with possible market failures and imperfections. If industrial policy can generally be linked with dynamic internal economies, dynamic external economies, investment complementarities, the existence of monopoly power in trade, and the need to provide a minimum standard of living, then it is possible to conclude that some sort of industrial policy was necessary. The more that specific policy measures can be linked to specific market failures and imperfections, the greater will be the likelihood that industrial policy was effective.

This matching of industrial policies with possible market failures will begin our evaluation of industrial policy in Chapter 4. Additionally, the stated intentions of policy will be matched with outcomes to provide further insight into the possible efficacy of industrial policy. While simple enumeration of policy, policy intention, and market imperfections forms a basis for evaluating policy efficacy, simple quantitative analysis can also contribute to our understanding of the importance of industrial policy. It is not possible to determine what the course of economic development in Japan would have been in the absence of industrial policy, and as a result, it is impossible to definitively determine the impact industrial policy has had on growth. However, it is possible to ascertain whether or not industrial policy did have an impact on the pattern of development by examining the relative magnitude of government subsidies and loans by industry. For instance, if government support was large relative to private sector financing or if subsidies were sizeable compared to corporate taxes, then industrial policy almost certainly affected investment in targeted industries.

This still leaves us some way from our final goal of evaluating the impact of industrial policy on Japanese economic development. Linking policy to market failure and providing empirical evidence that policy affected growth at the industry level are both necessary conditions that must be fulfilled if industrial policy was an important factor behind Japan's remarkable success. Still unanswered, however, is the question of whether Japanese industrial policy was instrumental in achieving rapid development. To address this issue, we shall examine whether policy increased Japan's growth potential through its impact on exports and total investment. If exports and investment as a percentage of GNP were higher in the post-war era than in the pre-war era, this will strengthen the case for the efficacy of industrial policy to the extent that increases can be attributed to policy.

Together these analyses help to provide a foundation from which to judge the importance of industrial policy in the course of Japanese economic development. Conclusions will necessarily be probable rather than definite: given our lack of data about how Japan would have developed in the absence of industrial policy, it is not possible to directly test any hypothesis that might be derived from an explicit dynamic model of development based on the discussion in Section 3.1, and it is for this reason that modelling was not pursued. It is also not feasible to fully measure the total costs and benefits derived from policy, because costs are inextricably linked with institutional factors, and benefits can never be proved to have occurred. However, correlating industrial policy to market failures and imperfections provides a valuable taxonomy to address policy efficacy, and linking policy to changes in Japan's export and investment behaviour adds further evidence about policy impact. This approach will help in answering whether Japan was better off implementing industrial policy than not.

3.3   Historical View of Industrial Policy

What those who made industrial policy thought at the time policy was implemented and the way in which policy was formulated further reinforce the already strong argument against the optimality of Japanese industrial policy. Quantitative information was not always used to determine the magnitude of policy intervention. Despite iterations across industry, government, and academia, final policy output could not have accurately addressed each problem. Perhaps more importantly, policy-makers in the government did not have any consistent rationale for implementing industrial policy. There was no ideology, unless a simple belief in the need for policy intervention constitutes such. There was certainly no single dynamic development framework, however simple, under which all types of industrial policy were explained, evaluated, and implemented.

Thoughts behind Japanese industrial policy were influenced by a variety of conflicting factors. The most important of these was the interaction between Japanese Marxist thought, the economic liberalism of the New Dealers in the Occupation, and the classical economic tradition of such Occupation figures as Joseph Dodge. Of course, Japan's own experience with economic policy during the war and prior to it also influenced the way in which bureaucrats in post-war Japan viewed and shaped industrial policy.

Japan's experience with economic controls in the 1930s and 1940s coloured the thinking behind immediate post-war policy. Economic controls had proved themselves practical, in that industry output could be controlled in the desired fashion. When faced with the problem of a balance of payments deficit or with extreme shortages of material inputs, the bureaucratic response was to control directly the allocation of inputs and imports. That direct control over resource allocation was viewed favourably by both the government and academia can be ascertained from the 1947 report on 'Basic Problems Facing Japanese Reconstruction' (*Nihon Keizai Saiken no Kihon Mondai*) by a special committee of the Foreign Ministry. The government acted directly to allocate funds to selected industries through the Reconstruction Finance Corporation from 1946 to 1949 and also directly set prices for many industries in the 1947–9 period. Legal support for the direct government control over trade was provided by the Law Concerning the Management of Foreign Exchange and Foreign Trade of 1949, which allowed the government to allocate imports not only by industry but also by firm.

Intellectually, the most persistent characteristic of Japanese industrial policy has its root in Marxist thought in Japan. That characteristic is the perceived need to protect and promote Japanese industry, which faced large capitalist competitor nations. Bureaucrats in Japan were profoundly influenced by Marx's perceptions of the strength of capitalism. By deduction, Japan needed protection from this strength lest domestic industry be overwhelmed, and protection would continue until Japan could encourage its own industries to develop enough to compete. It is tempting to hypothesize that the reason Marxism was so overwhelmingly popular in Japan was that it rationalized the deep-rooted feelings of inferiority that Japan so often exhibited over the centuries when exposed to other cultures. Whatever its origins, the Japanese Marxist view of the threat of the strength of capitalism affected Japanese industrial policy for at least two and a half decades. It was for this reason that Japan dragged its feet for five years after promising to liberalize foreign investment into Japan, and it is for this reason that the Japanese greeted the initial announcement of capital liberalization in 1964 as the 'second coming of the black ships'. It seems ludicrous now to compare the impact of capital liberalization to the first coming of the black ships, the event that ended 250 years of isolation, brought down the Tokugawa government, and resulted in the Meiji Restoration. Even in 1964 Japan had the third highest GNP of OECD nations, and had advanced to second place by the time liberalization began in 1969. However, the hyperbole does show just how strong and persistent were Japan's perceptions of its own weakness relative to the rest of the world.[13]

Marxism in Japan, together with past economic history, defined the role of the state in economic policy. The state was to be active in influencing resource allocation and economic development. This active role of the state was also reinforced by the Occupation through its early emphasis on the practicality of economic controls. First, Japan inherited if not a firm belief in democracy from the Occupation, then at least a strong belief in economic equality. In its economic dimension, the democratization of Japan began with land reform, granting workers the right to organize, and the dissolution of the *zaibatsu*, the giant Japanese holding companies. These measures attempted to create economic equality, promoting gains for the farmer and the worker while undercutting drastically the position of the wealthy landlord or corporate owner. This belief in economic equality has remained strong to the present day, and has shaped government policy in numerous ways. The concept of equality strengthened the rationale for agricultural price supports, and the diminution of wage differentials between small and large enterprises was an active policy goal until the late 1960s.

The Occupation's emphasis on democracy also influenced the way in which economic policy was to be formulated. Just as the government was expected to politically represent all of the conflicting interests of the voters, so too were all economic interests to be represented in policy. In

[13] While Japan's interpretation of Marxism may have focused attention on the strengths of a capitalistic state, less attention was paid to Marx's arguments about the inevitable decline of capitalism. Certainly from the bureaucratic perspective, there was little recognition of the supposed weaknesses of capitalism. Rather, the converse seemed to hold true: capitalism was to be emulated in order to create a strong economy. This belief certainly was reinforced by the intellectual legacy of the Occupation.

order to synthesize conflicting economic interests, Japan extended the consensus-building process from the chambers of the Diet to government advisory councils which included not only government officials, businessmen, financial leaders, and academics, but journalists, labour union officials, and members of consumer groups.

The second legacy from the Occupation was a belief in the market pricing mechanism. Occupation support for freely competitive markets reinforced the lessons the Japanese had learned about the excesses that could occur with strong state control over the economy, excesses that had led not only to fascism but also to corruption. These experiences made Japan welcome greater reliance on competitive markets. Of course, for Japan, with its long history of government intervention in the economy, this belief in the market pricing mechanism did not mean that resource allocation was to be left solely to market forces. However, it did mean that whenever government intervention occurred, such intervention was to be temporary. Subsidies to many industries did not continue indefinitely, but rather were gradually phased out as competition was encouraged. Belief in markets influenced the way in which policy was to be formulated: not the state alone, but the government in conjunction with private industries would determine policy. Additionally, commitment to the market pricing mechanism also influenced the way in which the government intervened in markets, encouraging it to utilize market forces when intervening. For instance, by keeping interest rates artificially low for most of the post-war period, policy caused loan demand to naturally exceed supply. However, instead of intervening itself to ration credit, the Japanese government relied on city banks and long-term credit banks to fulfil much of this function. Theoretically at least, these institutions could have faced bankruptcy, so the government did manage to introduce at least some market discipline in the determination of who would receive loans.

To Japanese policy-makers, free competition was an ideal to be achieved, but it was not a principle which could never be violated. That this was so can be seen not only from the numerous ways in which the government temporarily protected and promoted industries, but also from the government's worries about 'excessive competition' as well as a lack of concern about the dangers of economic concentration. The government regularly encouraged the cartelization of industries to adjust production. Moreover, firm size was associated with efficiency: the larger the firm, the more competitive it was expected to be. This belief can be traced back to the 1930s, when policy-makers in Japan identified its numerous small inefficient companies as a cause behind economic stagnation and turned to Germany's experience with rationalization and cartels as a model for economic restructuring. In post-war Japan, policy-makers felt that the competitive process in an industry with many small firms would inevitably lead to the bankruptcy of some as others grew at their expense. In the face of this 'excessive competition' the government felt the need to attempt to minimize the costs associated with these bankruptcies. In many cases, the existence of numerous firms in an industry was not tolerated. Through mergers and acquisitions, policy-makers hoped to raise the efficiency of industry more rapidly than if the industry had been left to market forces alone.

The government took this policy to its extreme in the 1960s, when it actively encouraged mergers between very large companies to deal with the perceived threat of trade and foreign capital liberalization. The government expressed very little concern about the possible detrimental effects of rising economic concentration, perhaps in the belief that with liberalization foreign companies would contribute to competition in the Japanese economy. Even if the active promotion of large-scale mergers did represent a temporary retreat from belief in the market pricing mechanism, this retreat was short-lived. Widespread criticism of government intervention to restructure Japanese industry through mergers and acquisitions resulted in the defeat of MITI's Law Concerning Temporary Measures to Promote Designated Enterprises, and reporting of the debate amongst academics, businessmen, and government officials arguably raised public awareness of the economic pitfalls of an oligopolistic market structure.

While belief in economic equality, the strength of capitalism, and the efficacy of the market pricing mechanism together with the experience of pre-war and wartime economic measures constitute the basis of thought behind industrial policy, the combination of these sometimes conflicting factors was in practice complex. None ever dominated the others entirely; it was from the unstable balance between them that industrial policy emerged. Belief in economic democracy did not prevent the government from viewing the worker as the provider of the necessary capital for reconstruction and growth. The Japanese worker was to pay the cost of economic development, as was clearly stated in the first Economic White Paper, published in July 1947. There were expectations that the worker would benefit from economic growth, but this certainly did not preclude temporary sacrifice on his part. Belief in the market pricing mechanism did not preclude government intervention or the encouragement of economic concentration. Similarly, the belief in the strength of capitalism did not prevent the government from sometimes exempting small companies and distributors from the forces of competition.

Of the two types of industrial policy, anti-growth policy has its strongest root in the concept of economic equality. Agriculture was subsidized to aid the farmer. Smaller enterprises were also subsidized and protected, in an attempt to narrow the wage gap between small and large companies. Competition in distribution was blocked, to provide jobs and reasonable standards of living for the large number of workers in that industry.

Pro-growth industrial policy owes most to Japan's experience with economic controls, while a commitment to the market pricing mechanism affected the length of policy intervention and in some cases the way in which intervention occurred. That pro-growth policy was felt to be necessary at all probably comes from the emphasis by Japanese Marxists on the strength of capitalist economies. Japan felt it had to respond to that strength in order to survive, and that it could best do so by the government actively taking part in building a capitalist state. Pro-growth industrial policy may also be correlated with neoclassical economic beliefs. However, Japanese policy-makers did not generally cite infant industry arguments as a justification for government intervention, especially in the 1945–55 period. In fact, discussions of promoting industries often asserted that industries should be selected on non-neoclassical grounds. For example, in regard to government support of the steel industry, 'the international division of labor suggests that a Japanese steel industry is not economical and that steel should be imported. . . . However, based on employment considerations, foreign currency constraints, its importance as a basic industry, and its ability to insulate Japan from world economic cycles, a steel industry of some size must be supported even if it is unprofitable . . .'.[14] Thus, even though infant industry arguments were utilized more generally after 1955, because pro-growth policy measures were already widely in use, such arguments could not have formed the initial basis for policy formation. Rather, it was the government's pre-war and wartime experiences in allocating resources that lay behind initial post-war attempts to promote the growth of certain industries.

This brief summary of the thinking behind industrial policy highlights one major limitation of the analysis which follows. While an evaluation of the economic costs and benefits of industrial policy measures can shed light on the role that policy played in Japan's rapid development, policy-makers themselves had no single world-view under which policy measures were implemented. Measures were often adopted because they were practical rather than because they satisfied economic criteria for theoretical consistency.[15] While industrial policy measures, particularly in the 1950s, often were in fact first-best solutions in an economic sense, this was

---

[14] Ōkita Saburō, 'Kokunai Kaihatsu ka Bōeki Izon ka', *Kokumin Keizai*, 6 (1949) (Tokyo, Kokumin Keizai Kenkyū Kyōkai). As quoted in Tsuruta Toshimasa, *Sengo Nihon no Sangyō Seisaku*, 30.

[15] For an excellent analysis of the dynamics of policy formation in Japan, see Kent E. Calder, *Crisis and Compensation: Public Policy and Political Stability in Japan* (Princeton, NJ, Princeton University Press, 1988).

largely the result of Japan's history and institutional interactions. In other words, luck played a major role in whatever success Japanese industrial policy may have enjoyed, a crucial point to other developing nations wishing to imitate Japan.

4

Evidence on the Efficacy of Industrial Policy During the High-Growth Period

This chapter correlates policy measures with the economic criteria which must have been fulfilled in order for industrial policy to have positively affected Japan's economic recovery and growth. If Japanese industrial policy is to be considered to have helped foster successful economic development, it must satisfy two necessary conditions. First, industrial policy must be rational. It must serve an economic purpose which in the absence of policy would be unfulfilled. Otherwise, government intervention can only lower the growth potential of an economy. The usual competitive economic paradigm is of little use in analysing this issue, since the assumption of perfectly competitive markets is equivalent to asserting that industrial policy cannot be important in economic development. However, the framework outlined in the previous chapter provides a basis from which to judge policy rationality. If industrial policy matched market failures and externalities, it was rational and possibly served a useful function.

A second necessary condition which industrial policy must fulfil if it is integral to growth is an impact on resource allocation. Industrial policy cannot be important to economic development if it does not affect the way resources are deployed. Moreover, resource allocation must be affected in the way which policy suggests. If industrial policy attempts to direct capital to a certain industry, it must to some extent succeed in its goal or policy effectiveness will be zero.

In addition to these two necessary conditions, policy must also be characterized by flexibility. Because policy-makers cannot forecast with perfect accuracy future changes in demand, technologies, and raw material prices, policy measures will need to be adjusted or reversed if unexpected developments occur. Without flexibility, the probability that industrial policy can contribute positively to development declines dramatically.

Unfortunately, fulfilment of these conditions, policy rationality, policy impact, and flexibility, does not suffice to determine whether Japanese industrial policy was actually important in achieving high growth. While policy may have been rational and may have directed resources in the way that policy planners intended, this does not refute the claim that economic growth would have been the same or faster in the absence of policy. Although we have no counter-example as to how Japan would have developed in the absence of policy, we will examine structural change in order to determine whether the Japanese economy in the 1950s and 1960s differed substantially from its pre-war version. If differences exist, if these differences increased growth potential, and if they can be attributed to industrial policy, then the case for policy effectiveness is increased.

4.1 The Rationality of Industrial Policy

In order to address the questions of policy rationality and policy impact, consider first what industries the Japanese government targeted. The overview of Japanese development presented in Chapter 2 provides a rough indication of what industries the government emphasized between 1951 and 1973, but that discussion was largely qualitative in nature. The allocation of government subsidized loans provides more objective criteria concerning industrial targeting; this information for the 1950s is summarized in Table 4.1.[1] According to these tables, industrial policy initially focused on electric power, coal, marine transport, and steel, and to a lesser extent, agriculture, textiles, general machinery, and chemicals. Later in the decade, industrial policy also came to emphasize designated equipment and synthetic rubber in addition to its earlier targeted industries. Small and medium-sized enterprises were also the focus of industrial policy: government loans through the Smaller Business Finance Corporation rose at an average annual rate of more than 25 per cent in the latter half of the 1950s and were of comparable size to loans granted through the Japan Development Bank.

Many of the industries targeted and policies adopted in the 1950s fit neatly in the framework proposed in Chapter 3. Of the industries selected, steel, chemicals, textiles, designated equipment, and shipbuilding may all be associated with dynamic internal economies. Despite the long history of the steel industry in Japan, technological change, such as the basic oxygen furnace and integrated manufacturing, revolutionized production methods and made previous experience obsolete. From this perspective, the steel industry in Japan in the 1950s could well have been an infant industry, and a similar argument can be constructed for shipbuilding. Chemicals and textiles provide clearer examples of infant industries, since the government supported new products within these sectors. It was not traditional textiles that were targeted, but rather synthetic fibres, a

---

[1] We will only examine in detail government loans granted through the Japan Development Bank. As this bank was the most visible channel for government funds to foster investment, a breakdown of its loans provides an outline of major policy intentions. Other government financial institutions, such as the Smaller Business Finance Corporation, were quite important to industrial policy but were more highly specialized in intent.

field in which Japan had had no commercial expertise before World War II. While government support for the chemical industry in the first half of the 1950s initially emphasized fertilizers, later measures promoted new chemical industries, including synthetic rubber and synthetic resins. Similarly, designated equipment covered products largely new to Japan; their selection may perhaps be justified on infant industry grounds.

Table 4.1. Breakdown of New Loans of the Japan Development Bank, 1951–1959 (%)

	1951	1953	1955	1957	1959
Electric power	11.93	52.89	45.19	46.68	35.98
Marine transport	22.85	25.82	32.25	29.33	27.30
Mining					
Coal	15.13	5.26	7.36	6.22	7.37
Other mining	4.20	0.86	0.72	0.00	0.28
Steel	17.50	4.71	0.20	3.85	1.67
Fertilizer	3.71	0.84	1.70	0.71	1.75
Petrochemicals	0.00	0.00	0.00	2.51	6.69
Synthetic rubber	0.00	0.00	0.00	0.00	5.82
Designated equipment	0.00	0.00	0.11	5.26	4.02
General machinery	4.75	0.75	2.31	0.48	0.38
Shipbuilding	2.28	0.00	0.14	0.06	0.26
Cars	0.66	0.24	0.61	0.00	0.00
Tourism	0.29	0.17	0.00	0.63	2.87
Infrastructure	3.28	0.45	0.00	0.11	3.31
Textiles	2.86	2.55	0.51	0.88	0.29
Land transport	0.00	0.32	0.00	0.30	1.16
Air transport	0.00	0.05	1.03	0.00	0.29
Chemicals	5.74	2.27	2.47	0.35	0.68
Gas	1.89	0.79	0.30	0.00	1.67
Agriculture, Forestry, Fisheries	3.25	1.16	0.53	0.06	1.21
New technology	0.85	0.70	0.15	0.71	0.78
Regional development	0.00	0.00	0.00	0.00	0.32
Economic aid	0.00	0.00	4.27	0.80	0.89
Others	1.75	0.41	0.97	1.13	1.09
TOTAL	100.00	100.00	100.00	100.00	100.00

Source: Nihon Kaihatsu Ginkō, *Nihon Kaihatsu Ginkō Nijūgonen Shi.*

Although it is impossible to ascertain definitely that steel, shipbuilding, select machinery, chemicals (synthetic rubber), and textiles (synthetic fibre) were in fact infant industries, that these industries were associated with foreign technology imports implies that they may have been subject to dynamic internal economies. (Of the cases of technology imported in the 1949–59 period, 10.9 per cent were for metal manufacturing (largely steel), 23.1 per cent for electronic machinery, 6.1 per cent for transport

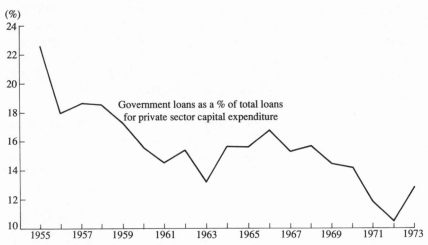

Fig. 4.1. Government Funding of Industrial Investment
Source: Sōmu Chō, *Nihon Chōki Tōkei Sōran*, 3.

machinery, 24.4 per cent for chemicals, and 4.6 per cent for textiles.)[2]
Learning by doing effects could well have been important; certainly the
cost of output per unit for these industries declined substantially over
time.[3] Not only might targeting of these industries have been appropriate,
but policies chosen often had first-best characteristics amongst the realm
of possible policy options. In the case of dynamic economies internal to
an industry, appropriate policy response is generally a subsidy. In practice, the use of subsidies was widespread: these were provided not only
through tax breaks, but also through low-interest government loans.[4]
Interestingly, these subsidies generally entailed low administrative costs.
Favourable tax treatment cost the government little to administer, and
the channelling of government funds through the Japan Development
Bank also helped to avoid the high disbursement costs that would occur
if a non-specialist government organ were in control.

---

[2] Kagaku Gijutsu Chō, *Kagaku Gijutsu Hakusho* (Tokyo, Ōkurashō Insatsu Kyoku,
1964), 347.
    [3] For example, between 1956 and 1960, production costs (labour and raw materials) for
crude steel fell 29%. Hugh Patrick and Hideo Sato, 'The Political Economy of United
States–Japan Trade in Steel', in Kozo Yamamura (ed.), *Policies and Trade Issues of the
Japanese Economy* (Seattle, University of Washington Press, 1982), 205.
    [4] Loans granted through government financial institutions such as the Japan
Development Bank generally had interest rates equivalent to the long-term prime rate. In
many instances, rates even lower than this were granted. Whatever rate applied, however,
loans from the Japan Development Bank were always less expensive than loans from private
sector banks since the JDB did not require compensating balances. (Nihon Kaihatsu Ginkō
Chōsa Bu, *Tōkei Yōran* (Tokyo, Nihon Kaihatsu Ginkō Chōsa Bu, various years).)

If the costs of implementing policy measures were held down through utilizing subsidies, the costs of formulating policy were also kept low, primarily because of a multi-layered system of checks and balances. While policy formation was largely the domain of well-trained bureaucrats, businessmen and academics also sat on policy committees, thus helping to avoid ill-conceived policy measures. Business views were also transmitted by industry organizations (*gyōkai*) which had regular, in-depth contact with bureaucrats, providing the government as they did with detailed data on output, inventories, shipments, and investment plans for members of these associations.[5] Another check on policy formulation occurred at the bureaucratic level: although MITI officials were directly responsible for much of industrial policy, government budgets were the domain of the Ministry of Finance, and other government ministries including the Ministry of Agriculture and the Ministry of Construction also had input into policy formulation.

Tariffs on imports were another policy measure used to support the targeted industries of steel, chemicals, synthetic fibre, and shipbuilding, allowing domestic manufacturers to capture sales that would otherwise have gone to foreign companies. While also low in administrative costs, tariffs did impose a direct burden on users of these products, and in this regard were not as optimal as subsidies such as tax incentives and government loans. Another problem associated with using tariffs as a means to support infant industries is a bias against exports. By insulating domestic producers from foreign competition, tariffs can prevent industries from becoming competitive enough to export. A third problem associated with tariffs is the issue of dynamic production complementarities. The profitability of investment in an industry such as shipbuilding or car manufacture may depend crucially on investment in the steel industry if imports of steel are blocked.

Japanese industrial policy responded to all of these problems associated with using tariffs. In order to reduce the additional cost to users of tariffed products, the government employed further tariffs and/or direct subsidies. Hence, the higher cost of Japanese steel to shipbuilders and car manufacturers was countered by tax breaks for these industries, trade restrictions, and, in the case of shipbuilding, low-interest government loans. The possible bias against exports arising from tariffs may never have been high in Japan's case, given that most manufacturers expected to eventually compete in world markets. This expectation on the part of

---

[5] These industry organizations also provided members with information about policy decisions, in effect acting as a two-way conduit at low cost to both the public and private sector. This function was enhanced by occasionally placing retired government bureaucrats in the management of industry organizations next to officials from companies in the organization.

industries was reinforced by government exhortation as well as by export promotion measures in the form of tax incentives whereby manufacturers could claim as a tax credit up to 50 per cent of export sales or 3 per cent of total sales, whichever was smaller.

Closely related to the possibility of an export bias is the bias against competition which trade controls can generate. This is clearest in the case of import quotas, through which the government essentially grants a monopoly position to quota recipients. Tariffs, however, can also impede competition by effectively removing foreign companies from the market-place. Domestic producers may find few reasons to compete in order to reduce prices below the combined total of the foreign price plus the fixed margin provided by the tariff. Japanese authorities avoided this problem by fostering intense competition amongst Japanese companies, ensuring that the tariff did not effectively generate a floor price. Competition was promoted through the allocation of foreign exchange: MITI granted foreign exchange to multiple companies in an industry rather than just one or two. Similarly, government loans were granted to several companies within targeted industries, and tax incentives applied to all. The government also spread the benefits of imported technologies across numerous firms. MITI also used this tool to selectively reward winners in an industry and punish losers. In short, the tools of industrial policy were used in such a way as to ensure that domestic competition was vigorous.

The third problem associated with tariffs, the generation of investment complementarities, was answered by drawing up and publishing long-term industry plans. Created largely by industries, these plans provided a general blueprint as to the future direction of output and investment. Thus, the car industry, for example, could refer to long-term plans published by the steel industry in formulating its own investment decisions. Moreover, the government helped to spread this information, informing industries about other investment plans as well as attempting itself to guarantee that investment plans were consistent across industries.

Costs associated with tariffs are far from negligible, as can be inferred by the numerous policies designed to offset these costs. Even so, tariffs may still be part of a first-best policy solution. Apart from the standard terms of trade argument for tariffs, one that policy-makers in fact did not use, tariffs over time may be more easily changed, providing flexibility in adjusting subsidy disbursement. It may be easier to fine-tune tariff rates than tax rates or government grants, giving the government more ability to gradually reduce actual support of industries. Control over this may have helped to offset the costs of tariffs.[6] Most importantly, tariff costs

---

[6] Despite the ease with which tariffs could have been adjusted, in practice Japan did not frequently change these rates, waiting until 1960 to begin trade liberalization on a wide scale.

may further have been offset by the control they gave to the Japanese government in negotiating the import of new foreign technologies.[7] The government acted to screen foreign technology, ensuring that the most appropriate technology was purchased by controlling the import process. In general, one technology would be selected from a variety of possibilities, and one company in an industry was selected to introduce a technology from abroad. Depending on the success of this trial, other firms might then be allowed to import the same technology, or another firm could be selected to introduce a different form of this technology. In cases where two competing foreign technologies appeared to be of equal effect, the government would encourage the introduction of both, allowing two domestic firms to compete with these technologies before finally choosing the winner and encouraging its diffusion throughout the industry.[8]

The government not only acted to screen technology, but it also helped Japanese industries obtain foreign know-how at very cheap prices.[9] It bargained directly with foreign companies, refusing to allow technology imports on terms it thought unfavourable to Japanese buyers. In practice, this meant reducing royalties paid as well as limiting agreed constraints on the export of goods produced by Japanese companies using foreign technologies. Of course, government control over the import of technology was made possible only by tariffs and constraints on foreign investment. With these avenues of extracting return on know-how blocked, foreign companies had an incentive to license technology. Since foreign companies were often monopoly suppliers of a technology, direct supervision of the Japanese government over the licensing terms may have helped prevent foreign companies from extracting monopoly gains.

Although policy-makers did not, at least initially, explicitly view steel, chemicals, select machinery, synthetic fibres, and shipbuilding as infant industries, that much of industrial policy was at least implicitly concerned with this issue can be inferred from the emphasis which policy-makers placed on the learning process associated with the introduction of new technologies. To the extent that these were infant industries, industrial policy towards them could have been economically rational. Support measures were often first-best policy solutions. While tariffs traditionally

---

[7] While it was capital controls that gave the Japanese government direct power over negotiating imports of foreign technologies, tariffs on imported products increased the motivation of foreign firms to sell their technologies to Japanese companies.

[8] For a general discussion of Japanese policy towards the import of technology, see Merton Peck and Tamura Shūji, 'Technology', in H. Patrick and H. Rosovsky (eds.), *Asia's New Giant: How the Japanese Economy Works* (Washington, DC, The Brookings Institute, 1976), 525–85.

[9] Ozawa Terutomo, *Japan's Technological Challenge to the West, 1950–1974: Motivation and Accomplishment* (Cambridge, Mass., MIT Press, 1974), 52–7.

do not fall into this category, they did provide a stimulus for technology imports and gave the government control over import terms. It is conceivable that the benefits which accrued from government control over the import of technology may have largely offset the economic costs of tariffs.

The rationality of another policy commonly used to influence resource allocation in designated industries, the formation of cartels and the encouragement of mergers, might also be questioned. Such policy cannot be part of any first-best solution unless it can be proved that efficiency did rise with firm size. The existence of economies of scale, whereby production costs fall as output rises, remains controversial although empirical evidence favours such a view.[10] Hence, rather than justifying cartelization and mergers as a means to obtain economies of scale, it suffices to note that the detrimental impact of such policies, the lessening of competitive forces, was at least partially offset through policies which specifically fostered competition between firms. Moreover, cartelization may have helped to disseminate information to small producers about the outside environment that they might otherwise have failed to receive as well as helping to facilitate the co-ordination of investment amongst firms. Therefore, even without assuming scale economies, cartelization and merger policy may have provided some useful functions; at the very least, the detrimental impact of this policy was limited by other measures designed to spur competition amongst firms.[11]

Unlike shipbuilding, steel, chemicals, select machinery, and textiles, policy towards the electric power industry cannot be fitted into an infant industry argument. Even so, most governments agree about the need to intervene in this industry. Power generation is a natural monopoly, requiring government control to ensure optimal investment and pricing. The electric power industry also lends itself to dynamic investment complementarities: the profitability of investment by users of electric power

---

[10] For empirical evidence on the existence of scale economies, see, for example, Ozaki Iwao, 'The Effects of Technological Change on the Economic Growth of Japan, 1955–1970', in Karen Polenske and Jiri Skolka (eds.), *Advances in Input-Output Analysis* (Cambridge, Mass., Ballinger Publishing Company, 1976), 93–111. Yoshioka Kanji has also provided non-parametric estimates of production functions in Japan which show that scale economies exist. (Yoshioka Kanji, *Nihon no Seizōgyō/Kinyūgyō no Seisansei Bunseki: Kibo no Keizaisei/Gijutsu Henka No Jisshō Kenkyū* (Tokyo, Tōyō Keizai Shinpō Sha, 1989).) However, constant returns to scale translog production functions also fit most Japanese industries quite well (Kuroda Masahiro, *Economic Growth and Structural Change in Japan*, 1 (Tokyo, Keio University, 1991)).

[11] The obsession of policy-makers with firm size suggests that they did believe in scale economies; this belief probably also reinforced their use of tariffs as a policy tool. However, if static scale economies did in fact occur, tariffs would be a second-best solution. Denying foreign firms access to the domestic market would allow domestic companies to capture scale economies, but at a cost to users of the tariffed products. Equal benefits at lower cost could have been obtained by larger direct subsidies to the targeted industries.

will depend upon the availability of electricity. For this reason as well, government intervention is needed.

Although many of the targeted industries may well meet criteria for rational intervention, the coal and marine transport industries do not. Despite improvements in shaft mining technology, it is difficult to argue that coal was in any real sense an infant industry, nor was it a natural monopoly. The marine transport industry also does not fit either of these categories. Government support of this latter industry had as its goal not only the fostering of marine transport but also the promotion of the domestic shipbuilding industry, since government loans to marine transport were used to purchase domestically produced vessels. Even as a policy to stimulate shipbuilding, subsidies to the marine transport industry are not a first-best solution. The most direct way to promote shipbuilding is to subsidize investment in that industry; this avoids the cost of excess capacity in marine transport that can result should subsidies there be designed to encourage ship orders.

Government intervention in marine transport and coal cannot be justified on infant industry grounds, on linkage effects, or on the grounds of a natural monopoly.[12] Hence, policy towards these industries can only be economically rational if general dynamic externalities were important to the Japanese economy. If industrialization created an atmosphere that was conducive to further industrialization, then the widespread use of trade barriers and subsidies would rationally exploit this opportunity. In turn, trade barriers across many industries will generate numerous dynamic investment complementarities. For instance, with imports of coal controlled, profitable investment in steel, electric power, and chemicals depended upon domestic coal output and investment. Similarly, the exclusion of foreign companies from the Japanese shipping industry made the profitability not only of Japanese shipbuilders but also of all exporters dependent on the domestic marine transport industry, necessitating the co-ordination of investment decisions amongst industries.

However, this reasoning is so general that it is unsatisfying and unconvincing. The assumption of general dynamic externalities and the resultant need for widespread tariffs and subsidies can be used to assert the rationality of policy intervention in almost any industry. It is the opposite extreme to the assumption of perfect markets: the latter assumes away any rationality for industrial policy while the former essentially assumes

---

[12] Undoubtedly one reason the government targeted these industries, particularly coal, was a shortage of foreign currency. In itself, this shortage could only necessitate support of a very inefficient industry with poor growth prospects such as coal if Japan had no other way to earn or borrow foreign exchange. The economy almost certainly would have benefited more had policy-makers devoted resources spent on coal to more potentially successful import competing industries.

that all policy may be rational. It seems more useful to assume that general dynamic externalities did not exist and investigate policy rationality in this stricter environment. In this case, subsidizing coal and marine transport and blocking foreign competition entailed a substantial cost on Japanese users of coal and shipping. The damage done by this was compounded in the case of coal, since it directed resources which might otherwise have been used elsewhere to an industry which would eventually prove uncompetitive. While the protection of the domestic marine transport industry has many precedents in other countries, as an economic policy it was certainly not rational. Although this may have helped to support the Japanese shipbuilding industry, it would have been less costly to increase subsidies to shipbuilding if that was indeed the policy goal.

The issue of the rationality of industrial policy in the 1950s has thus far been confined to measures designed to promote the development of industries which would be competitive in the future. These pro-growth policies were probably on average rational: excluding coal and marine transport, targeted industries may well have been subject to dynamic internal economies, and policy measures for these infant industries can be interpreted as generally making economic sense. However, industrial policy also targeted anti-growth industries, industries whose future prospects were not thought to be particularly bright but which nevertheless were supported because of the employment opportunities they provided. On these grounds, industrial policy targeted all small enterprises in addition to distributors. Policy towards agriculture may also be viewed at least partially as fitting into this category.

Anti-growth policy is economically rational if it leads to the survival of some portion of the population which otherwise would starve. Additionally, anti-growth policy is rational when labour relocation involves sizeable private and social costs and when there is the possibility of limited advances in productivity in these low-growth industries. It seems probable that conditions in the Japanese economy in the 1950s were such as to necessitate some form of anti-growth policy. There is widespread evidence of surplus labour in the 1950s. Agriculture had employed approximately 14 million in 1930; in 1950 it employed 16.1 million people. Not until very late in the decade did the agricultural population decline to pre-war levels, suggesting the existence of surplus labour at least from the end of the war into the 1950s. This existence is further reinforced by wage differentials between large and small companies, with large firms in 1955 paying workers 1.7 times the rate of medium-sized enterprises.[13]

The government supported this surplus labour through its agricultural

---

[13] Nakamura Takafusa, *The Postwar Japanese Economy*, 164.

policies, its policies towards the distribution sector, and policies towards small enterprises. Most of these measures could be considered economically rational. In regard to agriculture, the government provided subsidies through price supports, a policy which did not discourage technological innovation. In fact, agricultural productivity advanced rapidly: after increasing 10 per cent in 1954 and 20 per cent in 1955, productivity increased at about a 4 per cent annual rate in the latter half of the decade.[14] Had subsidies taken the form of wage supports, these not only would have been difficult to administer but would have reduced incentives for productivity advances.

Government policy towards agriculture was actually more positive in the 1950s than the discussion thus far indicates. Support of the fertilizer industry in Japan was provided in order to increase the use of chemicals in agriculture, thus raising productivity. Mechanization was promoted, and the government also provided funds for improving the infrastructure for irrigation in order to raise agricultural output. In short, it not only attempted to maintain employment in agriculture, but it targeted productivity increases as well even though it had no expectation of creating an export industry. Such policy was largely rational: the government tried to maximize potential gains in output in agriculture while minimizing the dislocation of rural workers in a surplus labour situation.[15]

Anti-growth policy in the distribution sector largely took the form of constraints on competition. Revisions of the Anti-Monopoly Law in 1953 permitted manufacturers to set retail prices, effectively blocking competition that otherwise might have arisen between small and large retailers. Fixed margins also supported the proliferation of numerous wholesalers, as did restraints on the expansion of large retailers.[16] While this blocking of competition was perhaps the only feasible way that the government could support employment in the distribution system, policy provided less incentive for technological innovation in distribution than in agriculture. Because restrictions limited increases in market share, incentives to improve efficiency were reduced.

Small enterprises in the 1950s were supported through government loans, through the cartelization of exporters, through tax breaks, and through limiting competition. As outlined above, the latter factor was

[14] This figure excludes the year 1956 when agricultural output fell 5.5%. (Sōmu Chō Tōkei Kyoku, *Nihon Chōki Tōkei Sōran*, 2: 100–1.)

[15] For agricultural policy to have been totally rational, it must be shown that domestically produced fertilizer is preferable to imports. This might be done on the grounds that the expertise gained in fertilizer production was useful in creating new chemical industries, a plausible if not entirely convincing argument. However, the reason the government promoted fertilizer probably had more to do with a shortage of foreign exchange and import constraints than it did with linkages to the chemical industry.

[16] In June 1956, the government implemented the Department Store Law (*Hyakkaten Hō*), which required government approval for the establishment of new stores.

particularly important for distributors, but more than 50 per cent of smaller companies were engaged in distribution.[17] Cartelization was a tool applied to small companies in industries such as spinning, clothing, table linens, and glass in order to promote exports in these industries.[18] This may have had some impact in diffusing information about foreign markets to smaller companies, but attempts to use cartels to guide investment by smaller companies were not successful.[19] Loans and tax breaks helped support the continued existence of many smaller enterprises: while not necessarily a plus for economic efficiency, these measures did support employment. Moreover, excluding small distributors, industrial policy did not act as a disincentive to competition.

It is also possible to classify policy towards the coal industry in the latter half of the decade as a type of anti-growth rather than pro-growth policy. Whereas policy initially promoted increased output, the Second Coal Rationalization Plan (1956–60) emphasized the closing of inefficient mines, and a reduction in production costs even at the expense of output.[20] The availability and low price of oil changed the long-term outlook for the domestic coal industry, and the government responded by shifting its emphasis away from growth and towards a managed contraction, providing funds to purchase and close small inefficient mines while maintaining as much as possible employment in the industry. Given the existence of surplus labour, this shift in policy towards coal made limited sense. However, it was only because the government had directed resources towards coal mining in the first place that employment was a concern at all. In other words, policy towards coal in the second half of the decade was designed to offset some of the policy mistakes that had occurred previously.[21]

Many of the anti-growth measures outlined above could well have been rational in the 1950s, since they helped to promote the survival of the surplus labour force. Administrative costs of these policies were extremely low, perhaps in contrast to the alternative of unemployment insurance, which would probably not have been feasible anyway given the size of this surplus pool of workers. Anti-growth policy towards agriculture and small enterprises did not eliminate incentives for technological innovation, another mark of policy rationality. Although distribution policies unfortunately did not share this characteristic, probably no feasible measure to support employment in distribution could have avoided this pitfall. There

[17] Chūshō Kigyō Chō, *Chūshō Kigyō Hakusho* (Tokyo, Ōkurashō Insatsu Kyoku, 1963), 48–52.

[18] Kōsei Torihiki Iinkai, *Kōsei Torihiki Iinkai Nenji Hōkoku* (Tokyo, Ōkurashō Insatsu Kyoku, 1971), 291–302.

[19] For such policy failure in the textile industry, see pp. 97, 197–9.

[20] Nihon Kaihatsu Ginkō, *Nihon Kaihatsu Ginkō Jūnen Shi*, 222–32.

[21] A similar argument holds for policy towards the marine transport industry.

were, of course, other significant costs associated with anti-growth policies. These were paid directly by the Japanese consumer in the form of
higher prices for food and goods. However, the benefit of these policies,
worker survival, may have outweighed the costs, just as overall benefits
to the Japanese consumer of rapid growth in the 1950s probably outweighed the costs paid to support inefficient industries.

If industrial policy in the 1950s, with a few notable exceptions such as
coal and marine transport, may have largely been rational, that rationality arguably lessened as time went by. True, industrial policy in the early
1960s was characterized by a wonderful flexibility: as the disappearance
of surplus labour lessened the importance of measures designed to support employment, policy towards distribution and smaller enterprises
focused increasingly on promoting modernization and technological innovation. At the same time, support given to older infant industries was
decreased, as new infant industries were identified and promoted.
However, this decrease in support towards older industries probably did
not occur quickly enough. Moreover, policy promoted over-investment in
many industries in order to offset the perceived threat of trade and capital liberalization,[22] increasing their dependence on exports. Finally, a high
level of support towards agriculture became entrenched despite a tighter
labour market, as the political power of the farmer rose.

The 1960s and the early 1970s witnessed a decreasing emphasis on
energy generation, indicated by the declining proportion of government
loans going towards the electric power and coal industries. At the same
time, the government emphasized new energy-related industries, including
petroleum and nuclear power. It also promoted other new manufacturing
industries, including computers, computer software, petrochemicals, and
anti-pollution equipment (see Tables 4.2 and 8.1). Infant industry arguments can again be applied to justify government intervention in all of
these new industries; measures adopted to support these industries
included the usual collection of tax breaks, low-interest loans, and trade
protection, and were generally rational, first-best policy responses.[23]

---

[22] For a discussion as to how policy at least indirectly promoted excessive investment in
the steel industry, see Ch. 5.

[23] One possible exception to the first-best rule was the establishment in Aug. 1961 of the
Japan Electronic Computer Corporation (JECC; *Nihon Denshi Keisanki Kabushiki Kaisha*)
which bought Japanese computers and leased them to domestic users at favourable rates. In
effect, this was an output subsidy (which totalled 750 billion yen over the 14-year existence
of JECC), potentially a second-best solution compared to the first-best policy of an investment subsidy. However, it seems unlikely that over-investment in computer production was
caused by the JECC or that the efficiency of firms using a JECC computer was weakened
compared to users of imported computers. Moreover, competitors such as IBM generally
subsidized the leasing of their computers. For further details, see Shinjo Koji, 'Konpyūtā
Sangyō', in Komiya Ryūtarō, Okuno Masahiro, Suzumura Kōtarō (eds.), *Nihon no Sangyō
Seisaku* (Tokyo, University of Tokyo Press, 1984), 297–323.

Table 4.2. Breakdown of New Loans of the Japan Development Bank, 1961–1969 (%)

	1961	1963	1965	1967	1969
Electric power	24.49	20.69	8.72	7.23	7.57
Marine transport	20.90	22.70	44.71	37.94	33.65
Mining					
Coal	10.51	8.78	7.09	6.52	0.60
Other mining	0.99	3.67	3.31	0.00	0.00
Steel	1.04	0.78	0.25	0.77	0.21
Fertilizer*	1.39	1.61	1.04	0.43	1.47
Petrochemicals†	0.58	1.65	2.65	5.88	5.61
Synthetic rubber	0.35	0.41	0.65	0.43	0.00
Designated equipment	8.45	6.61	3.26	3.58	3.24
General machinery	1.43	1.76	4.42	0.00	0.00
Shipbuilding	0.27	0.43	0.63	0.67	0.51
Cars	0.00	0.00	0.00	2.15	0.34
Computers	0.46	1.24	2.75	3.01	5.30
Tourism	3.41	5.11	1.75	0.70	2.33
Infrastructure	2.78	2.08	1.58	0.00	0.00
Harbour development	0.17	0.00	0.00	0.03	0.05
Warehouses/silos	1.09	1.20	0.79	1.28	0.54
Distribution centres	0.00	0.00	0.00	0.26	1.62
Distribution: equip. & improvement	0.00	0.00	0.00	1.28	0.82
Anti-pollution equipment	0.00	0.14	0.73	0.27	0.91
Textiles	0.08	0.00	0.34	0.28	0.96
Land transport	0.99	3.67	3.31	0.00	0.00
Air transport	0.99	0.74	0.13	0.00	0.00
Chemicals	0.25	0.00	0.00	0.00	0.46
Gas	0.07	0.00	0.00	0.17	0.08
Agriculture, Forestry, Fisheries	0.27	0.00	0.33	0.21	0.88
New technology	0.46	1.69	0.60	0.00	0.00
Regional development	18.49	19.91	17.04	16.02	15.42
Others	3.25	2.19	2.46	0.00	0.00
TOTAL	100.00	100.00	100.00	100.00	100.00

* After 1967, this includes ammonia as well as ammonium sulfate.
† After 1965, the petrochemicals category also includes the petroleum industry, which until that time had received no loans.

Source: Nihon Kaihatsu Ginkō, *Nihon Kaihatsu Ginkō Nijūgonen Shi*.

As the government promoted new infant industries, it also trimmed support granted to infant industries targeted in the 1950s. For example, government loans to steel were reduced, tariffs were cut, and tax incentives were decreased. This reduction is crucial for the rationality of any infant industry policy: support should decline as competitiveness rises. Despite meeting this criterion, it is not clear that support was reduced as quickly as it should have been. In practice, this is extremely difficult to judge: just as it is not possible to prove that a targeted industry was in fact an 'infant', so too is it not feasible to judge when support should be cut. Moreover, policy has a natural tendency to continue support for too long, since reducing government aid before an industry is truly competitive will greatly reduce that industry's chance of survival and thus waste all government aid spent to that point. Even so, the increased competitiveness of steel, indicated by its expanding share of Japanese exports, probably implied the optimality of a more rapid reduction in government support. Worries about the impact of trade and capital liberalization on all Japanese industries may have curtailed the speed by which tax incentives for steel were decreased, and a similar argument can be made for the machinery industry. Additionally, worries about liberalization prompted the government to encourage mergers amongst large steel and shipbuilding companies, the economic rationality of which is certainly in doubt. Efficiency gains from mergers amongst large companies are few unless economies of scale exist, and efficiency losses can be great if mergers reduce competition. Japanese merger policy did seem to avoid most efficiency losses, since government supervision ensured a high continuing degree of competition in steel[24] and shipbuilding, but it is not clear that merger policy was beneficial.[25]

The disappearance of surplus labour in Japan in the 1960s resulted in a shift in some of the measures used to maintain employment. Policy towards smaller enterprises and towards distribution became much more positive in nature, promoting rather than blocking competition. Modernization was actively encouraged, as can be seen from increased government loans to distribution as well as in the rapid rise in loans for smaller enterprises. In the case of distribution, some of this encouragement was passive: existing restrictions did not pertain to new types of stores including supermarkets and other large chain stores. However, the government still attempted to regulate competition, not promoting it to the point that numerous bankruptcies occurred.[26]

While policy towards smaller enterprises and distribution shifted as surplus labour disappeared, policy towards agriculture did not. Agricultural policy in the 1960s had two competing goals: improving productivity

---

[24] For a discussion of how government supervision promoted competition in the steel industry, see Ch. 5.

[25] According to a simulation analysis by Yamawaki, domestic Japanese steel prices would have been lower and export prices higher in the 1971–5 period had the merger between Yawata Steel and Fuji Steel not occurred. (Yamawaki Hideki, 'Market Structure, Capacity Expansion and Pricing: A Model Applied to the Japanese Steel Industry', *International Journal of Industrial Organization*, 2 (Amsterdam, North Holland Publishing Co., 1984), 29–62.

[26] That the government remained concerned with the costs of competition can be seen from its continued implementation of such laws as the Department Store Law as well as from the administration of loans through the Smaller Business Finance Corporation.

while at the same time maintaining the large agricultural work-force. The latter goal was the result of the rising importance of the rural voter to the ruling Liberal Democratic Party and would prove far more important than the former. In an attempt to buy rural votes, the government introduced a new price-fixing system for rice linked to urban wages in 1960, and raised the price it paid farmers for rice each year by a substantial amount. Trade protection was also strengthened. These measures largely negated efforts to raise agricultural productivity. Small landowners, expecting higher land prices and receiving government subsidies, did not sell their plots, although non-farm employment became increasingly important to their total income package.[27] The Agricultural Basic Law (*Nōgyo Kihon Hō*), which provided government subsidies for investment in new technology and new areas of production, did promote mechanization and specialized agricultural activities, but this did not compensate for the productivity constraints caused by the large number of small plots.[28] With the government reliant on rural voters and unable to encourage an increase in plot size, agricultural policy in the 1960s lost the rationality it may have had in the previous decade. Furthermore, by promoting the misuse of resources, agricultural policy became a constraint on potential growth of the Japanese economy. Certainly the purchasing power of the Japanese consumer was reduced through high prices for rice and other agricultural products.

Industrial policy in the 1960s and early 1970s also became more concerned with easing the adjustment costs of industries in a structural or cyclical downturn. Policy towards the coal industry continued to emphasize the closing of inefficient mines, but even more aggressively than in the past.[29] Coal output declined from its post-war peak of 55.4 million tons in 1961 to 50 million tons in 1965 as the number of mines active year round fell from 662 to 287.[30] Decreases thereafter were even more rapid, as output declined to 38 million tons in 1970 and 27 million tons in 1972 while the number of mines in full operation fell to 102 and then to 77.[31] At the same time that policy promoted the shrinkage of the coal industry overall, measures were also implemented to slow the pace of decline. For example, the government promoted the construction of coal-

[27] Nakamura Takafusa, *The Postwar Japanese Economy*, 193–206.

[28] Hayami Yūjirō and Yamada Saburō, *The Agricultural Development of Japan* (Tokyo, University of Tokyo Press, 1991), 88–105.

[29] The Miike coal strike, which began 25 Jan. 1960 and lasted 282 days, acted as a catalyst for a major rationalization programme in the coal industry. This programme combined regional assistance and worker retraining with reductions in employment and helped to act as a blueprint for measures towards other declining industries (Laura Hein, *Fueling Growth: The Energy Revolution and Economic Policy in Postwar Japan* (Cambridge, Mass., Harvard University Press, 1990), 323–8).

[30] Nihon Kaihatsu Ginkō, *Nihon Kaihatsu Ginkō Nijūgonen Shi*, 388–91.

[31] Ibid. 389.

fired electric power plants, encouraged the construction of vessels to carry coal more efficiently, and established designated prices for coal used in the generation of electric power.

This attempt to manage an orderly decline in the coal industry was probably rational. Although the disappearance of surplus labour makes it impossible to justify these measures on the grounds of employment alone, imperfect labour mobility probably necessitated government intervention in order to facilitate the transfer of miners to new jobs. From this perspective, government assistance to affected regions and measures to promote worker retraining were beneficial; programmes also may have helped to curtail the social unrest that accompanied the closing of mines.[32] However, it was industrial policy towards coal in the first place that caused the expansion of an unprofitable industry. Later attempts to manage the decline of the coal industry were rational and do illustrate the ability of policy-makers to reverse policy mistakes. Even so, the benefits of these later policy measures must be weighed against the costs of the initial policy failure.

Policy towards textiles also became increasingly concerned with promoting a decrease in capacity. By linking the allocation of cheap, profitable cotton imports to the production capacity of the cotton spinners in the early 1950s, government policy promoted over-investment.[33] This mistake was compounded with the passage in 1956 of the Law Concerning Temporary Measures for Investment in Textile Manufacturing (*Seni Kōgyō Setsubi Rinji Sochi Hō*), as manufacturers rushed to increase capacity ahead of controls. To deal with excess capacity in the textile industry in the 1960s and early 1970s, the government provided funds to purchase old textile equipment in addition to offering tax concessions to firms that scrapped capacity.[34] It is difficult to view these policy measures favourably: not only did they meet with limited success in reducing capacity, but these measures were necessitated by past policy mistakes.

Industrial policy in the 1960s and early 1970s did exhibit several unambiguous signs of rationality. Measures used to support infant industries in the previous decade were generally reduced, a necessary condition for the rationality of any infant industry policy. The government shifted its focus to the promotion of newer infant industries, often adopting first-best

[32] This marks one of the government's first attempts to orchestrate the decline of an industry. In the 1970s and 1980s, adjustment policy was used with increasing frequency, preempting the importance of traditional anti-growth policy. In practice, adjustment policy came to combine elements of both pro-growth and anti-growth policy as practised in the 1950s. For further details, see Ch. 8.

[33] Tsuruta Toshimasa, *Sengo Nihon no Sangyō Seisaku*, 194–5.

[34] Yamazawa Ippei, 'Seni Sangyō', in Komiya Ryūtarō, Okuno Masahiro, Suzumura Kōtarō (eds.), *Nihon no Sangyō Seisaku* (Tokyo, University of Tokyo Press, 1984), 345–67.

measures to address the causes of dynamic internal economies in computers, petrochemicals, and anti-pollution equipment. Moreover, as the labour market became tight, measures designed to block competition and ensure employment in distribution and in smaller enterprises in general were eased. This shift in policy, from constraining growth to promoting it, was not only rational in the light of the disappearance of surplus labour, but also reflected a remarkable flexibility on the part of policy-makers.

At the same time, industrial policy in several instances failed to exhibit rationality. Most damaging was agricultural policy, which became driven by political rather than economic considerations. As a result, measures largely blocked competition in the sector, even though the need to absorb workers in agriculture had dissipated. Secondly, worries about the liberalization of trade and foreign capital also probably caused the reduction in support for older infant industries to occur at a slower-than-optimal speed. Even after export performance showed that the Japanese steel industry had become one of the most competitive in the world, government support continued in the form of tax incentives. The rationality of policy to increase firm size is also questionable: perhaps the best that can be said about this is that such policy was balanced by measures to ensure that competition amongst firms remained strong. Finally, measures to control the decline of the coal and textile industries met with mixed results: policy towards coal may have been economically rational and successful, but policy towards the textile industry failed to meet stated goals in reducing capacity. Moreover, adjustment measures for both industries were made necessary because of past policy mistakes.

If the rationality of industrial policy became increasingly questionable from 1960, events in the early 1970s would call into question the basic aim of industrial policy. Crowded living conditions and growing pollution problems generated dissatisfaction with the goal of economic growth, and as a result industrial policy began to emphasize the quality of growth rather than simply its achievement. Moreover, specific past measures came to be viewed as responsible for the problems Japan faced, since the development of heavy industry in Japan generated much of the pollution in question. This mistrust of specific policies grew as the promotion of exports was linked to appreciations of the yen and the first oil shock found Japan highly dependent on energy-intensive industries.

4.2   The Impact of Industrial Policy on Resource Allocation

The matching of policy type to market failure in Section 4.1 does suggest that industrial policy could have been effective in promoting post-war development, albeit to a decreasing extent from 1960. Certainly many of the policies were probably economically rational, at least in the early stages of Japan's growth. This cannot be stated with absolute certainty, since it is not possible to verify that the hypothesized market imperfections and externalities did in fact exist. Targeted industries may not have actually been infant industries, despite their association with newly imported technologies and their sharp reductions in unit cost over time. They may only appear so, especially in retrospect to someone attempting to evaluate policy. The trade-off between minimizing the costs of unemployment through anti-growth policy and maximizing potential output through pro-growth policy is even more elusive. It is not possible to verify if the costs paid to support these low-growth industries were curtailed sufficiently, nor is it possible to empirically ascertain that these costs were in fact necessary.

While the above classification can be criticized as simply an ex post justification for industrial policy, it does favour the contention of possible policy rationality, albeit to a waning degree after 1960. Even if policy was rational, however, this still leaves us a long distance away from our goal of evaluating the efficacy of industrial policy. Another necessary condition that policy must fulfil if it was important to economic growth is an impact on resource allocation. Did industrial policy in Japan influence the way in which resources were allocated, thus affecting the pattern of economic development?

The answer to this is an unambiguous affirmative. Proof is provided first by the size of government finance relative to private sector lending. As shown in Table 4.3, government-subsidized loans accounted for over 30 per cent of total investment in agriculture, electric power, marine transport, and coal throughout the 1950s. Government loans initially accounted for over one-third of investment in steel, chemicals, machinery, and textiles, but decreased gradually as time progressed. Even so, government funding continued to account for more than 10 per cent of investment outlays for most of these industries throughout the 1950s. Direct government funding became less important in general in the 1960s and early 1970s, although it still accounted for a sizeable percentage of capital expenditure in many industries. Interestingly, government funding continued to provide most of the investment funds for coal, marine transport, and agriculture, industries facing problems caused by past policy mistakes or subject to a high degree of protectionism.

Through low-interest loans, the government directly influenced investment in recipient industries. Additionally, government funding also served to attract private sector funds to designated industries. Government loans probably acted as both a signal and a guarantee of government interest in promoting targeted industries; as such, the perceived risk on the part of

100   The Efficacy of Industrial Policy

Table 4.3. Government Funding as a Percentage of Capital Expenditure by Industry

	1952	1955	1956	1965
Coal	33	32.8	46.9	60.9
Agriculture	70	48.3	54.9	53.0
Textiles	46	19.6	12.6	14.6
Chemical	35	10.9	6.5	6.3
Iron/steel	32	4.3	3.9	2.9
Machinery	33	18.0	6.5	8.4
Electricity	50	43.0	24.2	20.8
Marine transportation	33	49.6	33.1	65.1
Land transportation	19	9.5	14.7	19.8
TOTAL		29.6	15.6	16.5

Source: Tsuruta Toshimasa, *Sengo Nihon no Sangyō Seisaku*, for 1952 figures.
All other data from Nihon Ginkō, *Honpō Keizai Nenpō*, *Keizai Tōkei Nenpō*.

private banks of lending to these industries was reduced. The direct effect of government loans together with the indirect effect of risk reduction helped to stimulate capital expenditure in recipient industries, with investment in many of these industries rising faster than the national average.[35]

That industrial policy influenced resource allocation and capital expenditure is also suggested by Fig. 4.2. This figure actually understates the true magnitude of these subsidies since it fails to take account of accelerated depreciation measures for which data are not available. By reducing the cost of investment, these tax breaks as a whole stimulated capital accumulation in targeted industries.

Further evidence that industrial policy did influence resource allocation, promoting investment in designated industries, is provided by the impact of technology imports on investment. Technology imports, controlled by industrial policy, clearly stimulated capital expenditure by importing firms. According to a 1962 MITI survey,[36] technology imports accounted for 27.7 per cent of investment by importing firms in the 1950–60 period. This represented 9.0 per cent of the total investment in the economy. Additionally, simple correlations between technology imports and investment by importing firms are positively significant as are correlations between technology imports and total investment.[37]

[35] Keizai Kikaku Chō Keizai Kenkyūsho Kokumin Shotoku Bu, *Minkan Kigyō Shihon Sutokku* (Tokyo, Ōkurashō Insatsu Kyoku, various years).
[36] Current Status and Problems of Foreign Technology Absorption (*Gaikoku Gijutsu Dōnyū no Genjō to Mondaiten*) (Tokyo, MITI, 1962) as quoted in Ozawa Terutomo, *Japan's Technological Challenge to the West, 1950–1974*, 37–44.
[37] Ibid. 41–3.

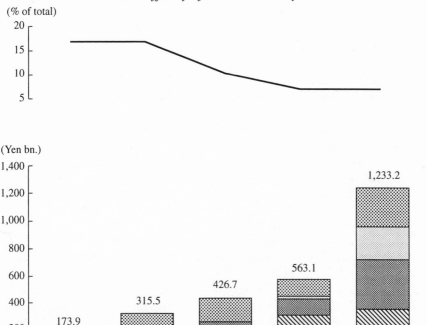

Technology promotion   Export promotion   Rationalization   Energy development   Other

Fig. 4.2. Government Subsidies to Industry by Purpose

Source: Tsuruta Toshimasa, *Sengo Nihon no Sangyō Seisaku*.

4.3   Policy Impact on Potential Growth

The likelihood that industrial policy in Japan was largely rational at least into the 1960s fulfils one necessary condition for policy to have speeded up economic development. The second necessary condition for policy effectiveness, an impact on resource allocation, was certainly fulfilled throughout the entire period. Moreover, policy showed enormous flexibility: support towards probable infant industries was gradually reduced, and in some instances such as coal, the goal of developing an industry was reversed to one of aiding the industry's decline. Measures to block competition in distribution and amongst small companies were also lessened as time passed. However, probable fulfilment of these conditions, at least in the 1950s, still does not provide proof that industrial policy was successful in that it fostered more rapid economic development than would otherwise have occurred. The impact of industrial policy on invest-ment in heavy industries may not have been that large, and the benefits of increased investment in these industries on total development may have been outweighed by the costs of misdirecting resources to some industries such as coal mining. Moreover, by directing resources to tar-geted industries, industrial policy could have reduced investment in other sectors of the economy.[38] Hence, it is not yet clear whether Japanese industrial policy really achieved its stated goal of maximizing the growth potential of the Japanese economy. Put differently, it is not clear that economic growth would have been slower without industrial policy. Growth could have been as fast or even faster without policy interven-tion.

It is not possible to provide direct evidence on this point, since there is of course no empirical evidence as to how Japan would have developed in the absence of industrial policy. Nevertheless, it is possible to address this issue indirectly. The initial constraint on economic growth in post-war Japan was its supply of savings and its ability to invest. A related con-straint was Japan's ability to import foreign materials and equipment, and its access to foreign exchange, which in turn was determined by Japanese exports. Hence, the question of the impact of industrial policy on potential economic growth can be rephrased as the relationship between industrial policy and export growth or industrial policy and the rates of savings and investment. If it can be shown that industrial policy raised Japan's ability to export or if industrial policy raised Japan's abil-ity to save and invest, then industrial policy probably increased Japan's potential growth, fostering more rapid economic development than would otherwise have occurred.

Concerning trade, it is not clear that industrial policy increased the ability of the Japanese economy to export, at least at the aggregate level. Exports as a percentage of GNP were actually lower after the war than prior to it. Earlier data reinforce this conclusion: between 1910 and 1930, exports as a percentage of GNP varied between 15 and 20 per cent, far higher than export ratios after 1950.[39] It is thus difficult to argue that industrial policy unambiguously raised the growth potential of the Japanese economy by increasing the relative magnitude of exports.[40]

---

[38] This assumes that Japan's investment funds were fixed by domestic savings. To the extent that Japan could borrow overseas, the constraint of domestic savings on investment was not absolute.

[39] Sōmu Chō Tōkei Kyoku, *Nihon Chōki Tōkei Sōran*, 3: 344–5.

[40] This argument might still be rescued by examining trends in value-added for Japanese exports. Value added rose as development progressed, and exports embodied relatively less raw material content. If Japan's move up the value-added ladder was substantially faster than the experience of other countries such as West Germany, the case for policy efficacy

The case for investment and savings is clearer: both rose dramatically during the post-war period. Which of these two variables, savings or investment, actually represents the true constraint on economic development is a matter of controversy in economic literature. Neoclassical growth models commonly emphasize domestic savings, and assume that the amount saved is transformed into investment. Hence, if savings rise, investment also increases, thus stimulating growth. However, if international capital flows are introduced, this result need not obtain. Domestic savings can flow overseas, thus possibly lowering domestic investment and consequently economic growth. Conversely, foreign capital may flow in, augmenting the domestic savings pool and raising the ability of the domestic economy to invest in plant and equipment. From this perspective, the desire to invest, which might more formally be called effective investment demand, holds the key to potential growth in a developing economy. In post-war Japan, effective investment demand probably determined growth, but limits on capital flows also meant that domestic savings played a key role in defining potential growth.

Industrial policy in Japan may have stimulated both savings and investment. The sharp rise after the war in gross fixed capital formation was the result of rapidly rising corporate investment rather than public or residential investment (Table 4.4). Since industrial policy targeted corporate capital formation, this increase in investment suggests that policy could well have contributed to an increased growth potential for the Japanese economy and a more rapid rate of development than would have occurred in its absence. Similarly, industrial policy could have had a positive impact on total savings by increasing savings in the corporate sector, thus helping to increase both potential investment and growth.

As already noted, industrial policy stimulated investment in specific industries through favourable tax breaks and government subsidies. These measures lowered the cost of capital accumulation in designated industries, and, through this cost reduction, raised investment in those industries if not the economy overall. Given limited foreign capital inflows, whether or not stimulating investment in targeted industries reduced investment in others depends on how industrial policy affected aggregate savings. Accelerated depreciation by definition raised savings in recipient industries, given that corporate savings equals depreciation plus retained earnings. Tax and subsidy policy may also have raised total savings. To the extent that these measures increased profits and redistributed funds from the personal to the corporate sector, and to the extent that the corporate sector may have had a higher marginal propensity to save than the

would be strengthened since industrial policy in Japan consciously attempted to raise value-added.

Table 4.4. Exports, Investment, and Savings as a Percentage of GNP

Year	Exports	Corporate investment	Government investment	Total fixed capital formation*	Gross savings
1930	19.50	3.86	3.49	8.50	11.94
1935	25.38	9.75	3.07	14.19	19.51
1940	18.47	16.82	3.08	21.07	26.89
1944	5.30	17.60	3.33	21.80	27.22
1950	11.88	9.88	6.18	17.58	28.17
1955	11.35	10.30	6.50	19.76	25.59
1960	11.45	18.78	7.38	30.15	34.05
1965	11.15	15.92	8.97	30.55	34.04
1970	11.70	20.13	8.17	35.03	40.33
1973	10.92	19.07	9.14	36.60	39.81

*Includes residential investment in addition to corporate and government investment.

Source: Sōmo Chō, *Nihon Chōki Tōkei S ōran*, 3.

consumer sector, total savings for the entire economy may have risen. If industrial policy helped to increase aggregate savings, its positive impact on investment in targeted industries was not necessarily accompanied by reduced investment elsewhere. In other words, industrial policy probably raised potential growth.

This latter argument can also be applied to analyse trade protection. If, through tariffs on imports, industrial policy raised profits in manufacturing, total savings in the economy may have risen if the marginal propensity to save in the corporate sector was higher than that of consumers. This result is far from definite, since tariffs could well lower the overall real income of the economy.[41] If real income falls because tariffs reduce wages more than they raise profits, then whether or not total savings increase depends on both how wide the differential is between the marginal propensity to save from profits and the marginal propensity to save from wages as well as the relative increase in profits compared to the fall in wages.

The Japanese government also attempted to promote investment by placing relatively low tariffs on capital goods and high tariffs on consumer goods. If these measures lowered consumption, they may have stimulated investment.[42] However, because the real income of the economy may drop because of the distortions from the tariffs, investment may fall even if consumption decreases. Even if such a tariff structure did help to raise investment in post-war Japan, it would have introduced distortions, acting to discourage investment in subsistence sectors, acting to discourage the development of a domestic capital goods industry, and acting to over-promote investment in manufacturing sectors. These former two problems were probably avoided through the measures designed to offset the distortions of a differentiated tariff structure, but over-investment in some manufacturing industries may have been exacerbated by tariff policy.

Industrial policy may also have raised effective investment demand by lowering risk. Certainly, industries targeted by industrial policy invested more than they would have otherwise, not only because of tax breaks and low-interest loans but also because industrial policy acted as insurance, effectively promising further government support should investment plans go awry. Furthermore, this risk reduction may have been general to all industries. Although industrial policy primarily concentrated on a few industries, measures affected many to some extent. Even those industries which received little government support may have felt that industrial

---

[41] Assuming that the terms of trade are constant and that there are no domestic distortions in markets, tariffs will reduce real income.

[42] Clearly, if consumption is inelastic, if it does not drop with price increases, then investment cannot rise.

policy effectively lowered the risk of investment and expansion. Industries that received no government aid may also have perceived reduced investment risk, given that it was common knowledge that the government wished to promote aggregate investment and growth. As such, industrial policy may have raised effective investment demand in general, stimulating economic development.

Just as industrial policy may have raised total effective investment demand by reducing risk, this increased investment may have contributed to higher aggregate savings. That is, investment to some extent may have generated its own savings, as rising investment increased profits. Additionally, to the extent that industrial policy raised the profitability of investment, corporations may have worked harder to implement investment plans, reducing leisure or lowering wages.

Through these above mechanisms, it is possible that industrial policy raised investment and savings in Japan, fostering more rapid economic growth than would have occurred in the absence of policy.[43] This conclusion must remain probable rather than definite: tariff policy may have reduced real income, acting as a possible drag on savings and investment. If industrial policy did not help increase savings, then measures to promote investment in some industries may have reduced total investment by directing resources away from capital investment in other industries. Finally, by shifting resources away from consumers to corporations, industrial policy could have lowered savings from what it otherwise would have been if the corporate sector did not have a higher marginal propensity to save.

Furthermore, the rapid rise in investment and savings in post-war Japan, while suggestive of a positive role played by industrial policy, does not constitute direct proof of policy effectiveness. These increases can be at least partially explained by other factors, such as the promotion of aggregate savings through the equalization of rural incomes resulting from land reform, the stimulus provided to savings by the need to rebuild housing stocks, or the impact of technological change on investment. Still, a positive role for industrial policy is consistent with the dramatic increases in savings and investment in post-war Japan, and it is theoretically possible that industrial policy could have promoted rapid economic development by affecting these variables. Its most important role might have been in reducing the risk of investment, thus raising effective investment demand for the entire economy.

Even if industrial policy did initially spur rapid economic development by stimulating increases in savings and investment, this policy was not costless. It could well have increased capacity in targeted industries past

---

[43] Personal savings could also have been increased by government measures designed specifically to do so.

optimal levels, both by reducing the relative cost of investment as well as by reducing the risk of investment. Moreover, if industrial policy did stimulate savings and investment in the 1950s, it may have contributed to the disequilibrium between the two that emerged from the mid-1960s. After 1964, Japan exhibited a chronic balance of payments surplus, indicative of an imbalance between domestic savings and investment. The excess of domestic savings over effective domestic investment demand suggests that potential growth of the Japanese economy was higher than realized growth. By promoting savings, industrial policy may have contributed to this problem.

4.4   Institutional Requirements for Policy Efficacy

This chapter has argued that post-war Japanese industrial policy probably fulfilled the economic conditions necessary for it to have stimulated economic growth, at least until the early 1960s. First, industrial policy had a clear impact on resource allocation. The absolute size of government loans and government subsidies provides proof of this, at least up to 1960. Thereafter, industrial policy may have had an impact more at the margin, but it certainly affected resource allocation. Direct government financial support, however small, signalled that investment plans had passed government evaluation standards. These evaluations had proved largely successful in the early 1950s, and it was therefore not unreasonable for private banks to consider these standards of value in making their own risk assessments. Additionally, private banks viewed government support of an investment project as an implicit guarantee that project failure would not result in loan defaults. Tax policy also influenced investment decisions at the margin: to assert that it did not would be equivalent to asserting that markets do not function, thus reinforcing the need for an industrial policy to achieve development.

Secondly, industrial policy in the early post-war period may well have been rational, serving economic functions which would not have been addressed in the absence of policy. Specifically, government measures probably helped to correct externalities associated with infant industries, promoting investment in industries new to Japan as well as in those where previous production methods had been rendered obsolete through technological change. It is impossible to ascertain definitely that these targeted industries were in fact subject to dynamic externalities, but their large share of newly imported technologies and substantial declines in production costs over time reinforce such an interpretation. Government measures also helped to address the dynamic investment complementarities which occur when the profitability of investment in one industry depends on investment in other industries. Policy may also have levelled bargaining positions in negotiating technology imports. Finally, industrial policy could well have acted to control the costs of development, trading off employment stability against the promotion of growth. Here again, it is impossible to fully prove that the labour population was in such surplus as to necessitate the blocking of competition in major sectors of the economy, although the number of displaced workers after the war, the rise in agricultural employment to unprecedented heights, and the decimation of Japan's capital stock provide evidence that this was so.

Measures adopted to address these issues were often first-best policy solutions. Investment in infant industries was stimulated directly through government loans and tax breaks. The active dissemination of information helped to co-ordinate investment across industries. What anti-growth measures were adopted did not totally discourage innovation. Only tariff and cartel policy measures may not have been first-best policy solutions, but tariffs may have been necessary to negotiate imports of technology and the government often attempted to mitigate the distorting impact of tariffs through additional measures. Most importantly, the potential negative effect on competition that tariffs and cartels can generate was avoided by policy measures that rewarded winners and punished losers.

The fulfilment of these necessary economic conditions is not proof that industrial policy actually stimulated economic development. Growth might have been as fast or faster without such large-scale government intervention. However, circumstantial evidence favours a contribution from industrial policy. Investment and savings as a percentage of GNP rose dramatically after the war. This break with past history may partially be due to industrial policy: measures could theoretically have raised aggregate investment and savings, although this cannot be definitely proved.

If the rationality of policy cannot be fully proved in the 1950s, the decreasing rationality of policy from the early 1960s is easier to show. The need for anti-growth measures disappeared as investment and growth created new jobs, but despite this, agricultural policy increasingly blocked competition. While previous measures to promote infant industries were reduced, they were probably not decreased as rapidly as the emerging competitiveness of these industries dictated. Consequently, industrial policy may have contributed to over-investment in targeted industries. As the economic rationality of industrial policy declined, so too did circumstantial evidence that policy may have contributed to a higher growth potential for the Japanese economy. Japan began to exhibit a chronic current account surplus from the mid-1960s, indicating that industrial policy may have been too successful in promoting domestic savings or not successful enough in stimulating investment.

Although the reasoning and evidence presented thus far is useful in assessing the economic impact of policy efficacy, the dynamic process of formulating and implementing industrial policy in post-war Japan has not yet been adequately addressed. To some extent, this issue lies beyond the scope of this work, the primary goal of which is to provide an informed judgement about the economic role played by industrial policy. Moreover, there already exist a number of valuable studies which investigate the dynamics of policy-making in Japan.[44] Nevertheless, any success enjoyed by Japanese industrial policy is inextricably linked to the ability to forge and implement appropriate policy measures, and several factors increased this ability.

Studies of institutional conditions needed for an effective industrial policy have emphasized three factors.[45] First is the need for a well-trained bureaucracy, capable of intelligently formulating policy. Second is the power to implement policy. Third and final is the ability to forge consensus about the goals of industrial policy. That Japan has had an extremely well-trained bureaucracy has been documented elsewhere.[46] However, policy was by no means dependent solely on the skills of these bureaucrats. The failure of government measures to contain inflation after the war and evidence that government officials could be corrupted led to the creation of an active role for businessmen, academics, and representatives of the public in policy formulation. Policy committees were mixed, with representatives from all of these groups having a say in how policy was made.

Non-government members of policy committees provided bureaucrats with information necessary to formulate successful policy. However, government access to necessary information was more greatly facilitated by the interaction between industry organizations (*gyōkai*) and the bureaucracy. The dissolution of the *zaibatsu* after the war fragmented business interests, greatly complicating the government's ability to easily obtain data. This problem was solved as corporations formed organizations to represent their industry, often at the behest of the government. By the end of 1946, organizations representing corporations in steel, textiles, cotton spinning, coal, and machinery had been formed;[47] such organizations today now number in the thousands. Industry organizations provided the government with detailed data on production, inventories, shipments, and

[44] For insight into the roles played by government bureaucracies, see Chalmers Johnson, *MITI and the Japanese Miracle*, and Daniel Okimoto, *Between MITI and the Market: Japanese Industrial Policy for High Technology* (Stanford, Calif., Stanford Univ. Press, 1987). The interaction between politics and policy is addressed by Kent E. Calder, *Crisis and Compensation: Public Policy and Political Stability in Japan*.

[45] John Zysman, *Government, Markets, and Growth*.

[46] See, for example, Chalmers Johnson, *MITI and the Japanese Miracle*.

[47] Tsūshō Sangyō Shō Tsūshō Sangyō Seisaku Shi Hensan Iinkai, *Tsūshō Sangyō Seisaku Shi*, 16 (Tokyo, Tsūshō Sangyō Chōsa Kai, 1992), 346–56.

investment, giving the information necessary for policy formulation as well as the compilation of government statistics. These industry organizations proved to be quite cost effective to the government, since they alleviated the need to increase the number of officials that would have been required had the bureaucracy been required to gather all data itself. Such organizations were also of benefit to corporate members, explaining both the intent of policy and likely policy changes. Furthermore, they lobbied for policy measures on behalf of their members: for example, the Cotton Spinners Association asked MITI to further curtail operations in their industry in November 1952; at the same time, the Coal Mining Association requested that MITI implement measures to improve their accounts.[48]

These organizations, specific to an industry, thus helped the government to gather information at low cost while they also enabled corporate members to press for policy changes and learn in detail what impact policy measures would have. Broader input about policy direction was given to the government by academics and outside committee members; this function was enhanced by general business organizations which represented the interests of many industries. These broader business organizations, such as the Federation of Economic Organizations (*Keizai Dantai Rengōkai*; commonly called the *Keidanren*) and the Japan Committee for Economic Development (*Keizai Dōyūkai*), acted as another conduit between members and the government, but concerned themselves with the general direction and formulation of policy rather than policy measures designed specifically for an individual industry.

The expertise of bureaucrats was thus augmented by business and other private sector expertise, enabling policy to be intelligently formulated. The second necessary institutional condition for policy success, sufficient power to enable policy-makers to implement industrial policy, was also fulfilled for the first two post-war decades. MITI's control over foreign exchange gave it enormous influence over corporations, since it could deny a firm access to needed imports of machinery or raw materials. MITI control over technology imports further augmented this influence; firms could not get access to new technologies without government approval. Government loans and tax breaks provided a third means by which bureaucracies could influence corporations, forcing them to accept policies.

A corollary to this condition of access to power is the need to prevent abuse and excess. This corollary was fulfilled by an extensive series of checks and balances in policy formulation at a variety of levels. First, interests of the public and the business community were represented by non-government committee members as already noted. The political

[48] Tsūshō Sangyō Shō Tsūshō Sangyō Seisaku Shi Hensan Iinkai, *Tsūshō Sangyō Seisaku Shi*, 404.

process in Japan also afforded another route for non-bureaucratic representation in policy-making, one that was particularly useful in addressing major problems neglected by policy, such as pollution and social welfare. Secondly, power to implement policy was not vested in one government ministry; MITI's primary role in implementing industrial policy was checked by the Ministry of Finance's control over government budgets, a factor which helped to lead to reductions in support for previously targeted industries. Spending excesses were also checked by placing the goals of macroeconomic policy ahead of those of industrial policy. MITI was further forced to co-operate with the Ministry of Finance because of the latter's role in the granting of tax breaks, and it also needed the co-operation of the Ministry of Construction to provide the necessary infrastructure for targeted industries. Other government ministries, including the Ministry of Agriculture and Forestry, the Ministry of Posts and Telecommunications, and the Ministry of Labour, also had substantial input into industrial policy, as did government agencies such as the Hokkaido Development Agency, the Science and Technology Agency, the Fair Trade Commission, and the Economic Planning Agency. The conflicting interests of these ministries and agencies often resulted in fierce debate, and compromise acted to check potential abuse of power.

The financing of industrial policy was also subject to checks and balances. Although the Japan Development Bank was under the jurisdiction of the Ministry of Finance, representatives of MITI were also on the board. More importantly, the Japan Development Bank took into account the criteria of potential profitability in granting loans; partial use of this market mechanism helped avoid waste. The market mechanism also determined the lending activities of long-term credit banks in Japan. With the passage of the Long-Term Credit Bank Law in 1952, the government created private sector institutions to supply funding for plant and equipment investment. The government could influence the lending activities of these banks through potential constraints on demand for their debentures, but these banks were also forced to emphasize the profitability of loans since they theoretically could have become bankrupt.

Another check on industrial policy was provided by the practice of retiring bureaucrats at a young age, most before they are 50 years old. These ex-bureaucrats 'descend from heaven' (*amakudaru*) to positions in business, finance, government corporations, politics, and industry associations. The reliance by bureaucrats on second careers obviously helped to prevent the implementation of totally inappropriate policy measures.[49]

---

[49] Possible conflicts arising from this practice, whereby a bureaucrat attempts to implement a policy favouring a firm which will later employ him, are minimized by regulation under law and supervision. Moreover, a retiring government official is generally given no choice as to his next position.

Furthermore, this practice also facilitated communication between government and business and provided another means for each to influence the other. Of 114 top MITI officials retiring between 1973 and 1984, fully 69 were hired by the private sector, 2 by industry associations, 4 entered politics, 25 were given jobs in special corporations, 8 received positions in public welfare corporations, and 6 found other employment.[50] As can be seen from Table 4.5, targeted industries such as steel provided the majority of private sector employment opportunities for former top MITI officials; positions in special corporations were also related to MITI's use of industrial policy.

The third and last institutional requirement necessary for the success of industrial policy is the ability to generate consensus about policy goals. Japan's success in this area undoubtedly owes much to the anti-growth characteristics of some measures adopted. That policy should promote growth was largely unquestioned in the two decades following World War II; not until pollution and urban overcrowding became serious problems did that consensus shatter. In other words, the goal of growth was accepted so long as policy had no significant negative effect on the living standards of any major group in Japan. Business interests accepted industrial policy for a protracted period of time because it generally did not impede profit growth. More surprisingly, consumers also accepted industrial policy. Even though they paid the cost of this policy through higher import prices, they also benefited from economic growth through higher wages, and these wage gains were more immediately apparent than were the costs of higher import prices.

The government also helped to placate potential opposition groups by promoting income equalization through efforts to eliminate the dual structure that characterized the Japanese economy in the 1950s. The government also regularly cut personal income taxes, ensuring that the contribution of consumers to public revenue remained roughly constant at about one-third of total taxes collected. That is, by reducing income taxes eleven times in the 1954–74 period,[51] the government passed on to consumers the benefits of growth. However, perhaps most important to

---

[50] The term 'top MITI official' includes all internal and external bureau chiefs as well as vice-ministers. The internal bureaus of MITI are the International Trade Policy Bureau, the International Trade Administration Bureau, the Industrial Policy Bureau, the Industrial Location and Environmental Protection Bureau, the Basic Industries Bureau, the Machinery and Information Industries Bureau, and the Consumer Goods Industries Bureau. External bureaus are the Natural Resources and Energy Agency, the Patent Agency, the Medium and Small Enterprises Agency, and the Industrial Technology Agency. (Seifu Kankei Tokubetsu Hōjin Rōdō Kumiai Kyōgikai, *Seirōkyō Amakudari Hakusho* (Tokyo, Seifu Kankei Tokubetsu Hōjin Rōdō Kumiai Kyōgikai, 1986), 73–96.)

[51] Joseph Pechman and Kaizuka Keimei, 'Taxation', in Hugh Patrick and Henry Rosovsky (eds.), *Asia's New Giant: How the Japanese Economy Works* (Washington, DC, The Brookings Institute, 1976), 317–82.

Table 4.5. Post-Retirement Employment of Top MITI Officials, 1953–1984

Employer	Number of MITI Officials
Special Corporations	25
Electric Power Development Corporation	3
Smaller Business Finance Corporation	3
Japan Development Bank	2
Small Business Credit Insurance Corporation	2
Small Business Promotion Corporation	2
Japan Petroleum Development Corporation	2
Export–Import Bank of Japan	1
Japan External Trade Organization (JETRO)	1
Japan Electric Metres Inspection Corporation	1
Research Development Corporation of Japan	1
Power Reactor and Nuclear Fuel Development Corporation	1
Overseas Economic Co-operation Fund	1
New Energy Development Corporation	1
Institute of Developing Economies	1
Industrial Relocation and Coal Production Areas Promotion Corporation	1
Osaka Small Business Investment Corporation	1
Tokyo Small Business Investment Corporation	1

Private Sector Companies

STEEL	14	MACHINERY AND CARS	13	PETROLEUM	13
New Japan Steel	2	Toyota	2	Arabian Oil	1
Nippon Kōkan	2	Isuzu Motors	1	Maruzen Oil	1
Sumitomo Metal	1	Hino Motors	1	Kyōdō	3
Kawasaki Steel	1	Mitsubishi Electric	1	Indonesian Oil	2
Kobe Steel	2	Sony	1	Shell	1
Mitsui Metal	2	Sumitomo Electric	1	Kyushu Oil	1
Daidō Special Steel	1	Matsushita Electric	1	Chubu Oil	1
Ishikawajima-Harima	1	Fujitsu	1		
Japan Special Steel	1	Furukawa Electric	1		
		Hitachi	1		
		Shōwa Denkō	1		
ELECTRIC POWER	8	CHEMICALS	11	COMMERCE	8
Tokyo Electric Power	2	Bridgestone Tire	1	Mitsui & Co.	1
Kansai Electric Power	2	Sumitomo Rubber	1	Marubeni	1
Kyushu Electric Power	2	Japan Synthetic Rubber	2	Jusco	1
Tohoku Electric Power	1	Takasago Thermal	1	Daiei	1
Chubu Electric Power	1	Central Glass	1	Itōchū	1
		Japan Petrochemical	1	Daimaru	1
BANKS	2	New Osaka Petrochemical	1	Sumitomo Shōji	1
Long-Term Credit Bank	1	New Japan Steel Chemical	1		
Sanwa Bank	1				

Public Welfare Corporation	8
Politics	4

Note: Figures for industry totals presumably are sometimes greater than the aggregation of those appointed to individual companies because individual company lists are incomplete.

Source: Seifu Kankei Tokubetsu Hōjin Rōdō Kumiai, *Seirōkyō Amakudari Hakusho*.

maintaining consumer support of industrial policy was government policy to ensure full employment. By blocking competition in some industries, the government's anti-growth policy effectively bought off the potential losers from economic growth. Through these efforts to control the process of modernization and employment loss in some industries and through efforts to slow the decline of other industries, the government helped to guarantee satisfaction towards industrial policy amongst consumers. Without anti-growth policy, consensus would probably have fragmented earlier, as the losers from growth would have agitated to maintain the status quo.

The waning of the rationality of industrial policy from the 1960s occurred simultaneously with an undermining of the institutional criteria necessary for policy success. From the early 1960s, the power to implement policy was gradually eroded as trade and capital flows were liberalized. Japanese corporate success also reduced the reliance of industry on government support measures. However, it was the collapse of national consensus about the goals of industrial policy from the late 1960s that really undermined policy effectiveness from an institutional point of view. As policy goals multiplied, the government's ability to achieve support for industrial policy deteriorated. Diminished support, together with reduced powers to implement policy, led increasingly to situations where policy was actively resisted by industries.

If the 1960s witnessed a deterioration of policy rationality, an emerging problem of surplus savings, reduced power to implement policy, and a fragmenting consensus about policy goals, the early 1970s witnessed a collapse in public confidence in industrial policy. Policy-makers were caught unawares by the appreciation of the yen and the first oil crisis. Industrial policy was blamed by some for promoting exports and causing the yen's appreciation, while there was general dismay at the energy-intensive nature of Japanese manufacturing, exacerbated by the expansion of heavy industry which was linked to industrial policy. Government policy also increased inflation in the early 1970s and arguably worsened Japan's economic performance in the first half of that decade. However, this failure and the collapse of public support would cause policy to change. Despite its much smaller role, industrial policy in the 1980s may have marginally supported Japanese growth.

5

Industrial Policy and the Japanese Steel Industry (1945–1990)

In order to better understand how Japanese industrial policy has actually functioned in the post-war period, this chapter examines in detail policy measures towards steel. Until the early 1970s, policy measures towards steel typify pro-growth industrial policy. Through government funding, tax breaks, import barriers, investment co-ordination, mergers, and the adoption of foreign technology, industrial policy attempted to build a world competitive industry. On the face of it, policy succeeded: output and investment soared through the 1950s, and by the mid-1960s steel had emerged as the largest export industry in Japan, a position it was to keep until 1977.[1] Japanese steel production had become the most modern in the world by the late 1960s, and Japan today is one of the world's largest steel producers.[2]

Despite apparent success, the development of the steel industry was not without problems. Capacity often outstripped demand, squeezing profits. The industry was heavily criticized as a polluter from the 1960s and, because production is energy-intensive, it was hard hit by the oil shocks. The industry's success at exporting also raised its vulnerability to appreciations of the yen. By overly stimulating investment, industrial policy probably contributed to these problems, exacerbating the difficulties in adjusting to higher energy costs, currency fluctuations, and sluggish world growth.[3] Industrial policy became increasingly concerned with correcting these difficulties, and during much of the 1970s focused almost exclusively on promoting capacity reductions, thus shifting from a pro-growth stance to one of anti-growth. Policy towards steel again changed in the early 1980s, as the government actively supported diversification efforts into new areas, thus combining to some extent pro-growth and anti-growth policies.

[1] Sōmu Chō Tōkei Kyoku, *Nihon Chōki Tōkei Sōran*, 3: 38–43.

[2] Excluding the year 1978, Japan was second only to the USSR in terms of steel production from 1974 to 1990. (Nihon Tekkō Renmei Tekkō Tōkei Iinkai, *Tekkō Tōkei Yōran* (Tokyo, Nihon Tekkō Renmei, 1991), 30–3.)

[3] After peaking in 1974 at 119 million tons, annual output of crude steel fell to a low of 102 million tons in 1978. Production has since fluctuated, but even in expansion periods it has not reached a new high since 1974. When output was declining, however, the industry was rapidly diversifying. After a generally poor performance in the 1970s, profits for the major steel companies set record levels in 1981 and have recently been about four times their 1970 average.

Before detailing the role that industrial policy has played in the development of the Japanese steel industry, it is worth noting why steel became a focus of government intervention. There are at least four plausible factors which influenced the targeting of steel. First, steel is a basic materials industry and is used as an input not only in construction but also in most manufacturing industries, notably machinery and automobiles. Strength in such a basic industry can favourably influence the development of these downstream users. The second factor which may have influenced the targeting of steel was simply force of habit. The government had long promoted the development of a domestic steel industry, sending technicians abroad, experimenting with foreign technology, and even going so far as to have state-run companies.[4] These previous experiences with industrial policy and steel probably influenced the choice of steel as a policy focus in post-war Japan. The third factor, a pool of knowledge, labour, and capital for steel production, obviously is related to the second. Resource accumulation in the steel industry also grew as a result of the wartime buildup. Despite the collapse of production after World War II, Japanese policy-makers probably viewed this accumulated technology, capital, and trained labour as providing a sound foundation from which to successfully build a modern steel industry. Finally, policy-makers probably targeted steel because of a shortage of foreign exchange. In order to save foreign currency, Japan hoped to replace imports of steel with domestic production, not an unreasonable expectation given Japan's past experience in the industry.[5]

5.1 Priority Production and the Japanese Steel Industry (1946–1949)

The Japanese steel industry was one of the very few to escape almost unscathed from wartime destruction. Despite existing capacity, output of crude steel fell to 0.56 million tons in 1946, less than 7.5 per cent of peak 1943 output of 7.65 million tons, and the number of blast furnaces in operation dropped from 35 to 3.[6] This collapse in output was the result of an acute shortage of material inputs, caused both by a sharp decline in domestic coal production as well as economic sanctions. In an effort to reverse this precipitous decline, the government at the end of 1946

[4] Yawata Steel was founded as a national company and began production in 1901. The government combined it with six other companies to form Japan Steel in 1934, and Japan Steel was also under government control. It was broken up in 1950 by the Occupation into Fuji Steel and Yawata Steel, which were re-merged in 1970 into New Japan Steel.
[5] These views are reflected in the quote by Ōkita on p. 79.
[6] Nihon Kaihatsu Ginkō, *Nihon Kaihatsu Ginkō Jūnen Shi*, 236.

adopted its priority production system. Under this programme, the government used special funds provided by the Occupation to purchase oil, coal, and coke and allocated these materials to the domestic steel industry. In turn, the increase in steel output generated by these imports was channelled to investment in coal mining, and increased coal output was then cycled back to the steel industry. Through these supply-orientated policies, the government hoped to generate a cycle of increasing production, thus raising the possible production frontier of the economy.

Aside from its allocation of imports, the government stimulated production in the domestic steel industry through subsidies and loans. As outlined in Chapter 2, the government established the Reconstruction Finance Corporation to channel funds to specified industries for investment in plant and equipment. Steel, with its production base largely intact, was not the main recipient of these loans. Even so, from April 1946 to March 1949, the RFC loaned the steel industry 3.926 billion yen, generally to repair existing facilities.[7] This amount supplied almost 80 per cent of the funds used for investment in the steel industry over that three-year period, although it represented less than 3 per cent of total RFC loans.[8]

Even more substantial than government loans to the steel industry were state subsidies. The government set steel prices, and to ensure continued production in the face of rising material costs, provided subsidies totalling 76 billion yen for fiscal years 1947–9.[9] These subsidies did result in stable steel prices and increased production: the output of regular rolled steel in fiscal year 1948 actually exceeded the government target of 1.2 million tons. However, these subsidies caused producers to increase output without regard to cost.

The Occupation halted lending by the Reconstruction Finance Corporation in 1949 and ended subsidies through price controls in 1950, effectively stopping the priority production system. Without government support, the steel industry went into recession. With the Dodge Line battering the economy, steel manufacturers refused to embark on new expansion plans. Even so, investment in facility repair actually increased as old plans were completed, supported in part by US aid provided through the US Aid Counterpart Fund (*Mikaeri Shikin*).[10]

---

[7] Ibid. 236–7.

[8] Ōkurashō Zaisei Shi Shitsu, *Shōwa Zaisei Shi: Shūsen kara Kōwa made*, 19: 572. Total outstanding loans of the RFC were 132 billion yen at the end of fiscal year 1948 (Mar. 1949).

[9] Nihon Kaihatsu Ginkō, *Nihon Kaihatsu Ginkō Jūnen Shi*, 237.

[10] Capital expenditure in the steel industry in fiscal year 1949 more than doubled from the preceding year, totalling 5.184 billion yen, of which the US Aid Counterpart Fund provided 27% (ibid. 237).

5.2 Rationalization and Modernization (1950–1960)

With subsidies ended, government policy towards steel switched from emphasizing increased output without regard for cost to promoting improved profitability. To achieve this end, MITI requested that steel manufacturers draw up a plan to rationalize the industry. In its June 1950 response, the industry stated that profitability could be achieved only through continued subsidies for coal costs.[11] The government rejected this negative view, adopting in August 1950 a rationalization plan for steel drawn up by MITI's Industrial Rationalization Council.[12] As demand for steel rose with the boom accompanying the Korean War, the pessimism of steel manufacturers faded, and individual companies began drafting their own aggressive expansion plans.[13]

Corporate motivation to invest was further enhanced by the more competitive environment of the industry. The Occupation in April 1950 broke up Japan Steel into Yawata Steel and Fuji Steel in one of its few applications of the Law on the Elimination of Excessive Concentrations of Economic Power (*Kadō Keizairyoku Shūchū Haijo Hō*), leaving the industry without a price leader. Moreover, the ending of government subsidies in the summer further levelled the playing field, placing all six major steel companies in the same difficulty.[14] This more competitive environment, together with the sharp increase in demand from the Korean War, stimulated investment. Individual corporate investment plans, checked by the government for consistency against its investment outline, formed the basis of a three-year investment plan (fiscal years 1951–3) to modernize the industry. This plan was extended to 1954 and 1955; together with revisions it constitutes the first rationalization period for the steel industry.[15]

While steel investment in the 1946–50 period concentrated on the repair of existing facilities, the First Rationalization Plan focused on investment

[11] Arisawa Hiromi (ed.), *Shōwa Keizai Shi: Fukkō kara Sekiyu Shokku made*, 2: 134.

[12] Tekkōgyō Oyobi Sekitan Kōgyō Gōrika Shisaku Yōkō (Nihon Kaihatsu Ginkō, *Nihon Kaihatsu Ginkō Nijūgonen Shi*, 440).

[13] Both Yawata Steel and Nippon Kōkan announced 3-year modernization plans in early Nov. 1950. These plans were followed almost immediately by Kawasaki Steel's announcement of the construction of a new integrated steel facility in Chiba.

[14] The six major companies were Yawata Steel, Fuji Steel, Nippon Kōkan, Kawasaki Steel, Kobe Steel, and Sumitomo Metal Industries.

[15] Under strict government control, individual company plans were aggregated into a general 3-year plan, which initially called for investment of 42 billion yen from Apr. 1951 to Mar. 1953. This total was revised up in MITI's 'Report on the Rationalization of the Steel Industry' (*Tekkō Sangyō no Gōrika ni Kansuru Hōkoku*) in Feb. 1952 to 62.8 billion yen. Further revisions because of demand changes and inflation pushed the total to 128.2 billion yen, and the plan was extended for 2 more years, given difficulties in raising funds and delays in importing equipment. See Nihon Kaihatsu Ginkō, *Nihon Kaihatsu Ginkō Jūnen Shi*, 239.

in new equipment and technology. This can be inferred first from the sharp rise in projected investment: the First Rationalization Plan called for a tenfold increase in capital expenditure over the five-year period. The plan also directly called for the installation of modern equipment, including strip mills to replace old-style pull-over mills and the introduction of basic oxygen furnaces for steel manufacture. Moreover, the First Rationalization Plan called for a high dependence on imported machinery, planning that 60 per cent of the proposed equipment investment consist of foreign goods.[16] The goal of investment in modern equipment was greater profitability through quality improvement and reduced costs, particularly for hot-rolled steel, which was the target of about 50 per cent of planned investment. There was little need to focus on capacity expansion, given that a number of old blast furnaces remained idle. Even so, some capacity increases were approved, such as Kawasaki Steel's plan for an integrated steel plant in Chiba.[17]

To support implementation of this rationalization plan, MITI provided subsidies through tax incentives. In April 1951 the government granted a

Table 5.1. Summary of the First Rationalization Plan, Fiscal Years 1951–1955

Investment by product	Yen bn.	Source of investment funds	% breakdown*
Regular steel production	122.8	Own company funds	23.2
Pig iron	16.1	Japan Development Bank	9.1
Steel manufacturing	13.7	Equity/bond issue	24.7
Rolling mills	64.1	Long-term credit banks	24.4
Other	28.9	City banks	11.1
Speciality steel	3.6	Other	7.5
Other	1.8		
TOTAL	128.2	TOTAL	100.0

* This breakdown of funds includes not only the 128.2 billion yen for investment but also the 60.3 billion yen needed to repay loans during this 5-year period.

Source: Nihon Kaihatsu Ginkō, *Nihon Kaihatsu Ginkō Nijūgonen Shi.*

[16] Yamawaki Hideki, 'Tekkō Sangyō', in Komiya Ryūtarō, Okuno Masahiro, Suzumura Kōtarō (eds.), *Nihon no Sangyō Seisaku* (Tokyo, University of Tokyo Press, 1984), 256.

[17] Given the unused if inefficient existing plant, Kawasaki Steel's proposal for a new integrated steel plant in Chiba was particularly controversial since it was to have an annual output of 500,000 tons of crude steel, equivalent to 20% of total 1950 production. (Yonekura Seiichirō, 'The Postwar Japanese Iron & Steel Industry: Continuity and Discontinuity', in Abe Tetsuo and Suzuki Yoshitake (eds.), *Changing Patterns of International Rivalry* (Tokyo, University of Tokyo Press, 1991), 193–241.) The famous statement '[Kawasaki Steel's Chiba] factory will be overgrown with weeds' (*kōjō shikichinai wa penpengusa ga oishigeru de aroo*), long attributed to Governor Ichimada of the Bank of Japan, who later denied it, colourfully summarized expectations about the profitability of this venture. (Kōsai Yutaka, 'Fukkōki', in Komiya Ryūtarō, Okuno Masahiro, Suzumura Kōtarō (eds.), *Nihon no Sangyō Seisaku* (Tokyo, University of Tokyo Press, 1984), 25–43.

50 per cent increase in depreciation for specially designated equipment for three years, as well as a tariff exemption for special imported equipment;[18] this was followed in October with a price fluctuation reserve account for steel manufacturers. In February 1952, steel companies were allowed to establish a loan reserve account, and in March 1952 the government provided a 50 per cent write-off in the first year for equipment purchased specifically to promote rationalization.[19] Finally, the government subsidized exports of steel, amongst other products, by granting tax exemptions for export income.[20]

Despite increased earnings from tax breaks and the Korean War boom, industry profits alone did not suffice to cover the scale of planned investment. Hence, the First Rationalization Plan called for a high dependence on outside funding; the steel industry itself was expected to provide only about one-fifth of the funds needed (Table 5.1). Some of the additional funds were provided by the government, with low-interest loans from the Japan Development Bank totalling 17.2 billion yen between 1951 and 1955.[21] Apart from these loans, the government directly encouraged bank lending, with the Ministry of Finance in October 1952 requesting financial institutions to emphasize loans to the steel industry amongst others.[22]

Tax and financing measures were only two of many tools the government used to promote the realization of the First Rationalization Plan. Government control over the allocation of imports affected the development of the industry, with MITI ensuring that all producers had access to foreign exchange for importing raw materials and equipment. In this way, the government reinforced competitive trends in the steel industry, keeping corporate desire to invest high. Government regulation of the import of foreign technology also promoted the development of the steel industry and a competitive environment. Because the initial import of a technology often helped the importing firm to reap windfall profits, the govern-

---

[18] *Nihon no Sangyō Seisaku*, 239.

[19] Nihon Kaihatsu Ginkō, *Nihon Kaihatsu Ginkō Jūnen Shi*, 239. This 50% allowance was granted under the Law to Promote the Rationalization of Firms initially passed in Mar. 1952. Later revisions of this and related laws changed the rate at which equipment could be depreciated.

[20] From 1953 until Mar. 1963, the government granted tax breaks to manufacturers who exported in the form of tax exemptions for up to 50% of export income or 3% of total sales. The government also promoted exports through reserve accounts for losses in exporting and accelerated depreciation for equipment in foreign offices. See Tsūshō Sangyō Shō Tsūshō Sangyō Seisaku Shi Hensan Iinkai, *Tsūshō Sangyō Seisaku Shi*, 6 (Tokyo, Tsūshō Sangyō Chōsa Kai, 1990), 332–3.

[21] This figure includes funds for plant and equipment investment as well as funds used to repay loans. (Nihon Kaihatsu Ginkō, *Nihon Kaihatsu Ginkō Jūnen Shi*, 239.)

[22] On 27 Oct. 1952, the Ministry of Finance requested that financial institutions provide loans to four industries, including electric power, coal, marine transport, and steel (ibid. 239).

ment staggered its granting of new import licences, thus ensuring that windfall benefits were spread across firms.[23]

Finally, industrial policy also fostered the development of the steel industry by raising barriers against the import of steel products. Not only did Japanese buyers of foreign steel require government approval to import, but steel imports were also subject to sizeable tariffs. Between 1952 and 1967, a 15 per cent tariff was levied on pig iron and steel materials (structural steel and rolled steel) while a 12.5 per cent tariff was applied to steel ingots.[24] These tariffs were substantially higher than those in the US and Europe, and were not lowered until after completion of the Kennedy Round in 1967. Tariffs and government control over imports kept foreign steel products from flooding Japan in the 1950s: steel imports in that decade were 3 per cent or less of the market even though production costs for Japanese steel exceeded those for US steel until 1957.[25]

This first rationalization plan and the incentives provided to realize it can be broadly characterized as supply-side measures. They directly influenced both the output of steel as well as the structure of the industry which produced it. However, the rationalization plan did not ignore demand: not only were tariffs used to guarantee markets for domestic producers, but output targets in the plan were set so as to be consistent with government estimates of the probable demand for steel.[26] Moreover, industrial policy also influenced steel demand through measures designed to stimulate the development of end users such as the domestic shipbuilding industry and the domestic machinery industry.

The Second Rationalization Plan (fiscal years 1956–60) was motivated not just by the fulfilment of investment targets under the first plan, but also by the sharp rise in steel exports in the autumn of 1954 and the strong growth in domestic demand from 1955.[27] These necessitated an increase in production capacity, and steel companies responded with aggressive expenditure totalling 622.7 billion yen in the 1956–60 period, five times that of the previous plan (Table 5.2). While the First

[23] Nihon Tekkō Renmei, *Tekkō Jūnen Shi, Shōwa 33 Nen–Shōwa 42 Nen* (Tokyo, Nihon Tekkō Renmei, 1969), 860–5. Also, see Table 5.4.

[24] Yamawaki Hideki, 'Tekkō Sangyō', *Nihon no Sangyō Seisaku*, 262.

[25] 1957 is excluded from these figures because of emergency imports of steel by the Japanese government to cover a shortage. Japanese production costs for regular steel were 21% higher than US production costs in 1957, 24% greater for cold-rolled steel sheets, and 31% higher for hot thin steel sheets. By 1959, however, Japanese costs for all three products were between 13% and 21% lower than US production costs (ibid. 263).

[26] Demand for steel changed dramatically after the war. Prior to World War II, the military accounted for about half of the total demand for steel, but this of course disappeared with Japan's defeat. Thereafter, demand for steel came largely from capital goods industries and, from the latter half of the 1950s, demand for steel from consumer goods industries also rose substantially. (Nihon Kaihatsu Ginkō, *Nihon Kaihatsu Ginkō Nijūgonen Shi*, 438–9.)

[27] Nihon Kaihatsu Ginkō, *Nihon Kaihatsu Ginkō Jūnen Shi*, 245.

The Japanese Steel Industry

Table 5.2.   Summary of the Second Rationalization Plan, Fiscal Years 1956–1960

Investment by product	Yen bn.	Source of investment funds	% breakdown*
Regular steel production	541.6	Own company funds	30.6
Pig iron	97.2	Japan Development Bank	1.2
Steel manufacturing	53.5	World Bank†	6.8
Rolling mills	261.7	Equity/bond issue	24.7
Other	129.2	Long-term credit banks	14.9
Speciality steel	49.0	City banks	18.9
Other	32.1	Other	2.9
TOTAL	622.7	TOTAL	100.0

* This breakdown of funds includes not only the 622.7 billion yen for plant and equipment expenditure but also the 137.5 billion yen needed to repay loans during this 5-year period.
† Because World Bank loans were granted through the Japan Development Bank and were guaranteed by it, a more technically correct (but misleading) breakdown would include World Bank Loans as a part of JDB loans.

Source: Nihon Kaihatsu Ginkō, *Nihon Kaihatsu Ginkō Nijūgonen Shi.*

Rationalization Plan had been basically formulated and implemented under government control, its successor was not officially debated and approved by MITI's Industrial Rationalization Council. Rather it came directly from the steel companies themselves. Despite this more bottom-up approach to creating the Second Rationalization Plan, it was nevertheless implemented under MITI's strict supervision, with the government inviting, adjusting, and guiding investment.

Investment under the Second Rationalization Plan addressed the need for increased output in two ways. First, investment concentrated on eliminating the imbalances in production that had arisen under the piecemeal approach to investment that characterized the First Rationalization Plan. The second plan concentrated in particular on striking a balance between pig iron and steel production, leading to the increased emphasis on pig iron in the fiscal year 1956–60 period compared to the previous five years.[28] With the construction of eleven new blast furnaces over the five-year period, the capacity for pig iron almost doubled. Expenditure on steel manufacturing focused on basic oxygen converters not only to reduce costs but also to reduce the content of imported scrap iron, which Japan, with its limited foreign exchange, was finding it difficult to import in sufficient quantities. Following Nippon Kōkan's import of technology for LD converters from an Austrian steel company, a total of thirteen LD converters were constructed during the Second Rationalization plan.[29] Rolled steel, while still the target of most of the investment,

[28]   Nihon Kaihatsu Ginkō, *Nihon Kaihatsu Ginkō Jūnen Shi*, 245–6.
[29]   Nihon Kaihatsu Ginkō, *Nihon Kaihatsu Ginkō Nijūgonen Shi*, 443.

decreased somewhat in importance. Nevertheless, five new hot-rolling facilities were constructed and twenty-three cold-rolling facilities were built. [30]

Capacity was also increased under the Second Rationalization Plan through outlays on integrated mills in coastal areas. Kawasaki Steel's success with its new plant in Chiba led the other major makers to invest in their own new integrated mills, and converters and blast furnaces in these facilities helped meet strong demand for steel while alleviating constraints imposed by a shortage of scrap iron. As a result, by fiscal year 1961 20 per cent of Japan's crude steel was produced by converters, up from 4 per cent in fiscal year 1956, and the ratio of coke used in production fell by 18 per cent.[31]

Sources for the funding of investment in the 1956–60 period reveal a growing importance for the firms' own capital, reflecting the improved earnings that arose from strong demand, both domestic and foreign, for Japanese steel. In the light of the increased financial strength of the industry, the need for government loans and loans from long-term credit banks in funding investment decreased. At the same time, there was a sharp increase in funds provided by the World Bank, but this too signified improved earnings prospects for the industry.[32] Equity financing remained unchanged, providing approximately one-quarter of the funds used for plant and equipment investment.

Despite an absolute decrease in size, government loans to the steel industry in the 1956–60 period nevertheless targeted two key areas. First, loans through the Japan Development Bank increasingly emphasized speciality steel, for which demand was rising as the machinery industry expanded. Out of the 9.5 billion yen provided in loans, the Japan Development Bank funded investment to modernize the production of speciality steel, including the construction of large-scale electric furnaces, the renovation of rolling equipment, the purchase of equipment for the manufacture of hot and cold stainless steel, and the purchase of equipment to manufacture steel for bearings.[33] Secondly, the Japan Development Bank also provided loans of 1.7 billion yen for the development of port facilities near the new coastal factories built by the steel companies.[34] These loans facilitated increased shipments of steel products, efficiently handled the greater import of raw materials, and reduced transport costs for both, thereby strengthening the competitiveness of the industry.

---

[30] Ibid. 444.   [31] Ibid. 444.

[32] For a discussion of MITI's lobbying efforts on behalf of the Japanese steel industry, see Tsūshō Sangyō Shō Tsūshō Sangyō Seisaku Shi Hensan Iinkai, *Tsūshō Sangyō Seisaku Shi*, 6: 436–9.

[33] Nihon Kaihatsu Ginkō, *Nihon Kaihatsu Ginkō Jūnen Shi*, 247–8.   [34] Ibid. 248.

Apart from loans, the government continued to utilize the same measures to promote investment that it had adopted earlier in the decade, including tax breaks, trade barriers, and control over the allocation of imports of raw materials and technology. Tax breaks alone were equivalent to 35 per cent of capital expenditure in the fiscal year 1956–60 period.[35] While these measures undoubtedly helped the government to guide industry investment, industrial policy towards steel was augmented by two new tools. The first of these, long-term plans for the entire Japanese economy, provided assurance as to future demand, reducing the risk of investment in all industries including steel. The second new measure was specific to the industry, a system to monitor and influence steel prices and production.[36] Although only effective between 1958 and 1962, this monitoring system for a time helped mitigate industry recessions, thus supporting investment and government control over that investment.

By the end of the Second Rationalization Plan, output of crude steel had climbed to 22 million tons, about 3.4 times the amount produced in 1951. Exports rose from 1 million tons in 1951 to 2.5 million tons in 1960, and production costs had fallen substantially below those in the US. Industrial policy affected this growth not just through tax breaks, loans, and infrastructure support, but also through measures which reduced risk. These included government adjustment of investment plans as well as the publication of long-term growth estimates for both the steel industry and the economy. Industrial policy also promoted the steel industry through trade barriers which suppressed imports.

Policy during this decade also promoted competition. Although the breakup of Japan Steel by the Occupation provided the corner-stone for competition, government control over the import of raw materials and technology contributed greatly to the development of a competitive environment. Raw material imports were allocated to all six major steel producers, thus ensuring that no dominant firm emerged. The government

[35] Yamawaki Hideki, 'Tekkō Sangyō', *Nihon no Sangyō Seisaku*, 260.

[36] In an attempt to offset the sharp decline in steel prices accompanying the economic downturn in 1958, MITI introduced the List Price System (*Kōkai Hanbai Sei*), under which companies were required to tell MITI the amount of steel sold each month and the amount unsold, with the latter to serve as a guide to production cuts. Companies were also required to provide information to MITI on the price paid by wholesalers for steel, and manufacturers were subject to fines should the price charged by wholesalers fall below a certain level. Originally applied to five steel products (steel plate, small bars, medium bars, medium sections, and wire rods) to prevent excessive price declines, the focus of the system reversed in May 1959 with economic recovery and rising steel prices. Utilizing similar measures, the government attempted to mitigate excessive price rises and the monitoring system was extended to cover thin steel sheet (hot-rolled and cold-rolled) and wide bands in Dec. 1959. Finally, in July 1960, the emphasis again changed, and the government monitored prices and outputs to ensure stability, attempting to avoid large price swings in either direction. Despite being somewhat effective in initially smoothing prices, that effectiveness ended in 1962 (ibid. 268–72).

also staggered its permission to import new technologies amongst the major companies, thus guaranteeing that no one company always enjoyed the benefits of first importing a new technology. Moreover, the government curtailed these initial benefits by promoting the diffusion of a successful new technology throughout the industry. These facets of government guidance in importing technology promoted competition, but policy also reduced the risk and the cost associated with technology imports. By limiting the importation of a new technology to only one or two firms, and by also allowing the importation of rival technologies, industrial policy ensured that inappropriate technology was not imported on a wide scale. In addition, because government approval was mandatory, the government was able to intervene directly in the negotiation process for acquiring foreign technologies, often insisting on more favourable terms than had first been agreed by the Japanese purchaser.

Despite this apparent success, there were already indications of problems to come. The government felt the need to try to control price movements late in the 1950s, as the economic downturn in 1958 caused dramatic price declines. By the end of the decade, it was concerned with the problem of price competition caused by excess capacity and would spend much of the 1960s trying unsuccessfully to avoid this. Government measures to adjust capacity would paradoxically increase it, as would the measures to reduce risk in the industry. By the beginning of the 1970s, the industry would be characterized by over-capacity, allegations of dumping overseas, and declining profitability.

5.3 Trade Liberalization, Mergers, and Excess Capacity (1961–1973)

Although investment activities in the steel industry from 1961 to 1973 are commonly referred to as the Third Rationalization Plan, there was not so much a plan as a simple aggregation of investment outlays by individual corporations. The government did not directly control investment activities as it did under the First Rationalization Plan; nor did it directly adjust investment to be consistent with long-term demand estimates as it did during the Second Rationalization Plan. The government did provide targets and advice about investment, but under the Third Rationalization Plan the steel industry itself was primarily responsible for adjusting investment outlays of individual companies to match these goals.[37]

Government and industry estimates for steel demand during the Second Rationalization Plan had proved very conservative, and by 1959 the steel

---

[37] Yamawaki Hideki, 'Tekkō Sangyō', *Nihon no Sangyō Seisaku*, 257–8.

companies were already formulating new long-term strategies. Although these formed the basis for the Third Rationalization Plan, the industry estimate in October 1959 that demand would rise to 38 million tons of steel by 1970 was quickly replaced by the government forecast for 1970 of demand for 48 million tons published in the National Income Doubling Plan in November 1960.[38] Investment activities under the Third Rationalization Plan which began officially in fiscal year 1961 were thus initially expected to meet this 48 million ton output target in ten years' time.

Apart from its autonomous nature, investment during the Third Rationalization Plan differed from that of the previous plans in three ways. First, almost half of the total investment outlays were funded by industry earnings. City bank loans also increased in importance while those of long-term credit banks continued to decline (Table 5.3). These trends reflected the strength of the industry, and in recognition of this, government loans through the Japan Development Bank for investment in regular steel production dropped to zero. Government loans were provided for technology development, for pollution control, and for the rationalization of speciality steel, but as a percentage of total funds, these were extremely small.

Table 5.3. Investment by Fund Source in the Third Rationalization Plan, Fiscal Years 1961–1973

	Yen bn.	% breakdown
Equity/bonds	795.5	14.4
Long-term credit banks	428.5	7.7
City banks	1,484.5	26.8
Foreign capital	95.3	1.7
Own capital	2,682.0	48.4
Other	57.7	1.0
TOTAL	5,543.5	100.0

Source: Nihon Kaihatsu Ginkō, *Nihon Kaihatsu Ginkō Nijūgonen Shi.*

Secondly, investment in the Third Rationalization Plan focused on raising capacity through increasing plant size. Between 1960 and 1973, eight new plants for crude steel, including one with capacity in excess of 10 million tons, were constructed. These new plants accounted for 46 per cent of total crude steel output in 1973. The scale of blast furnaces at these new plants increased. Of the six facilities completed after 1966, all

[38] Nihon Kaihatsu Ginkō, *Nihon Kaihatsu Ginkō Jūnen Shi*, 250–1.

but one exceeded 4,000 cubic metres. As the scale of blast furnaces rose so too did the size of converters: the average output for the seven new converters finished between 1965 and 1969 averaged 202.8 tons per time, while the four finished between 1970 and 1973 averaged 292.5 tons per time. Continuous casting facilities were built in ever increasing size, with output per hour of Kawasaki Steel's continuous casting facility completed at its Mizushima site in the early 1970s almost ten times that of Nippon Steel's Muroran facility completed in the mid-1960s.[39] Steel companies also invested in larger, faster strip mills as well as computer control technology.[40]

Finally, total investment under the Third Rationalization Plan far exceeded government targets. By 1966, the 1970 output target of 48 million tons had been reached, and steel output by 1970 had climbed to 93 million tons before advancing to 119 million tons in 1973 (Fig. 5.1). In part, this was the result of higher than anticipated demand. The steel industry was a principal beneficiary of the 'investment generates investment' phenomenon that characterized economic growth in the 1960s. As noted in the 1960 Economic White Paper, by reducing its own costs, the steel industry directly stimulated car investment and thus indirectly investment in the machine tool industry. As a result, domestic demand for steel rose, further driving investment in the steel industry. Despite recognition of this dynamic, the government nevertheless underestimated the magnitude of its impact, resulting in excessively low-growth estimates for the economy overall and for steel in particular. In addition, the boom in domestic car sales in the 1966–70 period created far greater demand for steel than had been anticipated in the early 1960s. Export demand also exceeded expectations, supported by both strong US economic growth as well as cost-reducing investment by Japanese steel manufacturers. As a result, exports rose from 2.5 million tons in 1960 to 18 million tons in 1970, advancing even further to 25.6 million tons in 1973. In turn, these strong exports, which accounted for about one-quarter of total output, helped to support further increases in investment.

Despite rising demand, the steel industry was increasingly plagued by excess capacity, reflecting the failure of investment adjustment during the Third Rationalization Plan. Several factors contributed to this failure, the

[39] Data in this paragraph were largely taken from Nihon Kaihatsu Ginkō, *Nihon Kaihatsu Ginkō Nijūgonen Shi*, 446–8.

[40] Investment in larger plants undoubtedly helped lower production costs, contributing to the 35% decline in labour and raw material costs in Japanese steel production between 1956 and 1970 (Hugh Patrick and Hideo Satō, 'The Political Economy of United States–Japan Trade in Steel', in Kozo Yamamura (ed.), *Policy and Trade Issues of the Japanese Economy* (Seattle, University of Washington Press, 1982), 197–238). In other words, at least at the plant level, there were substantial scale economies, with larger plants able to produce steel more cheaply than smaller ones.

The Japanese Steel Industry

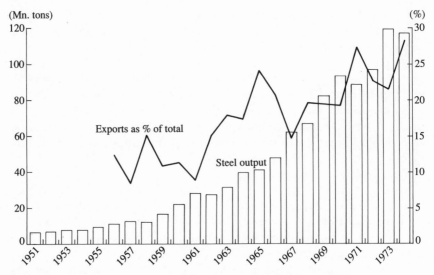

Fig. 5.1. Growth in Japanese Steel Production and Exports, 1951–1973
Source: *Nihon Kaihatsu Ginkō Nijūgonen Shi*; Nihon Ginkō, *Nihon Tōkei Nenpō*.

most important of which was the inability of the government to influence industry investment. Although the government had planned that the steel industry would autonomously adjust investment during the Third Rationalization Plan, the Industrial Rationalization Council of MITI nevertheless aggregated individual company expenditure plans and requested that the steel industry adjust these plans when total outlays were inconsistent with government demand estimates. This system failed to curtail investment,[41] and in 1967 the Steel Subcommittee of the Industrial Structure Council (*Sangyō Kōzō Shingikai Tekkō Bukai*) was established and given the task of formulating yearly and long-term demand estimates, debating yearly and long-term investments, and setting adjustment levels for investment. In the event that steel companies could not agree

[41] MITI initially advised the construction of 2 new blast furnaces and one hot strip mill in fiscal year 1960 (for completion in fiscal year 1962) while steel companies planned the construction of 5 new blast furnaces. Disagreement about how to adjust planned investment within the industry led to the construction of 3 blast furnaces and 2 hot strip mills, with the government agreeing in Dec. 1960 to the construction of another 3 blast furnaces. Government attempts to adjust investment again in fiscal year 1961 were also a failure, with all company investment plans going ahead except regarding the construction of cold strip mills and wire (or rod) mills. Although both the government and the steel companies initially agreed to halt investment in rolling equipment in fiscal year 1965, companies were free to decide investment in blast furnaces and converters. Moreover, in Nov. 1966, the government not only agreed to all industry plans for investment in rolling equipment for fiscal year 1967, it also agreed that rolling equipment investment which had been delayed by the moratorium could also go ahead. (Yamawaki Hideki, 'Tekkō Sangyō', *Nihon no Sangyō Seisaku*, 266.)

on how to allocate investment targets amongst themselves, then MITI would do so through administrative guidance. However, even this more rigorous system failed to constrain investment in the steel industry.[42]

The government's inability to curtail investment when the autonomous adjustment mechanism failed reflected its faltering control over the industry. The growing strength of the steel industry effectively ended its reliance on government loans. At the same time, tax breaks lessened in importance to the industry: while special depreciation measures were 12.7 per cent the size of investment in the steel industry in the 1956–60 period, that ratio dropped to 2.7 per cent in the 1961–5 period.[43] With the role of government financing and tax incentives reduced,[44] the government's ability to affect investment decisions faltered. State power was most weakened by the ending of foreign exchange allocations for the import of steel products and materials in 1960 and 1961:[45] without the ability to restrict or threaten a reduction in imported materials, the government lost its strongest stick to influence corporate behaviour.[46] The government's price monitoring system also lost its effectiveness after 1962 as excessive industry output resulted in widening deviation between market price (by wholesalers) and selling price (to wholesalers).[47]

While waning government control over corporate behaviour may have been a necessary condition for the sharp increase in investment in the steel industry, it was the steel companies themselves who chose to invest large amounts in new plant and equipment. Why they desired to increase industry capacity to such a great extent was the result of four factors. First was the structure of the industry itself: with six major firms and more than thirty smaller ones, the industry was only partially oligopolistic. Collusive profit maximization amongst so many firms is unlikely, and

[42] Government compilation of industry investment plans in fiscal year 1967 showed that firms planned to build 18 new blast furnaces by the end of fiscal year 1971. Administrative guidance did slightly affect the starting date for constructing some of these blast furnaces. However, the government was not only unsuccessful in reducing the total, but by the end of 1971, new blast furnaces constructed actually totalled 21 (ibid. 267).

[43] Ibid. 250.

[44] While reduced, some tax incentives remained substantial. Although the system of tax exemptions for export income (*yushutsu shotoku haijo seido*) was abolished in 1963, it was replaced by tax breaks for increases in export income (*yushutsu warimashi shōkyaku seido*) (which was abolished in 1972) and the reserve system for opening up foreign markets (*kaigai shijō kaitaku jumbikin seido*). Under the latter, a fixed percentage of funds earned in foreign transactions could be deposited in reserve accounts and treated as losses. Although firms capitalized at over 1 billion yen were excluded from utilizing this system after 1972, these reserves totalled 10 billion yen for the steel industry in fiscal year 1970 (ibid. 260–1).

[45] Ibid. 262.

[46] MITI did threaten Sumitomo Metal in 1965, stating it would halt the company's import of coking coal under a 1949 cabinet ordinance unless Sumitomo Metal limited production. This was a notable exception to the government's reduced role in controlling imports.

[47] Yamawaki Hideki, 'Tekkō Sangyō', *Nihon no Sangyō Seisaku*, 260–1.

firms in such an industry are more likely to follow one another in increasing investment even though this leads to excess capacity.[48] Secondly, since production costs fell as plant scale rose, steel companies invested in ever larger plants to reduce costs in an attempt to capture greater profits and market share. Thirdly, steel companies were optimistic about prospects for demand, having seen demand rise significantly in the past. Long-term government plans underpinned this optimism, as did the seemingly limitless prospects for exports. Finally, the steel industry, like others in Japan, felt the need to increase size in order to meet the potential competitive threat caused by foreign capital liberalization in the late 1960s.

In short, steel companies competed not only with each other through increasing investment but also with potential foreign rivals. Competition through investment can easily lead to excess capacity. A Japanese steel company could either choose to allow other Japanese companies to get ahead by investing, or it could choose to increase its own investment, thereby guaranteeing that capacity rises too much and all firms lose to some extent. The choice, then, for the company is to lose its own competitive position as its rivals reduce costs through investment or to ensure that excess capacity emerges and all firms suffer equally. Bankruptcy of any single company will not necessarily occur if all have relatively equal access to capital, and in any case, the government offered an implicit guarantee against the bankruptcy of any firm since the industry was highly targeted.[49] Naturally, this implicit guarantee against bankruptcy intensified investment competition in the industry, as did the government's autonomous adjustment system. Under this system, all firms were made aware in detail of their rivals' investment plans, and could therefore choose to increase their own outlays to prevent rivals from gaining an advantage. This they frequently did, even at the cost of excess capacity and poor industry profitability. Thus industrial policy, by reducing investment risks and providing information about corporate investment strategy to rivals, exacerbated excess capacity in the 1960s.[50]

While never officially recognizing its own culpability in reinforcing investment competition and creating excess capacity, the government did caution repeatedly about the problem of 'excessive competition' (*katō kyōsō*) in the steel industry.[51] Rather than highlighting the problems

[48] Frances Esposito and Louis Esposito, 'Excess Capacity and Market Structure', *The Review of Economics and Statistics*, 56 (May 1974) (Cambridge, Mass., Harvard University Press), 188–94.
[49] Although the major steel producers never fell into difficulty, the same was not true of the smaller speciality steel companies. Sanyō Special Steel and Japan Special Steel were reorganized with help from MITI in 1965.
[50] In other words, industrial policy to adjust investment was subject to moral hazard.
[51] Tsūsan Kōzō Shingikai Jūkōgyō Bukai Tekkō Kihon Mondai Shōiinkai, 'Kongo no Tekkōgyō no Arikata ni Tsuite', Nihon Tekkō Renmei, *Tekkō Jūnen Shi* (Tokyo, Nihon Tekkō Renmei, 1969), 831–7.

involved with the bankruptcy of a number of small firms, government use of this term for the steel industry essentially focused on the investment behaviour of large companies and the problem of excess capacity. By excessive competition, the government meant that no one firm was willing to allow its rivals to gain an advantage through investment. In this sense, the term signified competitive rather than collusive behaviour between market participants since only through collusion could the problem of excess capacity be avoided. In other words, the term 'excess competition' did not mean that there was in fact too much competition, but rather that there was competition at all. When demand increases, both highly competitive and partially oligopolistic industries tend to over-invest, causing excess capacity to emerge.[52] Only in a monopoly or in a tightly oligopolistic industry with collusion amongst firms can the problem of excess capacity be avoided.[53]

Although the government never explicitly recognized this interpretation for the term 'excess competition', its attempts to solve the problem were in fact consistent with this view. The government essentially attempted to raise collusion amongst steel companies by promoting mergers and by forming effective cartels. These measures were justified on other grounds: the government's encouragement of mergers was explained by its implicit

[52] Perfectly competitive markets are efficient when an economy is in equilibrium. However, the adjustment of such a market to change is not necessarily efficient. Consider a perfectly competitive market which is subject to an increase in demand. When demand shifts up from equilibrium, the price rises since supply is initially fixed. Existing firms and new entrants raise production in the expectation that this new price will be maintained. That is, because the market is perfectly competitive, firms do not expect their output to affect the price. In fact, assuming that the quantity demanded decreases with price, this behaviour will result in more output than is wanted at the new price, thus causing excess capacity. The subsequent decline in price will cause producers to cut back output and capacity assuming that there is no further shift in demand. This reduction will again be too large, generating a smaller price increase, and the process will continue until demand and supply are finally in equilibrium. (Tibor Scitovsky, *Welfare and Competition* (Chicago, Richard D. Irwin, 1951 and 1971), 229–37.) Similarly, firms in a partially oligopolistic market may not take into full account the effect of increased output on price and/or they may attempt to use the opportunity to increase their market share. In such a case, the initial increase in demand will also lead to excess capacity. This explanation, while quite simple, captures most of the important characteristics of the government's discussion of the relationship between competition and growth. It does not include the idea of economies of scale: if these in fact existed, then the problem of over-capacity would be intensified. This problem may also have been exacerbated by the length between the start of investment and the completion of new plants, as well as the strong probability that Japanese steel companies assumed that demand would keep increasing limitlessly into the future, given the very large rises in demand from 1946 to 1970.

[53] It is also possible that in its use of the term 'excessive competition' the government signified a concern that capacity excesses would eventually result in the bankruptcy of some firms. The remaining firms, with a larger share of the market, would act increasingly as oligopolies. In other words, the term 'excessive competition' may indicate a belief that normal competition over time might be unstable, requiring government intervention to prevent the formation of a tight oligopoly or monopoly.

belief that increased size raised a firm's ability to compete,[54] while cartels were viewed as a temporary expedient to promote price stability and capacity reduction. Whatever the reasons, the government did actively support mergers and cartels in the steel industry in the 1965–73 period. Initially, it focused on the speciality steel industry, which was rocked by insolvencies in late 1964 and early 1965. Deciding that the industry's troubles were structural in nature, MITI recommended that firms share both production facilities and investment projects, thereby fostering a consolidation of the industry.[55] The government next turned to regular steel, encouraging the merger of Yawata Steel and Fuji Steel in March 1970 into New Japan Steel. This essentially recreated Japan Steel, the firm that had been broken up by the Occupation, and created a dominant firm in the industry with more than 30 per cent market share in semi-finished steel and main steel materials.[56]

Although the government was instrumental in creating a tighter oligopoly in the steel industry from 1970, this alone proved insufficient to alleviate excess capacity. That it did not do so was probably the result of business cycle downturns, external shocks, and the turmoil of the 1970s that constrained demand for Japanese steel. The economy turned down in mid-1970, and if foreign demand for Japanese steel was little curtailed by the appreciation of the yen from August 1971, the stronger currency certainly reduced expectations about future growth in foreign demand. With investment projects already under way and expected to come on line in the next several years, the drop in the expected growth of foreign demand increased expectations that excess capacity would continue to plague the industry. In order to cope, the Japanese government formed recession cartels for crude steel and stainless steel sheets, offering incentives to reduce capacity.[57] Stimulative fiscal policy and the subsequent economic boom temporarily eased the excess capacity problem, and the recession

---

[54] In its Oct. 1966 publication, 'Concerning the Future Way for Steel' (Kongo no Tekkōgyō no Arikata ni Tsuite), MITI emphasized the need for large-scale investment, investment adjustment, and price stability in order for the Japanese steel industry to stay even with its foreign competitors. To achieve these goals, MITI recommended mergers, joint investments, and management exchange.

[55] Nihon Kaihatsu Ginkō, Nihon Kaihatsu Ginkō Nijūgonen Shi, 448.

[56] The proposed merger met with criticism from both the public and economists on the grounds that it would decrease competition and thus lead to inefficient allocation of resources. However, after a lengthy review by the Fair Trade Commission, the merger was approved under the stipulation that Fuji Steel sell one plant to Kobe Steel and Yawata sell one plant to Nippon Kōkan.

[57] These recession cartels, recognized under Article 24 of the Anti-Monopoly Law, provided funds to purchase and scrap equipment. The recession cartel for crude steel manufacturers using blast furnaces continued until Dec. 1972, as did the recession cartel for open hearth steel makers. The recession cartel for stainless steel plate was enforced until June 1973. (Kōsei Torihiki Iinkai, Kōsei Torihiki Iinkai Nenji Hōkoku (Tokyo, Ōkurashō Insatsu Kyoku, various years).)

cartel for crude steel was terminated at the end of 1972 while that for stainless steel ended in June 1973. However, another shock was just around the corner: the first oil crisis at the end of 1973 would hit a Japanese economy that was already experiencing serious inflationary pressures, and as a result GNP would decline in 1974. Stagnating domestic and world demand through the remainder of the decade created a chronic problem with excess capacity in the Japanese steel industry, a problem that was compounded by the much higher costs of this energy-intensive industry. Industrial policy towards steel had already moved from a pro-growth stance to one of temporary adjustment by the early 1970s. This adjustment became chronic, and government measures towards the steel industry for the next decade would closely resemble anti-growth policy. However, from 1983, government efforts to orchestrate a smooth contraction for the traditional steel industry were supplemented with efforts to encourage diversification into new business areas in what was effectively a synthesis between pro-growth and anti-growth policies.

5.4 Industrial Policy Towards a Declining Steel Industry (1971–1990)

With the first oil crisis, any hopes that Japan's high-growth period would continue were dashed. Steel was particularly hard hit by the surge in energy costs,[58] although the 13.7 per cent depreciation of the yen between August 1973 and 1974 helped to mitigate partially the blow to the industry. That is, even though this move in the currency further raised the price of oil to domestic steel users, the weaker yen also increased the competitiveness of steel exports. In part, yen depreciation helps to explain Japan's strong export performance (Fig. 5.2), but Japanese producers were nevertheless subject to charges of dumping.[59]

In the aftermath of the first oil shock, policy-makers concentrated on trying to curtail inflation by implementing price controls and monitoring the distribution of goods.[60] The steel industry was not directly affected by

---

[58] From 1973 to 1975, energy costs rose from 5.7% of total steel output to 9.9%. In relation to value added in the industry, the increase was even sharper, with energy costs rising from 18.7% to 46.2%. (Tsūshō Sangyō Daijin Kanbō Chōsa Bu, *Kōgyō Tōkei Hyō: Sangyō Hen* (Tokyo, Ōkurashō Insatsu Kyoku, 1973 and 1975).)

[59] For details on trade friction in steel in the 1970s, see Hugh Patrick and Hideo Satō, 'The Political Economy of United States–Japan Trade in Steel', *Policy and Trade Issues of the Japanese Economy*, 197–238.

[60] Worries that price controls would be applied to a broad range of products tempted many firms to collude and raise prices before the controls were implemented. For further details on policy in the aftermath of the first oil crisis, see Section 7.1.

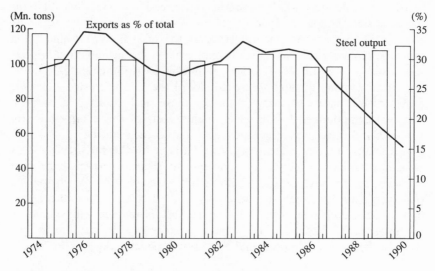

Fig. 5.2. Recent Trends in Steel Output and Exports
Source: Nihon Tokkō Renmei *Nihon Tekkō Yōran*.

these measures, but public anger over price collusion by firms hampered the government's ability to utilize cartels as a tool to help Japanese industry adjust to the oil shock. Hence, the government did not attempt to aid the steel industry by forming recession cartels, a measure which in any case had proved unsuccessful in helping the industry to reduce capacity in the early 1970s.

As inflation abated and price controls were eased, the government began to develop a comprehensive strategy to facilitate adjustment in industries such as steel that had been particularly hard hit by the oil shock. These efforts resulted in a series of new laws, the most important of which was the Law Concerning Emergency Measures for the Stabilization of Specially Designated Depressed Industries (*Tokutei Fukyō Sangyō Antei Rinji Sochi Hō*) passed in 1978. This law called for government funds to subsidize capacity reductions for steel as well as other depressed industries, and in this regard was quite similar to past policy measures used to facilitate decline. However, the law specifically called for an active role for the government in planning how capacity was to be scrapped. Moreover, in instances where adjustment did not proceed as planned, the law called for the government, in consultation with the Fair Trade Commission, to form a cartel to promote capacity reductions. Hence, the Law Concerning Emergency Measures for the Stabilization of

Specially Designated Depressed Industries partially offset the limitations placed on policy by the 1977 revision of the Anti-Monopoly Law.[61]

Although steel was targeted under the Law Concerning Emergency Measures for the Stabilization of Specially Designated Depressed Industries, it was not one which used available government funds to scrap capacity[62] nor did the government find it necessary to cartelize the industry to achieve adjustment.[63] Despite this lack of government support, the steel industry was apparently quite successful in reducing capacity, since by 1981, the blast and electric furnace manufacturers had eliminated fully 95 per cent of the 2.85 million tons of capacity called for in the government's reorganization proposal for 1978–83. This represented 13 per cent of the capacity that these manufacturers had had before reorganization efforts were begun.[64] Despite this apparent success, it should be noted that these numbers include capacity that was mothballed rather than scrapped and hence overstate the extent to which the industry had truly contracted.

Government efforts to help the steel industry shrink shifted in 1983 with the passage of the Law Concerning Emergency Measures to Improve the Structure of Designated Industries (*Tokutei Sangyō Kōzō Kaizen Rinji Sochi Hō*) which replaced the expiring Law Concerning Emergency Measures for the Stabilization of Specially Designated Depressed Industries. Not content simply to orchestrate capacity reductions, this law also called for government supervision of R&D investment and government suggestions about product specialization in order to help declining industries regain competitiveness. Under this new legislation, the government also had an active role in promoting the diversification of declining industries into new business areas.[65] The new legislation continued to designate electric furnace steel manufacturing as a troubled industry, and although blast furnace steel was not so designated, semi-finished steel was.

---

[61] This revision was the result of public dissatisfaction about collusive price-setting activities amongst firms in 1974. Dissatisfaction with government support of mergers also contributed.

[62] Sekiguchi Sueo and Horiuchi Toshihiro, 'Bōeki to Chōsei Enjo', in Komiya Ryūtarō, Okuno Masahiro, and Suzumura Kōtarō (eds.), *Nihon no Sangyō Seisaku* (Tokyo, University of Tokyo Press, 1984), 327–44.

[63] Kōsei Torihiki Iinkai, *Kōsei Torihiki Iinkai Nenji Hōkoku*, 1975–90. The government did allow small manufacturers of steel tube to form a recession cartel under Article 24 of the Anti-Monopoly Law from Sep. 1975 to Sept. 1977, after which time the cartel was continued under the auspices of the Law Concerning the Organization of Small and Medium Enterprise Groups (*Chūshō Kigyō Dantai no Sōshiki ni Kansuru Hōritsu*). However, the government did not attempt to use cartels to help the large steel companies adjust to the first oil crisis.

[64] Sekiguchi Sueo and Horiuchi Toshihiro, 'Bōeki to Chōsei Enjo', *Nihon no Sangyō Seisaku*, 336.

[65] To promote these ends, the law called for new subsidies and tax breaks.

Similar to the plan to reduce capacity in the 1978 to 1983 period, policy towards steel in recent years appears to have achieved its objectives. Diversification in the steel industry has been rapid, even more so than the average for Japanese manufacturing as a whole (Fig. 5.3). This does not constitute proof of policy efficacy—it is not clear that industry efforts to reduce capacity and to diversify were stimulated by government policy measures. Individual steel companies formulated their own plans to scrap capacity following the appreciation of the yen in 1985, and also have been highly self-motivated in forming individual diversification strategies. Moreover, the industry's financial ability to adjust was supported by the unexpected boom in the domestic steel market from 1987, a boom which also eased the need in the short term to scrap capacity. Finally, the success of diversification, whether self-motivated or policy driven, is also questionable given the continuing strong correlation between total industry profits and crude steel production (Fig. 5.3). Yet despite these qualifications, it also seems equally probable that government policy did not hamper reorganization efforts. Given the very small extent of government subsidies and tax breaks to the industry in the 1980s, even if policy impact was tiny, policy as measured in terms of cost effectiveness could have been very successful.

5.5   Evaluating Industrial Policy Towards Steel

For more than a quarter of a century after World War II, Japanese industrial policy aggressively promoted the expansion of the Japanese steel industry. From the early 1960s, however, policy began to focus on the problem of excess capacity, and by the early 1970s this had become such an overriding concern that industrial policy can be characterized as consisting primarily of anti-growth measures. Judging policy on the basis of meeting its goals, it is tempting to conclude that it was successful, at least prior to 1970. Between 1951 and 1970, steel output rose 14.4 times. Production costs were dramatically reduced, to the extent that steel emerged as Japan's largest export industry in the mid-1960s, a position it would maintain for more than a decade. However, as the aim of policy shifted to capacity reduction, its efficacy was initially lost. It probably contributed to the surge in inflation in 1973–4 by limiting the output of the industry, and it had no definite effect on reducing capacity for most of that decade. Policy may have become more effective in the 1980s, as efforts to reduce capacity were coupled with the promotion of diversification.

The same methodology outlined in Chapters 3 and 4 can be used to examine policy impact in more detail. For economic development in

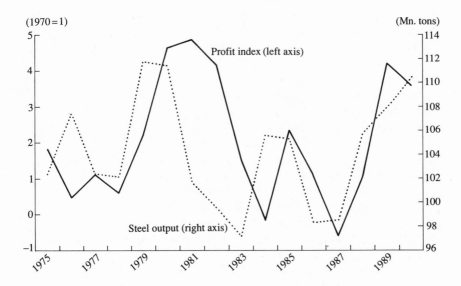

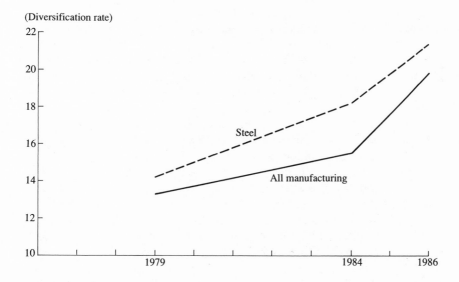

Fig. 5.3. Recent Trends in Diversification, Profits, and Steel Production, 1975–1990
Source: Nihon Renmei Tekkō, *Tekkō Tōkei Yōran; Kōsei Torihiki Iinkai; Nikkei Database.*

Japan to have benefited from policy to expand the steel industry depends both on whether steel was an infant industry and whether measures adopted to foster the infant industry were optimal. The former is crucial since if steel was not an infant industry, then it did not require government support. In that case, the resources used to support steel were wasted and better utilization of those resources could have accelerated economic development. Although the question cannot be answered with total certainty, available evidence strongly supports the contention that the Japanese steel industry after World War II was in fact an infant industry. Technological advances and more than a decade of economic isolation had left the Japanese steel industry so far behind the rest of the world that the import of new equipment and production processes on a very large scale was necessary if the industry was to survive. Japan essentially had to scrap existing facilities and start anew with unfamiliar technologies such as the basic oxygen furnace. Because learning new technologies was crucial to survival, steel was for all practical purposes an infant industry.

Not only was steel probably an infant industry, but measures adopted to support the development of the industry were in many cases optimal. Productivity increases in steel production could be expected as the industry adopted and learned new production techniques, and to realize these gains, the government directly subsidized investment in the industry through accelerated depreciation, reserve accounts, and low-interest government loans. These low-interest government loans were also the ideal policy response to capital market imperfections. The government directly promoted the adoption of new production techniques through subsidizing the import of foreign equipment, and domestic R&D was also stimulated through direct government support. The profitability of investment in the steel industry was initially dependent on investment in both the coal industry and the electric power industry, and the government responded to these investment complementarities by disseminating information as well as by funding steel industry investment in its own power generation.

The government also attempted to promote the domestic steel industry by shutting foreign steel products out of the domestic market. These trade policies most likely were not optimal, since they placed substantial costs on the very end users of Japanese steel, consumers in Japan.[66] Additionally, trade protection in steel and in other industries also widened the problem of investment complementarities. Finally, trade protection in steel also had the potential cost of stifling competition within the domestic industry, thus creating a bias against exports of steel.

[66] To offset steel tariffs, the government placed higher tariff rates on products made by manufacturers who used steel as an input, including, for example, machinery. Hence, tariffs were eventually paid by consumers in Japan rather than manufacturers.

Table 5.4. Japanese Imports of Steel Production Technology

Japanese company	Technology	Date imported	Imported from
Fuji Steel	Flat-rolled sheet produced in strip mills	Apr. 1951	Armco International
Yawata Steel	Hot-rolled silicon steel	May 1951	Armco International
Yawata Steel	Zinc-coated steel	May 1951	Armco International
Fuji Steel	Coating technology and plant control (information exchange)	June 1951	William S. Vaughan
Yawata Steel	Flat-rolled sheet produced in strip mills	Jan. 1952	Armco International
Nippon Kōkan	Rollers and large-scale coating equipment	May 1952	Charles Francis, Ralph Porter
Nippon Kōkan	Rolling equipment	July 1952	United Engineering and Foundry
Kobe Steel	Specially forged iron	Mar. 1953	Compagnie des Forges and Aciéries de la Marine and de St Étienne
Yawata Steel	Insulated arc welding rods	June 1955	Holding Intercito Ltd.
Fuji Steel	Extension utility poles (steel or aluminium)	July 1955	Josef Pfisteshemmer
Yawata Steel	TH-type frame steel	Dec. 1955	Bochumer Eisenhuette Heintzmann
Yawata Steel	Metal surface stripping equipment	May 1956	Union Carbide
Nippon Kōkan	Basic oxygen furnace	June 1956	Oesterreichisch-Alpine Montangesellschaft
Kobe Steel	Hot-extraction method for metal manufacturing	July 1956	Comptoir Industriel d'Étirage et Profilage de Métaux
Sumitomo Metal	Hot-extraction method for metal manufacturing	July 1956	Comptoir Industriel d'Étirage et Profilage de Métaux
Sumitomo Metal	Magnetized metal oxide	Oct. 1956	N.V. Phillips' Gloeilampenfabriken
Yawata Steel	Can production	Oct. 1956	American Can
Yawata Steel	Cold-rolled silicon steel	Feb. 1957	Westinghouse Electric
Yawata Steel	Hot-extraction method for metal manufacturing (also imported by Sanyō Special Steel at same time)	May 1957	Comptoir Industriel d'Étirage et Profilage de Métaux
Yawata Steel	Continuous casting	May 1957	Concast A.G.
Yawata Steel	Cast iron magnesium alloy (imported by Hitachi Metals in Oct. 1956)	June 1957	Canadian Nickel Products Ltd.
Kawasaki Steel	Regular-rolled sheet produced in strip mills	Sept. 1957	Republic Steel

Source: Tsūshō Sangyō Shō, *Gaishi Dōnyū: Sono Seido to Jittai.*

Rather than trade barriers, it probably would have been better to increase subsidies to the level at which Japanese steel products were competitive with foreign steel, thus avoiding these costs.

That Japan chose to use trade barriers can still be justified if these barriers were so beneficial in reducing the costs of imported technology that the costs of trade barriers were dwarfed in comparison. There is some anecdotal evidence in support of this contention. Control over trade and foreign capital inflows reinforced the government's ability to extract foreign technology on favourable terms to Japanese buyers. Not only were these purchase costs reduced, but by allowing only one or two Japanese companies initially to import a new technology, the government was able effectively to screen out inappropriate technologies that would have been costly had they been adopted on a wide scale. Moreover, this process also allowed the Japanese government to screen for the best technology, since it would often compare rival production processes by allowing the import of both on a trial basis (Table 5.4).

Despite this anecdotal evidence, it is far from clear that the benefits arising from trade barriers, namely support of the steel industry together with cheaper, more effective imports of technology, outweighed the direct costs to steel users and the potential costs to investment efficiency and domestic competition. Even so, industrial policy did explicitly attempt to offset the costs associated with trade barriers. First, the government ensured that domestic users of steel were not punished by the high prices for these inputs. It did so by putting even higher tariff rates on finished products such as cars and machinery, guaranteeing that domestic products were not more expensive than competing imports.[67] Secondly, trade controls created investment complementarities, where the profitability of investment in steel depended upon the investment in other industries. The Japanese government minimized this potential problem by co-ordinating investment activities across industries as well as by formulating long-term economic plans for the entire economy. Investment activities in steel were initially determined by the government, and the government made sure that these investment plans were consistent with those in electric power, shipbuilding, cars, and machinery. Even as direct government control over investment in the steel industry declined, it continued to provide growth forecasts for the economy and for industries through its long-term economic plans. These probably helped to prevent completely inappropriate investment in steel and in other industries.

[67] Of course, this tariff structure produced a bias against consumption. If the economy grows, this reduction in consumption at present can be offset by higher future consumption. Additionally, this bias against consumption in the short term can help to increase savings, thus providing funds to fuel investment and growth. These goals can generally be accomplished more directly and at a smaller cost through income taxes.

Finally, the government also adopted measures to offset any bias against competition in the steel industry that trade barriers might have produced. Export subsidies were one tool utilized to this end: by encouraging Japanese steel companies to market overseas, the domestic industry was not only kept aware of the activities of foreign rivals but was motivated to improve domestic productivity in order to capture a larger share of foreign markets. The government also promoted domestic competition in steel through the way in which it allocated imports of raw materials and technologies. The Occupation helped to level the playing field for the steel industry by breaking up Japan Steel, the dominant firm, and by ending price subsidies; the Japanese government furthered these measures by ensuring that the six major steel companies all had equal access to imported machinery, imported raw materials, and foreign technology. By not consistently favouring any one firm, industrial policy promoted competition amongst companies. Moreover, the government had the power to encourage or demand management changes when a company was falling behind, and this too acted to stimulate competition amongst all companies. In effect, government policy until the end of the 1960s kept the number of major steel companies constant at six, a large enough number to ensure that competition prospered.

The government's promotion of domestic competition produced great benefits. It stimulated investment in the most modern production techniques, supporting the introduction of foreign technologies. As a result, costs in the industry fell dramatically, dropping more than one-third between 1956 and 1960. Cost reductions stimulated further growth in the steel industry as exports rose and new domestic applications for steel were opened up. There were also enormous spill-over effects, since cost and quality improvements in the domestic steel industry increased the competitiveness of other domestic industries including cars, machinery, and shipbuilding. In turn, this greater competitiveness for users of Japanese steel further raised the demand for steel, thus supporting additional productivity improvements in the industry. In other words, the investment generates investment phenomenon that characterized Japanese development for much of the high-growth period was closely related to government measures to stimulate competition in the steel industry.

These policies in support of competition were not totally without cost. They naturally led to the issue of over-capacity which became the focus of policy from the early 1970s until the present. In an industry better characterized by competitive rather than oligopolistic behaviour, increased demand can lead to over-capacity in the short run since makers will not take into account what effect an increase in their output will have on prices. This problem is intensified by economies of scale in production, since expanding output would reduce production costs and intensify competition for market share. Additionally, continuous increases in demand for steel over time will exacerbate the problem of excess capacity in temporary downturns because steel manufacturers will view their output as being able to expand without limit. In other words, steel manufacturers will not worry about any temporary fall in demand but will invest to increase capacity to capture future demand. Finally, the problem of excess capacity is exacerbated by the long lags between the start of investment projects and their completion.

These characteristics of the Japanese steel industry created excess capacity, but the benefits of promoting competition outweighed the costs. Had policy towards steel simply stopped with promoting competition, it could well have been close to optimal.[68] However, it did not end at this point. Policy gave implicit guarantees against bankruptcy, and these exacerbated the problem of over-investment. More seriously, it also attempted to lessen the problem of excess capacity by encouraging the co-ordination of investment amongst firms from 1960. Paradoxically, this intensified excess capacity by ensuring that each firm in the steel industry was made aware of its rivals' strategies. This undoubtedly increased those instances where firms chose to increase their own investment rather than allowing rivals to get ahead.

Policy then made another error. Concern that competition could produce excess capacity caused the government to label this competitive investment behaviour as excessive. The term 'excessive competition' is highly misleading, at least in its application to the Japanese steel industry. There it seems to signify the excess capacity which can be naturally generated by simple competition; the term ignores all of the benefits that competition itself bestows in the form of price decreases and the rapid adoption of new technology.[69] In other words, the government reversed its support of competition in the industry. Worries about 'excessive competition', coupled with the perceived threat to the industry caused by foreign capital liberalization, drove the government to recommend the

---

[68] This issue is far from simple. While a competitive market is totally efficient in a static sense, competition in a dynamic model need not result in an optimal growth path since competition can temporarily generate excess capacity. Despite this caveat, it is possible that competition may produce as close to an optimal growth path as can ever be realized, given the ability of competitive markets to disseminate new information and the inability of a state-controlled economy to forecast technological change.

[69] That competition can generate excess capacity has been empirically verified (see, for example, F. Esposito and L. Esposito, 'Excess Capacity and Market Structure', *The Review of Economics and Statistics*, 56 (1974), 188–94). The term 'excess capacity' may also be misleading. It might not be optimal for an industry to operate at full capacity during an economic upturn, since this will lead to price pressures. Just as economists have discussed a natural rate of unemployment which signifies the trade-off between inflation and employment, so too might there be an equivalent concept for capital. An economy which does not have some sort of 'natural excess capacity' (perhaps because competition is constrained) may be more readily subject to periods of inflation and downturns in business cycles.

merger of the two largest steel companies into a single entity with dominant market share. With the formation of New Japan Steel in 1970, the government greatly increased the oligopolistic characteristics of the Japanese steel industry. While this may have reduced the rate at which excess capacity was being created, it did so at substantial costs to users of steel. Had the merger not been accomplished, domestic steel prices in the 1971–5 period would generally have been lower than actual prices, in some cases by as much as 14 per cent.[70] Moreover, the formation of 'excess capacity' might have improved the price performance of the overall economy, and policy may have deprived the economy of this benefit.

If industrial policy towards steel gradually lost its effectiveness in the early 1960s, it reached a nadir in the early 1970s. Industrial policy towards steel, like policy towards other industries, was criticized as promoting growth that was overly dependent on foreign markets and overly dependent on energy. These flaws were highlighted by the appreciation of the yen in 1971 and the first oil crisis. Moreover, the hyper-inflation of 1972–4 also made questionable government efforts to limit steel output since these efforts may have exacerbated price increases. From this nadir, the rationality of policy towards steel gradually improved. Recognizing that the industry had grown too much, policy from 1978 attempted to orchestrate an orderly retreat under government supervision. Some capacity reductions were achieved, and at zero direct cost to the government. From 1983, the government not only tried to facilitate the decline of the traditional steel industry, but it also tried to revitalize the industry, supervising R&D plans and product specialization. Through subsidies and tax breaks, the government also encouraged diversification into new product areas. Assuming that labour and capital lack mobility, many of these policy measures are first-best policy solutions. In fact, policy measures after 1983 were designed to be consistent with OECD guidelines on industrial adjustment, and thus the rationality of these measures is natural.

As rationality returned to policy formulation, the impact of measures decreased since the need for government intervention was limited. Capacity reductions in the 1978–83 period were achieved without any direct government aid, and tax breaks and subsidies to promote diversification have not been large. This stands in sharp contrast to the early development of the industry. The emergence of the Japanese steel industry as the most efficient in the world probably owes a great deal to industrial policy in the 1950s: in the absence of government funding and tax incentives, investment could not have occurred as quickly as it did and Japanese economic development would probably have occurred at a

[70] Yamawaki Hideki, 'Market Structure, Capacity Expansion and Pricing: A Model Applied to the Japanese Steel Industry', *International Journal of Industrial Organization*, 2: 29–62.

slower pace. The scope of market imperfections and externalities then meant that the role of industrial policy was much greater. At present, successful development has reduced the need for government intervention, and while the impact of industrial policy on the steel industry is very much less than in the past, it is notable that the government has been able to successfully reduce its involvement with the industry. Of course, this was not accomplished easily, as the policy mistakes of the 1960s and early 1970s show.

This evaluation of industrial policy towards steel is of course influenced by its being made in 1991. Judgement of policy a decade ago could well have concluded that measures were a failure: although policy had acted as a catalyst for early development, in the end it had apparently created an uncompetitive albatross. In 1991, such a judgement seems overly pessimistic. The costs inflicted on the Japanese economy in the 1970s by inappropriate policy measures are now offset by early policy success and the recovery of the industry in the 1980s. Yet this judgement too is subjective and may be reversed in another decade. In other words, a final judgement of industrial policy depends not only on the costs and benefits accrued through time but also on the future policy outcome. Because this future outcome cannot be known at present, a final evaluation of industrial policy is difficult.[71]

[71] This assumes that the steel industry in Japan would not have developed in the absence of policy. If steel would have developed anyway, the period of time that policy affects the economy is finite and the evaluation of industrial policy is greatly simplified.

6
Lessons for Developing Countries

Japanese industrial policy had a substantial impact on the allocation of resources during the three decades following the Second World War. Although this impact lessened over time, industrial policy clearly affected the pattern of economic development during Japan's high-growth era. By contributing to greater savings and investment, industrial policy may actually have increased the tempo of development, at least through the 1950s. Moreover, policy to maintain employment by blocking competition in select industries probably helped to create a stable base from which development could smoothly take place. Industrial policy may also have been crucial to the development of steel, chemicals, select machinery, and other industries subject to dynamic internal economies.

Even if industrial policy did contribute to Japan's successful development after the war, that contribution largely ended in the 1960s. The rationality of policy faded, as policy towards agriculture shifted to aggressive protectionism despite the declining need to support employment. Industries which had been promoted in the previous decade continued to receive some support in the 1960s even though these industries had achieved international competitiveness. Government encouragement of mergers also undermined the overall efficiency of the economy. Nevertheless, industrial policy in the 1960s did offer limited benefits. New infant industries, such as computers, were subject to generally appropriate policy response, and there was some disengagement of support for older infant industries. In addition, policy towards distribution and smaller enterprises shifted from blocking competition to promoting it, an appropriate reaction given the emerging shortage of labour.

By the second half of the 1960s, the balance between the benefits arising from appropriate policy and the costs of inappropriate policy response probably shifted towards the latter. Inappropriate industrial policy set the stage for the sudden appreciation of the yen in the early 1970s, an event which battered those government-targeted industries that had become increasingly dependent on exports for growth. The energy dependency of these industries was also highlighted by the oil crises. As will be shown in Chapters 7 and 8, policy response extended the period of adjustment to these events, increasing economic costs. Not until late in the 1970s did rationality return to industrial policy and its role, while strikingly smaller in scope, could have contributed marginally to favourable economic growth in the 1980s.

The probable success of Japanese industrial policy in the 1950s offers useful insight to developing nations at the present time, particularly Eastern European countries and the former Soviet republics. Equally, there is much to be learned from Japanese policy mistakes in the 1960s and the arguably complete failure of industrial policy in the first half of the 1970s. Section 6.1 of this chapter summarizes these economic lessons, providing a reference for those developing nations today who wish to emulate Japan. However, this summary alone does not suffice, since Japan's success with industrial policy owes much to historical and institutional accident. Section 6.2 thus outlines how Japanese industrial policy was shaped by its own past and its own place in the world economy. With these qualifications in mind, a tentative attempt at general rules for an effective industrial policy for developing countries is presented in Section 6.3.

6.1 Policy Success and Failure: Economic Insights

The most valuable lesson of Japanese industrial policy lies in its management of employment. The disruptions that followed the war were such that the government had to intervene to ensure the survival of the workforce. Thus, the government supported increases in agricultural output and at the same time fostered greater production of basic materials and energy. In the 1950s the government continued to strike this balance by subsidizing the modernization and development of select industries while protecting the distribution sector and small companies in general from market forces.

Implicit in these policy measures is the recognition that development is not without cost. These costs are the bankruptcy of uncompetitive industries and the subsequent emergence of unemployment. For an industrialized nation, such costs are generally outweighed by the benefits of competitive markets, but for a nation which has been isolated from the global economy, this will often not hold in the short run. Immediately after the war, Japan's stock of capital was so depleted that in the absence of policy intervention, full employment could only have been achieved at below subsistence wages. In order to prevent widespread starvation, Japan had no choice but to subsidize. After the early 1950s, starvation was no longer a threat, suggesting that the government could theoretically have eliminated all measures to support employment, relying instead on a programme to provide welfare benefits to those workers who would have lost their jobs in the absence of government intervention. However, such an alternative would probably have generated widespread social instability, both because of the magnitude of potential unemployment as well as the heavier tax burden on corporations and workers that would have been required to fund unemployment benefits. As it was, the costs of supporting employment were less visible, since they were reflected only in the higher prices resulting from the blocking of competition in distribution and amongst smaller companies.

Japan's anti-growth policy measures had one very important characteristic: they did not discourage limited technological progress and modernization. The scale of benefits may not have been great, but distributors and small enterprises nevertheless could capture gains from improved productivity. In other words, even these sectors had incentive to develop. This characteristic helped to minimize the costs of anti-growth policy and also acted as insurance against general economic stagnation. Moreover, it was because of familiarity with the benefits to be obtained from further modernization that small enterprises and the distribution industry did not resist the phasing out of anti-growth policy in the 1960s. The government's success in eliminating anti-growth measures is a major achievement of Japanese industrial policy. Unfortunately, this success was not absolute: policy towards agriculture shifted to aggressive protectionism in the 1960s, just as the need for anti-growth policy faded. This shift was the result of the rising political importance of the farming lobby and the inability of policy to further improve agricultural efficiency given the small size of plots under cultivation.

Industrial policy may also have contributed to higher rates of savings and investment, thus stimulating economic development. Policy directly increased corporate savings rates through accelerated depreciation, a measure which also stimulated investment. Investment was also stimulated by other tax breaks and subsidized loans. In addition, industrial policy raised the cost of consumption through higher prices, the result of tariffs and measures to guarantee employment. Thus, it may have increased household savings by decreasing the cost of savings relative to consumption. Similarly, it favoured corporate interests over those of the consumer, and to the extent that the marginal propensity to save was higher out of profits, this bias may have also stimulated aggregate savings.

Policy also responded well to the problem of capital market imperfections, establishing the Japan Development Bank to provide funds for industries. Like most developing countries, capital markets in post-war Japan were underdeveloped and tightly controlled, factors which undermined their efficiency. Compounding this problem was a shortage of private sector capital. Private financial institutions probably had an aversion to investing in projects which required a lengthy period before they would become profitable, so that in the absence of government intervention only immediately profitable investments would have received funding. In order to overcome this, the Japanese government created the Japan

Development Bank in 1951 to channel loans for long-term investments in recipient industries.

The Japan Development Bank replaced the Reconstruction Finance Corporation, which had been in existence for two years prior to the halting of its lending activities by the Occupation in 1949. The RFC had not been adequately regulated and had been allowed to issue bank debentures. The combination of these factors resulted in an excessive amount of lending which fuelled hyper-inflation in the latter half of the 1940s. In the light of this past experience, the Japan Development Bank was initially not given the right to issue bonds, and the bank's lending activities were under the strict supervision of the Ministry of Finance.[1] Moreover, the Japan Development Bank only provided loans in cases where it could expect repayment, thoroughly examining the financial conditions of a company and the feasibility of its investment plans before granting a loan. The Japan Development Bank Law was revised in July 1953, allowing it to issue debentures, guarantee debt, and borrow money from the government and foreign financial institutions, but these activities were also subject to the approval of the Ministry of Finance. As a result of strict supervision and high lending standards, loans of the Japan Development Bank never exerted excessive inflationary pressures on the economy.

The functions of the Japan Development Bank were supplemented by those of long-term credit banks and city banks, private sector institutions generally ruled by considerations of profitability. Even so, the government could exert some influence over their lending practices given the regulated state of the Japanese financial market. Long-term credit banks were the only private financial institutions allowed to issue debentures, and as such were important sources of funding for corporate plant and equipment investment. Through its ability to influence demand for these debentures, the government could potentially affect their lending practices, while the reliance of city banks on central bank credit left them subject to government pressure as well. However, these institutions had full responsibility for the loans they granted, ensuring that market principles determined most of their loans.

Industrial policy also probably served an important function in coordinating investment across industries. In a developing country, the profitability of investment in an industry such as steel will depend on the

---

[1] Although the Ministry of Finance had final jurisdiction over the Japan Development Bank, it was not the only bureaucracy to have important input into the allocation of JDB loans. Lending activities of the JDB were expected to broadly follow outlines laid down by the Economic Planning Agency in its yearly 'Basic Policy Concerning the Management of Government Funds for Industrial Investment' (*Seifu Shikin no Sangyō Tōshi ni Kansuru Unyō Kihon Hōshin*). This report was drawn up in consultation with other government bureaucracies such as MITI and the Ministry of Agriculture.

availability of power and transportation facilities. The same argument holds true for investment in other industries utilizing these inputs, and it is important that investment in the entire economy does not increase more quickly than the infrastructure can handle. It would have done the Japanese steel industry little good to raise capacity if power and transportation had not been available, and the government helped to ensure that this did not occur by supervising and controlling industry investment in the decade following the Second World War.

The benefits of industrial policy outlined thus far could probably have been obtained without implementing measures on as wide a scale as did Japan. Ensuring full employment may require some subsidies and a general blocking of competition in a few industries; measures to stimulate savings and investment may be adequately implemented at the macroeconomic level through a high consumption tax, lower corporate taxes, and savings incentives. Establishing and funding a development bank does not require extensive intervention once the institution has been formed, and the co-ordination and guidance of investment activities of all industries may only be crucial in very early development stages when a country lacks a basic infrastructure.

Hence, Japan's widespread use of industrial policy was not based on these problems and benefits alone. Rather, it was also predicated on a belief that state support was necessary to help industries grow. If an industry does learn over time, if productivity rises the longer that output continues, then the promotion of individual industries does make economic sense. Although the existence of infant industries cannot be empirically verified, that new technologies and new machinery are not mastered overnight supports the case for infant industries. Moreover, reductions in production costs over time are consistent with the existence of learning-by-doing effects. Even so, insights to be obtained from Japan's extensive implementation of measures to promote growth in various industries are highly dependent on the actual existence of infant industries. Were industries in Japan not in fact subject to dynamic external or internal economies, then the measures outlined below to promote growth would have been largely unnecessary. Development would have occurred more quickly and efficiently in the absence of pro-growth policy.[2]

That caveat noted, Japanese pro-growth industrial policy had several valuable characteristics which contributed to its probable beneficial impact on economic development through the 1950s. First, support was often provided through investment subsidies in the form of tax breaks. Not only do tax breaks involve relatively few administrative costs, but

---

[2] Even if policy allocated resources in exactly the same way as would have market forces, in the absence of market failures or externalities, industrial policy can only impede growth since implementing policy involves administration costs.

they also avoid corruption problems which can plague a large state programme that directly disburses funds. When providing funds directly, administrative costs were held down by having a specialized bank allocate industry loans rather than entrusting this function directly to the government. Problems were also minimized by reliance on private sector financial institutions. In instances where the Japanese government attempted to promote an industry through subsidizing output rather than investment, policy was often not as effective. For instance, the government supported shipbuilding through subsidizing the purchase of ships by the marine transport industry. While this policy did stimulate the shipbuilding industry, it also created excess capacity in marine transport. This example reinforces the conclusion of economic theory that it is best to support infant industries through investment subsidies as this minimizes distortions accompanying policy intervention.

While Japanese pro-growth industrial policy provides examples of how to implement low-cost subsidies, perhaps its most unique feature was its utilization of competition to shape the development of industries. As previously noted, market principles were applied to the funding of industry investment. Additionally, policy never consistently favoured any single firm. Until the early 1960s, support was spread more or less equally across enough firms to prevent the emergence of a monopolistic or strongly oligopolistic structure in any targeted industry. This is clear from the government's allocation of imports and foreign technologies as well as the allocation of government-subsidized loans. As a result, industrial policy promoted competition among firms in an industry.

Moreover, policy also rewarded corporate success and punished failure. By tying tax breaks to the amount a firm exported or to the increase in a firm's exports, policy provided incentives for companies to expand sales. The government also sometimes used its ability to influence investment to reward companies with high or increasing market share. On the other hand, policy threatened firms that failed to keep up with rivals with the replacement of their management. The government might temporarily favour a firm that fell behind with increased loans or approval for aggressive investment plans, but if these carrots did not suffice, the government would sometimes make the receipt of future support conditional on management changes. In one famous example of this, MITI insisted that unless the chairman of Maruzen Oil stepped down, permission to accept a loan from Union Oil would be denied.[3]

Finally, the government also used foreign competition as a tool to pro-

---

[3] Chalmers Johnson, *MITI and the Japanese Miracle*, 260–2. Intervention in corporate management by the Japan Development Bank was even more common. The bank would often place its own representative in management to ensure that plant and equipment investment was made according to plan.

mote domestic competition, although it only did so in overseas markets. Through trade barriers, the government insulated Japanese firms from foreign competitors in domestic markets. Industrial policy countered the potentially stagnating effect this could have had on domestic competition through implementing the export subsidy programme noted above. Not only did these subsidies permit Japanese firms to face foreign rivals overseas, but by linking the extent of the subsidy granted to the magnitude of exports, the Japanese government provided incentives for domestic firms to surpass foreign competitors. This exposure to foreign competition was crucial: without it, the motivation to compete would have been sharply curtailed.

Probably the most contentious characteristic of Japanese industrial policy was its reliance on trade barriers. Tariffs, quotas, and control over imports did draw resources into import-competing industries, thus promoting their growth. Moreover, the negative impact on domestic competition caused by shutting foreign firms out of the Japanese market was avoided by introducing export subsidies. Nevertheless, it could well have been more efficient to subsidize domestic firms to the point at which they were competitive with foreign rivals, since such a programme would not have distorted the use of protected products. It is possible that the benefits of trade barriers helped to offset at least partially their higher cost. Trade barriers increased the government's ability to extract foreign technologies, since foreign firms could not easily market their products in Japan or set up their own production subsidiaries. These limitations also helped to lower the prices foreigners were willing to accept for technologies, as did the government's direct involvement in all negotiations for technology imports. While such benefits were substantial, it is nevertheless far from clear that they outweighed the distortions generated by tariffs.

Whether or not trade barriers can be justified on the grounds of the benefits they created, their use magnified the problem of investment complementarity. When trade barriers are not present, the profitability of investment in an industry will depend on capacity increases by producers of non-tradable goods such as electric power and land transport but it will not be dependent on capacity increases by producers of tradable goods since the industry can choose to use either domestic or imported products. In Japan's early stages of post-war development, investment complementarities did exist because of infrastructure bottlenecks, but these complementarities would have disappeared as Japan's infrastructure improved. However, trade barriers increased the extent of these investment complementarities by effectively raising the number of non-tradable goods. Thus, the profitability of investment in machinery, shipbuilding, and cars, for example, depended on investment in the domestic steel industry since imports of foreign steel were restricted. Similarly, the profitability of investment in the steel industry was affected by the investment plans of these end-users of steel.

Just as the government alleviated the problem of investment complementarities arising from an underdeveloped infrastructure by directing and adjusting investment plans for select industries, so too did it initially use these powers to correct investment complementarities arising from trade barriers. However, as investment complementarities spread across the entire economy, the government lost the capacity to effectively correct complementarities by controlling investment levels.[4] Instead, it responded by making public the investment plans for key industries such as steel, thus providing necessary information to users of products made by these industries. It extended this function in 1955 when it began to publish long-term economic plans for the entire economy. Although these plans were not operative in the sense that they included detailed industry strategies which were implemented by the government, the plans nevertheless disseminated general information about the direction of growth in total and by industry, providing a valuable foundation from which investment plans could be formulated.

Much of Japanese industrial policy was concerned with fostering the development of infant industries, and measures adopted to do so were often both rational and optimal. Assuming that there were in fact infant industries in Japan during this time, then another important lesson can be derived from the trade-off between pro-growth policy for infant industries and anti-growth policy for highly labour-intensive industries. Given the limited resources at its disposal, the government could not hope to maintain the survival of its work-force simply with pro-growth policy. Instead, it was forced concurrently to block competition in select labour-intensive industries in order to achieve this aim. Under this constraint of guaranteeing employment, the government devoted as many other resources as possible to promoting growth in infant industries. This trade-off between anti-growth and pro-growth measures was not simple: it was complicated both by the possibility of limited productivity gains in labour-intensive industries and by the inability of labour and capital to move freely from one industry to another. Nevertheless, it was the active management of this trade-off that is the most striking feature of Japanese industrial policy and one that perhaps is of most interest to developing nations today. Anti-growth policy was implemented in such a way as to obtain some productivity increases, and anti-growth policy measures towards distribu-

---

[4] In fact, the government never attempted to regulate investment in every industry, recognizing from the start that it did not have the resources or the information to do so successfully.

tors and small enterprises were reduced as successful development gradually increased the demand for labour. This freed more resources for pro-growth policy, but the government also decreased support of infant industries after they had gained international competitiveness, thereby increasing its ability to target new infant industries.

Japan's experience with industrial policy was by no means a complete success. Measures to promote the coal industry were incorrect: although the government showed flexibility in reversing these, initial mistakes raised the cost of future adjustment. Policy measures for the textile and marine transport industries were also poorly designed. More seriously, policy towards agriculture became increasingly protective from 1960, even as a tighter labour market reduced the need for anti-growth policy. Support for increasingly competitive industries was gradually decreased, but pro-growth policy was also not disengaged quickly enough. Tax breaks fuelled greater investment which contributed to export growth, as did the continuation of export subsidies, setting the stage for the appreciation of the yen in 1971 that highlighted the increased industry dependence on foreign markets. By also dragging their feet on abolishing trade and foreign capital restrictions, policy-makers contributed to the abruptness by which the international community forced currency appreciation upon them. Finally, policy to promote mergers in the Japanese economy from the early 1960s probably reduced economic efficiency by undermining competition. As a result, Japanese industrial policy lost its rationality from the 1960s and arguably acted as a drag on development for much of the 1970s before policy rationality was regained.

The economic insights provided by these failures generally reinforce those that can be derived from probable policy successes. First, it is dangerous to reduce competition in industries that already have a secure place in international markets, as Japan did for steel in the 1960s. Secondly, it is counter-productive to reduce competition once unemployment is no longer a threat to worker survival. Thirdly, policy measures need to be designed to respond specifically to market failures and externalities to avoid such problems as occurred with coal, textiles, and shipping. Given that policy mistakes will almost inevitably occur, it is even more important that policy be flexible. Finally, it is necessary to attempt to establish some objective measure to assess the progress of infant industries. This is quite complicated, since governments are unlikely to possess quantitative data on production costs of domestic companies and foreign rivals. Moreover, there is a natural tendency to protect such industries too long, since a precipitous elimination of support threatens the survival of targeted industries and potentially wastes funds spent to that point. Even so, data on export performance and import penetration of targeted industries might provide criteria for decreasing government aid.

6.2   The Favours of History

While the economic evaluation in Section 6.1 provides a basis from which
to outline possible lessons for other developing nations, whatever success
Japan may have had with industrial policy owes much to historical and
institutional accident. Policies were not chosen solely on economic
grounds but were more importantly influenced by bureaucratic thought,
institutional interactions and constraints, the world environment, the
impact of the Occupation, and Japan's own economic past. The flexibility
of industrial policy, the ability to decrease support for targeted industries,
and the ability to maintain consensus about industrial policy were all the
result of Japan's history. Without these characteristics, industrial policy
could not have successfully promoted development.

The consensus that industrial policy should promote rapid economic
growth was maintained for almost twenty-five years after Japan's surrender; its surprising endurance derives both from the Occupation and from
measures implemented by the Japanese government. That the initial goal
of policy should be growth was determined by Japan's desire to recover
from the devastating effects of World War II coupled with the two US
goals of creating a strong ally in the Far East and reducing the costs of
the Occupation. Without the Cold War, the Occupation probably would
have carried out initial reparations plans, leaving Japan at a greatly dis-
advantaged level from which to develop.

The Occupation's equalization of the distribution of assets in Japan
created the key to forging initial policy consensus. Had land reform and
the dissolution of the *zaibatsu* not taken place, it is unlikely that most
Japanese would have viewed economic growth as in their own interest.
Moreover, Japan's interpretation of democracy as the equalization of
income helped to prolong the pro-growth consensus of industrial policy.
The government actively attempted to promote income equalization
between workers and farmers throughout the 1950s, contributing to the
belief that growth was beneficial to all. The strengthening of labour
unions by the Occupation also supported this belief by improving worker
wage settlements.

Government tax policy also fostered the general view that growth was
beneficial by cutting personal income taxes every year but one in the
period between 1954 and 1973. These tax reductions essentially helped to
distribute the benefits of growth amongst consumers, keeping the public
in favour of growth, but to some extent these measures were accidental as
well. Tax cuts occurred primarily because the government continued to
adhere to the tenet laid down during the Occupation that tax revenues
should derive in equal portions from personal tax revenues, corporate tax

revenues, and indirect taxes. Because personal tax revenues grew more quickly, these were reduced more to keep the balance than because of the state's desire to share the spoils of successful development.

Not surprisingly, Japan's ability to maintain consensus about the pro-growth nature of industrial policy was derived from measures which ensured that the benefits of growth were spread across the entire population. However, this consensus about industrial policy may also have been strengthened by the government's attempts to obscure policy costs. By keeping the public in the dark about the actual costs of industrial policy, the state pre-empted possible opposition to industrial policy. The most support provided by industrial policy was given through tax breaks, trade barriers, and measures to block competition in labour-intensive industries. All of these were hidden from public view—tax breaks involve no direct government disbursement of funds, and the higher prices caused by trade barriers and the blocking of competition are opaque in that the public did not know how much lower prices would be in the absence of these measures.

That the government chose to support infant industries through tax breaks rather than direct subsidies is due to the Occupation rather than a reliance on textbook economic optimality. The opposition of Joseph Dodge to the disbursement of subsidies through price controls in special accounts and his insistence that all funds disbursed by the government be made plainly visible probably caused the Japanese government to utilize tax breaks as a way to support industries. Since these involved no government handling of funds, the state could adhere to Dodge's beliefs while at the same time providing material support to industries.[5] Thus, the government was pushed accidentally into implementing the optimal measure to foster infant industries. Tax breaks involve few administrative costs and also avoid the problem of corruption that can accompany the direct government disbursement of subsidies. At the same time, they stimulate investment in targeted industries.

If Japan's ability to maintain consensus about the goals of industrial policy owes much to the accidents of history, so too does the government's limited success in disengaging policy. Not only was support for infant industries decreased as the competitiveness of those industries rose, but many anti-growth measures were phased out as the labour market tightened. Two factors contributed to the disengagement of policy, one internal and one external. Domestically, the power of policy-makers was far from total, being vested across ministries and subject to internal

---

[5] The implementation of tax breaks for select industries did violate the precept of uniform corporate tax treatment laid down by Occupation tax authorities under Carl Shoup. This probably reflects the stronger impact that Joseph Dodge had on Japanese authorities as well as their own desire to obfuscate the costs of industrial policy.

checks and balances. Although MITI had control over the formulation of most industrial policy measures, the power over formulating the government budget rested with the Ministry of Finance. This ensured that the funds MITI had at its disposal for industrial policy were limited. The Ministry of Finance naturally opposed any waste in government outlays, questioning all expenditure requests and in practice curtailing increases. In effect, this meant that should MITI wish to increase support for one industry, it needed to reduce support for other industries. As a result, MITI cut support measures for older infant industries such as steel that had improved productivity as it targeted newer infant industries such as computers. This check on industrial policy through government outlays also affected loans through the Japan Development Bank, and without it, it seems improbable that support measures, once introduced, would have been decreased.

Japan was thus lucky in its institutional legacy. Not only did it have a highly trained and capable bureaucracy, but the division of power amongst competing ministries promoted disengagement of industrial policy and checked potential abuse. However, it was not accident alone that gave Japan its institutions: industrial organizations were created after the war to facilitate communication between bureaucrats and businessmen. These organizations gave the government detailed data necessary to implement policy, lobbied for policy changes at the request of corporate members, and provided businesses with information about policy intent. The practice of government officials to retire to positions in private or public enterprise also increased communication amongst groups, serving to check inappropriate policy responses.

External pressure also helped the government to disengage policy. Foreign demands for trade liberalization resulted in the elimination of controls over import allocation in the early 1960s and the reduction in trade barriers which accelerated in the early 1970s. Tax incentives for exports were reduced due to foreign complaints in 1964 and finally abolished in 1972. These moves towards free trade dismantled much of the apparatus for pro-growth policy, and without external pressure it seems probable that the government would have continued to foster many industries even longer than it did. As it was, despite internal checks and foreign pressure, industrial policy continued to support many industries after they had achieved international competitiveness, and because of the political power of the agricultural lobby, policy blocked competition in this sector when the need to support employment had evaporated. In short, the disengagement of industrial policy was not an unmitigated success, and what success it did enjoy derived largely from institutional constraints and foreign pressure rather than active decisions on the part of policy-makers themselves.

Related to the decrease in intervention is the flexibility shown by policy-makers in changing the focus and direction of industrial policy. If government measures to stimulate the development of an industry failed, as happened with the Japanese coal industry, that industry was eventually abandoned. The pride of policy-makers in their infallibility was countered by the reality of both budget limitations and the input of industries in formulating policy. Additionally, this flexibility on the part of policy-makers was enhanced by their having no overwhelming ideological convictions. Neither the belief in state-controlled growth nor the belief in free-market competition ever totally dominated the other, although the government arguably exhibited a firm commitment to the free-market paradigm in the long run. Thus, belief in government intervention did not lead policy-makers into the trap of viewing the failure of policy towards coal as resulting from insufficient intervention. Nor did a belief in free markets lead policy-makers to abandon measures which supported employment before the economy was capable of providing jobs for all workers.

Policy disengagement and flexibility were closely linked to plurality in policy formulation. This plurality arose not just from institutional factors but also from specific design. Having previously experimented with state-led policy during the war and policy dominated by business interests prior to this, the government determined that industrial policy in post-war Japan should be formulated with input from academia, business, and the general public. This plurality in policy formulation, reinforced by the Occupation's emphasis of democratic precepts, facilitated appropriate policy response. It also limited the growth of the government. Government intervention can easily lead to more intervention, in some cases because the initial intervention necessitates other measures (i.e. trade barriers creating the need to co-ordinate investment across industries) and in other instances simply because intervention becomes a habit. With intervention fuelling more intervention, it would not have been surprising to find that the bureaucracy expanded to implement additional measures. Of course, a growing bureaucracy would have greatly impeded the ability to disengage policy. That the bureaucracy did not expand was largely due to the use of external groups in policy formulation, including advisory councils, industry organizations, and business groups. In other words, without a diverse base for formulating policy, growth in the bureaucracy could have undermined the rationality of industrial policy in Japan.[6]

---

[6] Although industrial policy in Japan largely managed to avoid the trap of ever increasing intervention, policy did maintain disequilibria in markets for foreign exchange and interest rates, necessitating further policy measures to counter these disequilibria. Inflation accompanying the Korean War caused the Japanese yen to become over-valued, but policy-

Historical and institutional accident benefited industrial policy in ways other than contributing to policy consensus, policy flexibility, and policy disengagement. First, Japan's choice of which infant industries to target was conditioned by her own past as well as the examples of other nations. Initially, Japan targeted material and capital goods industries because of previous expertise in these areas (steel, shipbuilding), because of past expertise relevant to targeted industries (synthetic fibres, chemicals for synthetic fibres), or simply because the industry was crucial to development (electric power). The selection of these industries was also influenced by the history of the development of other nations. As other nations had moved from light to heavy industry in the course of economic development, so too did Japan plan on progressing from textiles towards material industries that it thought would become competitive.

Japan's particular selection of targeted industries probably contributed to rapid economic development. With limited resources at its disposal, the targeting of material and capital goods industries meant that Japan could not devote much effort to promoting consumer goods industries. These latter are highly dependent on consumer tastes, which tend to change over time. In other words, consumer goods industries are highly dependent on market signals about demand, whereas demand for material inputs and capital goods tends to be more stable since products in these industries are often much the same. Because the success of industrial policy could be undermined by demand fluctuations, it was fortuitous that Japan chose to support industries where demand shifts could be forecast with some degree of accuracy. What few attempts the government made to guide consumer-related industries often met with failure, as is shown by policy towards the car industry in Japan.

Demand factors and Japan's capital markets could well have made government support of heavy industries indispensable. While demand for steel and ships, for example, may be more stable than demand for consumer goods, this demand is also cyclical. These cycles are not only long but also cannot be predicted with absolute accuracy. Moreover, new plant in heavy industry can take up to several years to build. Some uncertainty over the timing of demand cycles together with the need to

makers refused to consider depreciating the currency. This necessitated import controls to ensure that the trade deficit did not get out of control, and the government then used these import controls to promote the aims of industrial policy. While subsidies stimulated exports, the over-valued yen may have intensified competition amongst Japanese exporters by forcing them to increasingly aggressive efforts to raise productivity in order to match the challenge presented by foreign products abroad. Industrial policy in Japan also utilized disequilibria in financial markets to achieve its own ends. To counter deflationary measures implemented by Dodge in 1949, the Japanese government encouraged private bank lending, and as loans outstripped deposits, banks became increasingly dependent on the central bank for funds. This over-loaned nature of city banks continued for the next several decades, giving the government some ability to direct private sector lending to targeted industries.

invest several years ahead of demand increases can easily lead to periods of excess capacity. Japanese firms may have been particularly vulnerable to such excess capacity because of their heavy reliance on bank borrowing, itself the result of the stock market collapse caused by the Dodge Line. In other words, these factors could have combined to prevent the successful growth of some heavy industries in Japan in the absence of government intervention.[7]

That these targeted industries grew and contributed to Japan's rapid development may have more to do with expanding world trade than with industrial policy. Industrial policy promoted the expansion of plant size and the introduction of capital-intensive techniques. In the absence of growing world demand for Japanese products, the domestic labour force could not have been absorbed by these capital-intensive industries. Employment in manufacturing would not have risen as quickly or at all, curtailing the expansion of domestic demand and overall economic development. Hence, it was not only lucky that Japan targeted industries that were subject to stable (if cyclical) demand, but it was equally fortunate that the capital-intensive industries which were targeted benefited from strong world growth.

Japan's ability to utilize competition as a tool of industrial policy was also influenced by historical and institutional chance. First, the foundation for competition in the Japanese economy was laid by the Occupation's dissolution of the *zaibatsu*. Had Occupation authorities not eliminated the tightly oligopolistic market structure in Japan, competition between firms would have remained weak, greatly undermining the government's ability to use market forces to shape the development of industries. Secondly, the government induced competitive behaviour amongst firms in a targeted industry by threatening firms with eventual liberalization and the disengagement of government support. That is, to promote the development of an industry, the government temporarily exempted firms from market forces by erecting trade barriers and by providing subsidies. To create competition amongst firms in such an environment, the government needed to make firms believe that its eventual goal was the creation of freely competitive domestic and international markets. To make this goal credible, it occasionally had to eliminate support measures in order to make Japanese industries painfully aware of what a freely competitive structure entailed. The government certainly succeeded in this, but largely thanks to the Draconian policies implemented under the

[7] As argued in Ch. 5, excess capacity can arise naturally from competition, even without the problem of demand cycles and investment lags. Such a natural occurrence of excess capacity would not necessarily require government intervention, except to the extent that corporate reliance on bank borrowing has been excessively high because of capital market imperfections (the lack of a mature equity and corporate bond market). In such a case, the optimal policy intervention is to subsidize capital costs for firms in the industry.

Dodge Line in 1949. Industry subsidies were slashed drastically, causing over 40 per cent of small firms to declare bankruptcy.

Without the painful experience of Dodge's policies, the government's credibility in threatening eventual competition would have been reduced. As it was, the Occupation placed a very effective tool in the hands of Japanese policy-makers. With the end of the Occupation, the Japanese government tended to use this stick less drastically, keeping industry support measures in place until the development of targeted industries was well under way. Nevertheless, no industry from its own experience could expect support measures to continue indefinitely. Subsidies were reduced, protection was gradually lowered, and industries were finally exposed to market forces. In this fashion, despite temporarily blocking some competitive forces, industrial policy in Japan managed to convince firms that only the most efficient would survive, thus promoting competition amongst firms and helping to raise efficiency.

6.3   Implementing Industrial Policy in Other Developing Nations

Japan's successes and failures with industrial policy in the three decades following the Second World War offer important insights to other developing nations. Probably the most important of these is the recognition and treatment of the costs accompanying economic development. While a developing nation may choose to utilize resources to stimulate growth, the benefits that arise must be balanced against the costs that development incurs, the dislocation of labour and capital from industries which lose competitiveness. In practice, these dislocation costs can be enormous, including a dramatic decrease in the real wages of enough workers to undermine the stability of the government if not the non-survival of a substantial portion of the population.

Many developing countries today have been isolated from the world economy because of high trade barriers, internal economic controls, or the external imposition of trade restrictions and sanctions. The maximization of future growth and the benefits accruing from development will entail the elimination of these walls and controls. Yet for many countries, the immediate abolition of all barriers and the introduction of market economies would create economic hardship on such a wide scale that revolution could well occur, potentially disrupting future growth prospects. To prevent this, measures to support minimum living standards are appropriate since only in this way can a country develop in a smooth fashion.

Japanese post-war development provides an example of how to trade off the benefits of growth against the costs of development. Japan succeeded by spreading those benefits equally over most of the population, by having clearly defined goals, and by utilizing competition to ensure that economic stagnation did not accompany the measures which controlled the introduction of free markets. However, Japan did not have to deal with the problem of entrenched interest groups which might have opposed the initial economic reforms that laid the foundations for development. Land reform and the dissolution of the *zaibatsu* were forced on Japan by the Occupation; without these, competition in the economy would have been curtailed to such an extent that the Japanese government would not have been able to use market forces as a tool to shape industrial policy.

If a developing country can overcome entrenched interests to introduce the rudiments of a market economy, or if the developing country can be pushed into doing so, then it may be able to emulate Japanese industrial policy to foster more rapid growth. To ensure that its population supports development, the benefits of growth should be widely spread. The more equally such benefits are diffused, the longer will support in favour of development last. These benefits will occur naturally through wage gains, so long as the bargaining position of workers is not weaker than that of employers. Hence, government support of the right of workers to organize is probably crucial to fostering consensus towards economic growth. At the same time, the benefits of growth accrue not only through increases in income but also through rising asset prices, and an unequal asset distribution will eventually undermine public commitment to growth. In this sense, Japan not only benefited from the redistribution of assets under the Occupation but also has attempted to maintain equitable asset distribution through a steeply progressive inheritance tax system. In regard to the equal distribution of income and assets, South Korea now presents a sharp contrast to Japan's experience. It seems probable that opposition to government policies promoting growth in South Korea probably has a great deal to do with the less equal diffusion of the benefits of development than occurred in Japan.

The danger of economic stagnation always accompanies a government's exemption of select industries from market forces. Government attempts to minimize the dislocation costs arising from economic development can lead to the entrenchment of such measures; to the extent that this occurs, economic stagnation will result from the permanent blocking of competition in selected industries. Japan's avoidance of this trap probably derived from clearly defined policy goals, the plurality of policy formulation, and the visibility of the potential benefits of competition. Anti-growth policy in Japan was explicitly linked to surplus labour. As labour markets tightened, the government's rationale for protecting select sectors in the economy evaporated, leading it to recommend liberalization. The plurality of policy formulation also helped to ensure that anti-growth policies were phased out since most industries and the public were not in favour of their continuation. Finally, some firms within protected industries themselves were also in favour of the abolition of government control, having witnessed the benefits of competition in other industries.

While Japan's experiences in controlling the costs of development and avoiding economic stagnation have relevance to developing countries today, probably so too do pro-growth policies. Assuming that infant industries did in fact exist, whatever success pro-growth policy may have enjoyed in Japan was dependent on both the industries selected and the policies implemented to stimulate growth. Like any other developing country, Japan had numerous examples of technologically more advanced industries in industrialized nations from which to select targets. However, Japan did not choose to promote its most backward industries but rather emphasized industries where it had some expertise, thus improving the chances of successful growth. It also generally targeted industries which produced standard, similar products, thus ensuring that volatile swings in preferences and tastes would not have a negative impact on selected industries. By avoiding most consumer industries where demand was highly dependent on volatile tastes, the detrimental impact of interfering with market signals was minimized. Furthermore, by consciously selecting industries where demand was on a generally rising trend, industrial policy helped to ensure that the increased output of targeted industries could find buyers.

If a developing country chooses to implement its own pro-growth policy, it should be aware not only of these criteria in selecting industries to target but also of the relevance of standard economic analysis in selecting which policies to implement. Measures to support infant industries in Japan were often first-best textbook solutions. Subsidies were provided largely through tax breaks, the most efficient way to stimulate investment. What government funds were disbursed were allocated through an industrial bank, thereby overcoming the probable bias against funding projects that showed return only in the long run. However, the criterion of profitability was used in granting government loans; it was also emphasized because of reliance on private sector institutions to provide funding. In instances where Japan adopted second- or third-best policies to promote an industry, results were generally not as favourable, as was shown by the over-capacity in marine transport that arose from government subsidies of ship purchases to promote the shipbuilding industry.

Policy also addressed the problems of imperfect information well. The issue of investment complementarities, heightened by Japan's use of trade barriers, was solved by disseminating information about the investment strategies of various industries and the growth prospects for the economy overall. Not only was this information made available through the publishing of various plans, but regular contact between bureaucrats and businesses, often through industrial organizations, also facilitated the transfer of information. Unknowns about newly imported technologies were offset by study missions abroad, by government intervention in the negotiating process, and, in cases where competing technologies appeared of equal use, by importing both. The government also guaranteed that benefits from new technologies were widely diffused.

The largest violation of textbook policy optimality occurred in Japan's utilization of trade barriers. These may have helped Japan to extract foreign technologies at favourable prices and they also may have been useful in hiding the real costs of policy intervention. However, a developing country today will not find it easy to utilize trade barriers on a wide scale. As world trade has risen, so too has opposition to protectionism increased even for countries in an early stage of development. Additionally, this rise in world trade has arguably increased competition amongst industrialized nations, making it easier for a developing country today to obtain foreign technology than was possible in the past. Finally, trade barriers proved costly even for Japan: by disguising the costs of industrial policy, trade barriers may have helped to maintain consensus towards growth for too long a time, thereby contributing to policy excesses and the disruptions of external shocks in the early 1970s.

Perhaps the most valuable lessons concerning pro-growth industrial policy for developing economies today lie in Japan's utilization of competition as a tool to shape the direction of growth. Japanese industrial policy rewarded winners and punished losers, a necessary function if government intervention is to promote efficiency. Policy also exposed domestic firms in targeted industries to foreign rivals, if only in overseas markets, thus providing objective examples against which Japanese firms could measure themselves. The credible threat of eventual liberalization then guaranteed that Japanese firms would strive to obtain comparable or better levels of productivity.

Competition policy at both the micro and macro level entailed one notable characteristic. While losing firms were punished, industrial policy nevertheless supported the continued existence of a sufficient number of firms to guarantee natural competition in the long run. That is, the government did not permit bankruptcies to occur to such an extent that an industry became highly oligopolistic or monopolistic. Of course, this sometimes entailed temporarily interrupting competition between firms and providing financial support to the weak, but these short-term costs were more than offset by the long-term benefits of highly competitive industries. It most probably does not make economic sense for a developing country today to allow market forces to create a monopolistic industry which will stagnate in the future.[8] Rather, it may be in the country's interests to ensure the survival of a sufficient number of firms to capture the dynamic gains of competition in the future.

Japan's limited success with disengaging pro-growth policy also holds lessons for developing countries. To some extent, this disengagement was again a function of clearly defined policy goals. By setting concrete targets for policy, such as the creation of self-sustaining growth or the achievement of a certain degree of competition, there was a reason to reduce government support once these targets had been achieved. More importantly, a system of checks and balances helped to guarantee that support was decreased. Plurality in policy formulation contributed to this, as did the separation of powers between bureaucracies in Japan. Policy-makers' access to funds to provide support for industries was greatly restricted by separating control over the budget from policy implementation, a separation which forced policy-makers to cut support for some industries if they wished to promote others.

Not only was policy checked by dispersing powers across competing ministries, but it was also balanced by the close and competing relationship between bureaucrats and businessmen. Communication between industry organizations and the government was very frequent; channels were further enhanced through retired government officials with positions in corporations. Plurality in policy formulation provided another check against inappropriate policy response. Economic factors provided further checks and balances on policy in addition to these institutional ones. Industrial policy was placed second to macroeconomic policy priorities, ensuring that the former did not produce results such as inflation that ran counter to the economy overall. Reliance on private sector funding and the use of market principles in determining government loans also helped to guard against inappropriate industrial policy measures.

This system of checks and balances and clearly defined policy goals contributed to the flexibility of Japanese industrial policy. Policy mistakes will inevitably occur, but the damage from a mistake will increase dramatically the longer the policy is pursued. Clearly defined goals can help limit such damage by quickly identifying where policy results are less than initial expectations. To that end, constant review of industrial policy is also useful. Moreover, by spreading policy evaluation over diverse

---

[8] Some developing countries may be so small that economies of scale in select industries can be captured only under monopolistic production. Although it is theoretically possible for a single firm to act competitively if it is forced to compete aggressively with foreign firms, in practice this competition may be difficult to achieve. If so, small developing countries may be better off not promoting industries where large-scale economies at least at the plant level exist, such as aircraft or semiconductors.

groups representing government interests, public interests, and business interests, mistaken policies may be rapidly reversed. Practicality on the part of policy-makers is the key to the entire problem, and this practicality will decline the more driven policy is by political or ideological concerns.

While the successful characteristics of industrial policy in Japan hold lessons for other developing nations, there are also extremely useful insights to be gained from Japan's policy mistakes and failures. Japan was unable to prevent some politicization of industrial policy, and this resulted in the costly protectionism of agriculture from the early 1960s. Industrial policy will lose its economic rationality unless it can be isolated from special interest groups, and will consequently act to slow rather than accelerate the pace of development.

Secondly, Japan failed to disengage policy quickly enough, despite plurality in policy formulation, clearly defined goals, and various checks and balances. This failure highlights the true difficulties of implementing industrial policy, and in order to do better, a developing economy today would have to introduce even more rigorous and objective controls and reviews. In practice this might prove quite difficult, particularly since imperfect information can undermine the evaluation of industrial policy, limiting the usefulness of having clearly defined policy goals. For example, policy-makers in Japan lowered the risk of investment in targeted industries. This was probably necessary to stimulate expansion: the importation of a new technology often necessitated a substantial increase in investment in the targeted industry, and the subsequent rise in investment capacity often exceeded domestic demand in the short run. Since exports also could not expand immediately, the resulting excess capacity and faltering expected demand would have decreased investment in the absence of government support. Such investment decreases would not have been appropriate, since it was assumed that the targeted industry would become internationally competitive as investment continued. However, it is extremely difficult to determine precisely what amount of investment the government should support. Without accurate information as to the competitiveness of the targeted industry, policy can continue to promote the industry longer than it should, creating a severe problem with over-capacity.

A third problem which industrial policy in Japan did not totally overcome is one of moral hazard. Although the shock of the Dodge deflation and the government's disengagement of policy measures did help to convince industries that support would not continue indefinitely, government assistance did in some instances create expectations that further support would be forthcoming in downturns. Such expectations undermined government efforts to alleviate excess capacity. That is, belief that help would be forthcoming in a downturn led many industries to over-invest in an upturn. Although this problem may have been at its worst in the 1970s, adjustment measures even today are not totally immune from it.

While it may be difficult in practice to improve upon Japan's system of checks and balances, goal definition, and decision plurality, one mistake that Japan made contributed to the less than optimal disengagement of industrial policy. The government hid the true costs of industrial policy, providing most support through tax breaks and trade barriers. Disguising these costs to some degree may be useful in maintaining consensus towards policy, but arguably the process went too far and resulted in too slow a disengagement of policy. Developing countries today that wish to implement policy through tax breaks might be better off announcing publicly the magnitude of these tax breaks in order to keep the population aware of policy costs. Trade barriers, probably not an optimal policy in Japan, should be avoided as a policy tool, particularly since they would not be tolerated today by the rest of the world. In their place, a developing country should consider alternative subsidies, perhaps larger tax breaks. As long as these are made visible, the public would be aware of the costs of industrial policy, and would oppose policy that did not seem to be in their best interests. This check might contribute to a more optimal disengagement of industrial policy.

Related to the issue of optimal disengagement of policy is the natural tendency to over-control the process of change. Attempts to control the costs arising from development and efforts to spread those costs over time can constrain economic growth if measures adopted are unduly prolonged. It is not the minimization of these costs themselves which is desirable but rather the balancing of these costs against the benefits of growth. However, once measures to regulate change are introduced, the force of inertia will almost always guarantee that change is promoted at a suboptimal rate. Japan succeeded in not totally succumbing to inertia, phasing out anti-growth policy when it was no longer needed. Even so, these measures were abandoned too slowly. The sluggish pace at which trade and foreign capital controls were lifted provides another example of the over-regulation of change, and the government's promotion of mergers is another damaging instance of an excessive emphasis on controlling the costs generated by change and development.

Although much of it was accidental, Japanese industrial policy probably contributed to rapid development, particularly in the 1950s. Yet industrial policy itself is neither the sole explanation nor the single most important explanation of Japan's success. Without a highly trained labour force, development would have been slower. Because Japan's defence burden was borne by the US, the government could devote all of its resources to economic development. The strong expansion of world

trade greatly increased growth prospects and also ensured that employment opportunities increased in the capital-intensive industries targeted
by industrial policy. Appropriate macroeconomic policy contributed more
to stability than did industrial policy and may have played a larger role
in promoting savings and rapid economic development. In other words,
industrial policy should not be viewed as the single key to successful
development. More important to the development process is well-
informed macroeconomic policy, general incentives to invest, and general
incentives to train labour. The Japanese experience indicates that industrial policy can augment these, but successful implementation is difficult.
In the absence of a highly trained bureaucracy, a certain degree of
income and asset equality, and the rudiments of a market economy in
place, attempts to formulate and implement industrial policy cannot contribute to more rapid development.

Despite these qualifications, developing countries in the world today
can benefit from the Japanese experience, particularly those in Eastern
Europe. Given their previous economic history, these nations should also
be able to easily identify potential growth industries, as should the former
Soviet republics. The magnitude of the transformation required in these
nations also makes relevant Japan's use of anti-growth policy. Rather
than immediately freeing all sectors of their economies, some should be
protected in order to maintain stability until growing industries expand
sufficiently to provide better employment opportunities. At the same
time, these nations will need to introduce basic elements of a market economy in order to successfully develop potential growth industries. Only
by doing so can nations use competition as a policy tool, one that was
invaluable to Japan.

In implementing industrial policy, countries will also need to introduce
a strict system of checks and balances. Not only must industrial policy
interests come second to macroeconomic policy goals, but industrial policy must be determined by diverse interest groups and policy costs must
be made totally transparent to all. Moral hazard in industrial policy can
also be avoided by making clear through actions that support measures
are temporary. If the benefits of development are spread equally and governments are firmly committed to the eventual liberalization of all industries, then industrial policy can aid them in achieving feasible, fast
development.

Whatever potential developing countries today may have to utilize
industrial policy measures depends crucially on their existing institutions
and their ability to create new ones. Without a highly trained bureaucracy, policy cannot be intelligently formulated. Moreover, in order to
avoid the stagnating impact that an enormous bureaucracy would have, it
is essential to develop a system that enables the expertise of the business

community to be utilized, most probably by forming industry associations as Japan did. Additional input in decision-making is also necessary, guaranteeing that consumer interests are represented. Even Japan, blessed in its historical and institutional legacy, was unable to prevent the policy mistakes in the 1970s that undermined her economic performance. This should serve as a warning to developing nations today: although there may be gains possible from implementing industrial policy, institutional requirements are so strict as to preclude many countries from success.

7

External Shocks, Industrial Policy, and the Search for Balanced Growth

This chapter summarizes Japan's more recent experience with industrial policy, of interest because Japan's economic performance continues to surpass that of other major OECD nations. Although recovery from the first oil crisis was both difficult and protracted, the economy had largely adjusted to higher energy costs by 1978, and the second oil crisis presented few serious difficulties. Even the sharp appreciation of the yen from the autumn of 1985 caused only a brief downturn in growth. Between 1973 and 1990, real GNP rose at an average annual rate slightly in excess of 4 per cent, less than half the rate of the previous two decades but quite favourable for any developed nation.[1]

During this period, industrial policy underwent a dramatic change. The government increased intervention following the first oil crisis, utilizing price controls and cartels. Constraints on competition in distribution were also tightened, a strengthening of traditional anti-growth policy. However, this increase in intervention proved to be short-lived, as it was derailed by public dissatisfaction, foreign pressure, perceived policy failures, and reduced powers to implement policy. Traditional anti-growth policy was relaxed, as the government promoted competition in distribution, transport, and warehousing. More efforts were devoted to helping industries adjust to a changed environment; measures to that end came to combine elements of anti-growth policy with those of pro-growth policy. Finally, the scope of pro-growth policy was limited almost solely to the promotion of new technologies.

[1] In contrast, the US economy grew at an average real growth rate of 2.7% between 1973 and 1988, while West Germany grew at a 2.3% rate. (Nihon Ginkō, *Kokusai Hikaku Tōkei* (Tokyo, Nihon Ginkō Chōsa Tōkei Kyoku, various years.) Of course, an excessive easing of monetary policy and the subsequent asset inflation contributed to Japan's rapid growth in the latter half of the 1980s, and the downturn which began in the autumn of 1991 was the direct result of past policy mistakes. Although growth during the 1987–90 expansion was thus inflated at the expense of the early 1990s, Japan's potential to mitigate the detrimental effects of asset deflation may keep her 10-year average growth performance above that of the US and Germany.

7.1   Adjusting to the Oil Crises (1973–1981)

The first oil crisis marked the end of Japan's high-growth period. Relying almost entirely on imported oil, the 4.5 times increase in dollar-denominated oil prices between January 1973 and January 1974 rapidly eliminated Japan's trade surplus, especially since the yen also depreciated, falling from 265 against the US dollar in September 1973 to 299 by year end.[2] Inflation soared, fiscal and monetary policies were tightened, and domestic demand collapsed, resulting in the worst recession in post-war history. The economy actually contracted in 1974, declining 0.8 per cent,[3] and the Japanese economy required fully four years to overcome totally the negative effects of the first oil crisis.

That the Japanese economy performed so poorly in the face of the sharp increase in oil prices had more to do with previous policy mistakes than anything else. Excessively lax monetary and fiscal policies had over-stimulated the economy, causing inflation to soar from the second half of 1972. Nevertheless, the government delayed tightening, waiting until the second quarter of 1973 to move aggressively.[4] Even then, tightening was not a one-way process. Although monetary policy became increasingly restrictive, the anti-inflationary impact of cuts in government outlays was at least partially offset by tax reductions of 2 trillion yen in the autumn of 1973. Because policy failed to check inflation, speculative demand rose, whereby both consumers and producers stockpiled goods ahead of expected future price increases.[5] A vicious circle was soon formed, with speculative demand leading to higher prices as consumers and producers stockpiled goods. Price rises then increased speculative demand which in

---

[2] The demand for oil is little affected by price changes in the short or medium term, since energy is necessary to the manufacture of goods. Hence, the amount of oil Japan consumed did not decline by much despite the sharply higher yen cost for oil, and exports were not sufficiently stimulated by the currency move to offset this. Japan's current account balance fell into the red by 1.2 trillion yen in 1974.

[3] Real GNP growth measured in 1985 prices. (Keizai Kikaku Chō, *Kokumin Keizai Kessan Nenpō*, 1991.)

[4] The Bank of Japan did raise the Official Discount Rate by 75 basis points in the first quarter of 1973, but waited until after the 1974 budget was approved by the Diet in Apr. 1973 to move further. This budget, incorporating Prime Minister Tanaka's plans for rebuilding Japan, called for a 32.2% increase in public works expenditure. However, after adoption, the government delayed implementation of spending given the over-heated state of the economy.

[5] The halting of soybean exports to Japan by the US in Feb. 1973 acted as a catalyst to speculative demand, creating expectations of shortages of soy sauce, tōfu (bean curd), and miso. Worries about shortages and price rises then spread to other products. (Nakamura Takafusa, *The Postwar Japanese Economy*, 227–31.)

turn increased inflation. By September 1973, consumer prices were rising by 14.6 per cent while wholesale prices were growing by 18.7 per cent.[6]

It was against this background of rapidly rising inflation that the first oil crisis hit in October 1973. The 4.5 times price increase in petroleum together with the very real worry of a supply shortage fanned the fires of inflation and fuelled speculative demand for all products.[7] Inflation at the wholesale level exceeded 35 per cent in early 1974, its highest level since the hyper-inflation following World War II. In response, the government further tightened monetary and fiscal policy, and these actions finally helped lead to price stability from 1976. However, the economic costs of the surge in inflation and the overly expansionary fiscal policies which preceded it were enormous: total output actually shrank in 1974, as both public and private sector investment fell.

While the overheated state of the Japanese economy and sluggish policy response exacerbated the impact of the first oil crisis, high wage gains also increased the severity of the downturn. The 1974 Spring Labour Offensive resulted in a wage settlement of 32.9 per cent. Even in real terms, the wage settlement exceeded productivity gains, and this, together with the deterioration in Japan's terms of trade, greatly constricted corporate earnings. In turn, this decline in profitability caused real corporate investment to decrease in magnitude not only in 1974 but for the next three years as well.[8]

Although complete recovery from the oil shock would not occur until 1978, adjustment grew easier as time passed. The depreciation of the yen from the autumn of 1973 helped to stimulate export growth, as did expansionary US policies in 1975 and 1976. To this export growth was added in 1975 a recovery in personal consumption, aided by features of the Japanese labour market which helped to limit the rise in unemployment to the 2 per cent level.[9] Expanding consumption and exports

[6] Inflation rates reflect the change from the previous year. The base year for both the consumer and wholesale price indices was 1970. See Nihon Ginkō, *Keizai Tōkei Nenpō* (Tokyo, Nihon Ginkō Chōsa Tōkei Kyoku, 1973).

[7] The most well-known example of the problem of speculative demand from this period is the toilet paper shortage in the fourth quarter of 1973. This shortage arose as rumours of supply problems caused consumers to stockpile toilet paper, thus soon creating a shortage of toilet paper for sale on the market.

[8] For an elegant presentation of this argument, see Yoshitomi Masaru, *Nihon Keizai: Sekai Keizai no Arata na Kiki to Nihon* (Tokyo, Tōyō Keizai Shinpō Sha, 1981), 47–66.

[9] Unemployment in Japan after the first oil crisis only reached 2.3%, up from a low of 1.1%. Four factors helped to curtail the rise in unemployment. First, 1974 legislation called for government subsidies to firms to maintain employment. Second was the corporate practice of lifetime employment and third was the increased absorption of workers by the service sector. A fourth factor was the reduction in the labour force, the result of discouraged workers dropping out of the job search process. (Yoshitomi Masaru, *Nihon Keizai: Sekai Keizai no Arata na Kiki to Nihon*, 59–66.) The first three of these factors not only curtailed unemployment but also supported consumption, while the reduction in the labour force clearly only curtailed unemployment. It should also be noted that to the extent that labour

The Search for Balanced Growth

brought an end to the economic downturn that had lasted from November 1973 to March 1975, and despite continued declines in capital expenditure, real GNP rose 2.9 per cent in 1975 and 4.2 per cent in 1976. From January to October of 1977, the economic expansion again faltered, as yen appreciation, caused by the rising trade surplus, threatened further advances in exports. However, fiscal policy turned expansionary and became even more so by the year end, when foreign pressure on Japan to act as a locomotive to the world economy found sympathetic ears, and the combination of stable consumption and rising government expenditure resulted in real GNP growth of 4.8 per cent. Growth accelerated to 5 per cent in 1978, as a recovery in capital expenditure joined consumption and government outlays in driving the economy, offsetting the contraction in exports that occurred that year.

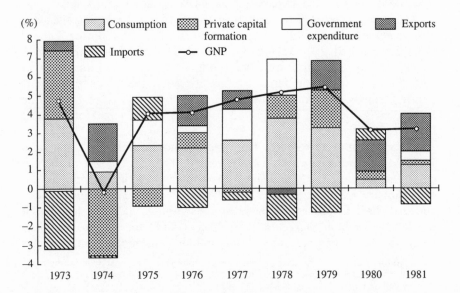

Fig. 7.1. GNP Growth and Contribution by Principal Component, 1973–1981
Source: Keizai Kikaku Chō, *Kokumin Keizai Kessan Nenpō*, 1991.

The recovery in capital expenditure was sparked by two factors. First, from 1976 real wage gains were held below productivity advances, and from 1978, even nominal wage increases fell below gains in productivity. As a result, corporate profitability improved, increasing the ability of corporations to invest. This increased ability was met with higher corporate demand for new equipment when the yen began to appreciate sharply in

is a fixed cost to Japanese firms, the recovery in consumption may have been at the cost of capital expenditure.

1977.[10] In order to protect the competitiveness of exports, Japanese manufacturers upgraded plant and equipment. Price stability was enhanced by
both the yen appreciation and the curtailment of wage gains, causing
inflation to fall to pre-oil shock levels.

Japan's recovery from the first oil crisis had not been easy but it would
prove to be durable. In April 1979, the second oil crisis struck, less than
one year after Japan had fully recovered from the first. This second oil
shock proved surprisingly easy to overcome, even though its initial
impact was equal to the 1973 shock.[11] Real GNP growth in 1979 was a
robust 5.6 per cent, while 1980 and 1981 witnessed expansions of 3.5 and
3.4 per cent respectively. As before, the depreciation of the yen accompanying the oil crisis supported strong export growth. This time, however,
capital expenditure expanded briskly instead of contracting, and consumption, although strong in 1979, was sluggish in 1980 and 1981.

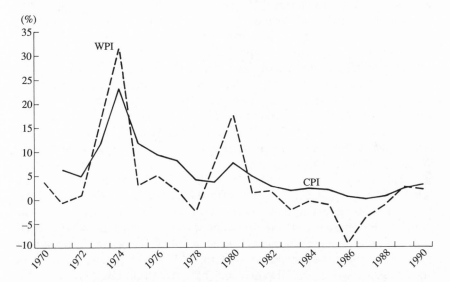

Fig. 7.2. Price Trends, 1970–1990 (Yearly averages)
Source: Nihon Ginkō, *Nihon Tōkei Nenpō*.

[10] The yen rose from 293 against the US dollar in Jan. 1977 to 238 by year end. It rose
to a high of 175 in Oct. 1978.

[11] Oil prices rose only about 2.4 times between the beginning of 1979 and the spring of
1980, far less than the 4.5 times increase that occurred between the beginning of 1973 and
the beginning of 1974. Despite the less dramatic rise in prices, however, the increase in oil
import costs as a percentage of GNP was approximately the same for the second oil crisis
as it was for the first. (Yoshitomi Masaru, *Nihon Keizai: Sekai Keizai no Arata na Kiki to
Nihon*, 247–9.)

Not only was economic growth less affected by the second oil crisis, but price performance was also substantially better. Inflation at the wholesale price level peaked at 24 per cent in April 1980 compared to over 35 per cent following the first oil crisis, while consumer price inflation only rose to 8.9 per cent compared to the 25 per cent level following the first oil crisis. Moreover, by 1981 wholesale inflation had subsided to below 2 per cent, evidence that price stability had been regained slightly more than two years after the second oil crisis in comparison to the four years required after the first.

Appropriate macroeconomic policy response undoubtedly contributed to the remarkable resilience shown by the Japanese economy to the second oil shock. The Bank of Japan moved quickly to tighten monetary policy, raising the Official Discount Rate five times from the spring of 1979, and tightening its monitoring of bank lending. Fiscal outlays were also curtailed: in real terms, government investment fell 1.8 per cent and government consumption showed its lowest growth in fifteen years.[12] However, policy response alone cannot account for Japan's rapid recovery, since monetary and fiscal policies were also tightened after the first oil crisis, albeit not as quickly and effectively as would have been optimal. Rather, differences in initial starting conditions, muted wage demands, and shifts in industrial policy account for Japan's relatively easy transcendence of the second oil shock.

In contrast to late 1973, the Japanese economy in 1979 was in no danger of overheating. The labour market was not at all tight, as shown by the low value of 0.65 for the ratio of job offers to applicants, a sharp contrast to the value of 1.86 in late 1973.[13] Inflation was stable, with wholesale prices flat before the second oil crisis compared to the 20 per cent inflation experienced in the autumn of 1973. In other words, the Japanese economy was at the beginning rather than the end of a business cycle, a cycle that was being led by a rebound in corporate investment after a four-year decline. Because of this difference, Japan had none of the problems with speculative demand that arose from late 1973.

Modest wage demands in 1980 also contributed to Japan's speedy recovery from the second oil shock. More bluntly, the decline in real employee income helped to keep corporate costs under control, preventing a decline in capital expenditure. Union acceptance of a modest nominal wage in 1980 was proof of the change in their behaviour. Although the increase in unemployment caused by the 1974 contraction of the economy was very small, that jobs were lost at all nevertheless undermined belief in lifetime employment. Hence, job security came to replace wage gains as the number one union priority. Unions in 1980 explicitly stated

[12] Keizai Kikaku Chō, *Kokumin Keizai Kessan Nenpō*, 1991.
[13] Yoshitomi Masaru, *Nihon Keizai: Sekai Keizai no Arata na Kiki to Nihon*, 252–5.

that 'our wage demand . . . aims at a real wage increase lower than the real GNP growth; in setting the 1980 wage demand we have given due consideration to restraining inflation'.[14] The 1980 Spring Labour Offensive thus ended in a wage increase of only 6.7 per cent; adjusted for inflation, this meant a decline in real wages of 1.2 per cent from the previous year. Corporate profits were supported by cuts in workers' living standards, and high earnings in turn supported corporate investment.

Japan's experience with the second oil crisis differed greatly from that with the first, but not only because of different starting conditions and a willingness on the part of workers to sacrifice wages for job security.[15] A third factor, the shifting role of industrial policy, also contributed to variations in economic performance. Direct interference with the market mechanism in 1974 and 1975 may well have exacerbated inflation, as could have the excessive promotion of cartels. Government avoidance of these mistakes in 1979 may have contributed to more rapid adjustment to the second oil shock, as might continued government support for energy-saving investment.

Industrial policy from the early 1970s had already moved from emphasizing the maximization of growth to focusing on growth management. Growth remained desirable, but not at the expense of the quality of life. Hence, industrial policy shifted from fostering basic industries to promoting knowledge-intensive industries, including electronics, industrial robots, and office automation equipment, since such knowledge-intensive industries did not worsen problems of urban overcrowding and pollution but nevertheless benefited from rising productivity and a high income elasticity. Interestingly, MITI in 1971 made explicit the scope of industrial policy, stressing that policy should be limited to instances of market externalities or failures.[16] Amongst these, MITI called for industrial policy to help correct pollution, promote technology development, aid infant industries, and assist declining sectors.

Despite the government's recognition of the need to limit intervention and its pledge to place more reliance on the market mechanism, policy response did not always agree with these precepts. First, the government increased constraints on competition in distribution in March 1974, when

[14] Shinkai Yoichi, 'Oil Crises and Stagflation in Japan', in Kozo Yamamura (ed.), *Policy and Trade Issues of the Japanese Economy* (Seattle, University of Washington Press, 1982), 183–4.
[15] This change in the behaviour of organized labour is quite important: although it may initially have facilitated adjustment by supporting capital expenditure, labour unions at present are perhaps more willing to sacrifice the interest of workers than they should be. That is, passive behaviour on the part of unions probably contributed to sluggish consumption in the 1980s and the record high trade surplus. This issue will be examined in further detail in Section 7.2 of this chapter as well as in Ch. 9.
[16] Sangyō Kōzō Shingikai, ''70 Nendai no Tsūshō Sangyō Seisaku', *Tsūshō Jaanaru*, 4.3 (1971), 1–67.

the Large-Scale Retail Store Law (*Daikibo Kouri Tenpo ni Okeru Kourigyō no Jigyō Katsudō no Chōsei ni Kansuru Hō*) replaced the Department Store Law. This new law gave the government power to check the advance of all large retailers in order to protect the smaller ones, difficult to justify under arguments MITI gave for policy intervention. More seriously, policy response to the first oil crisis directly contradicted those precepts. The government not only fostered numerous cartels to help industries adjust to the surge in oil prices, but it also directly set prices for a variety of commodities and determined operating rates in select industries. The extent of direct government intervention in the economy reached levels unprecedented since economic controls had been lifted in the early 1950s. With more than two decades of market experience behind them, Japanese industries discovered numerous means to circumvent or undermine this government intervention, with the result that controls probably worsened inflation in 1974.[17]

After the first oil crisis hit in October 1973, the Japanese government moved quickly to impose direct controls over prices and production. The Law Concerning Emergency Measures for the Stabilization of the People's Livelihood (*Kokumin Seikatsu Antei Kinkyū Sochi Hō*) and the Petroleum Supply and Demand Normalization Law (*Sekiyu Jukyū Tekiseika Hō*) were introduced to the Diet in early December and passed by year end. These laws gave MITI power to set prices for designated commodities as well as the right to demand reports from wholesalers and retailers to ensure that no one was involved in cornering markets for goods. While the Law Concerning Emergency Measures for the Stabilization of People's Livelihood was originally applied to three products,[18] the wording of the law was so vague as to make very easy its extension to other goods.[19] Consequently, many industries, worried that they would be targeted under this law, moved pre-emptively against it, entering into illegal cartels to fix prices at high levels before government action. The rise in such illegal price-fixing behaviour is apparent in the sharp increase in the number of cartels found guilty of illegal activities by

[17] Many industries attempted to increase prices ahead of the expected implementation of government controls, thus increasing inflation. Inflationary pressures were further increased by past policy mistakes. For example, the promotion of recession cartels in the early 1970s probably helped spark inflation from 1972. The extension of cartels such as that for high-temperature blast furnace steel from 1971 to 1972 and that for stainless steel plate from 1971 to June 1973 probably kept production down, thus contributing to price rises.

[18] Covered were lamp oil (Jan. 1974 to June 1974), LPG (Jan. 1974 to May 1975), and toilet paper (Jan. 1974 to May 1974). The Petroleum Supply and Demand Law regulated prices for gasoline, naphtha, and heavy oil.

[19] *Roppō Zensho*, 2 (1990), 3885–7. Not only was the wording of the law vague, but the government was using administrative guidance to regulate prices for 59 other products, including aluminium, high-density polyethylene, cement, cardboard, sheet glass, nylon textiles, synthetic rubber, light bulbs, fertilizer, soy sauce, sugar, beer, butter, and pharmaceuticals. (Kōsai Yutaka, *Kōdo Seichō no Jidai*, 207.)

the Fair Trade Commission, which totalled 129 cases in 1973 and 1974 compared to only 71 cases during the previous two years.[20] Investigations into illegal cartels covered a diverse range of industries, including not only milk processors and toilet paper manufacturers but also makers of raw concrete and agricultural machinery.[21]

Price-fixing cartels rose in number even before the Law Concerning Emergency Measures for the Stabilization of People's Livelihood was passed, as the possibility of government intervention in markets caused firms to raise prices. The most infamous example was the cartel formed by the petroleum refiners. On 27 November 1973 officials of the Fair Trade Commission raided offices of the petroleum refiners and distributors, unearthing evidence of collusion in the rapid rise of domestic oil prices. Most damaging were industry claims that the price rises had received unofficial sanction from MITI,[22] raising public dissatisfaction towards an industrial policy which seemed to unjustly favour corporate interests. Public anger was so great that it fuelled momentum for a strengthening of the Anti-Monopoly Law, which finally passed the Diet in 1977.[23]

Not only did industrial policy stimulate price rises through the threat of price controls,[24] but the threat of government rationing of oil through the Petroleum Supply and Demand Normalization Law probably deepened the recession following the first oil crisis. Firms facing the possibility of a decreased supply of power would have expected operating rates to fall, thus increasing unit costs.[25] Because of government monitoring, firms

---

[20] Kōsei Torihiki Iinkai, *Kōsei Torihiki Iinkai Nenji Hōkoku* (1977), 360–1.

[21] Tsuruta Toshimasa, *Sengo Nihon no Sangyō Seisaku*, 337–9.

[22] Oil industry officials claimed that MITI, which monitored the industry closely, had tacitly agreed to large price rises. The Fair Trade Commission took the companies involved to court, and in its 1980 decision, the Tokyo High Court did find the companies guilty of price collusion. The ruling also found indirectly against the legality of administrative guidance to the extent that it violated the Anti-Monopoly Law.

[23] Initially proposed revisions to the Anti-Monopoly Law were criticized as being too limited, but the revisions actually adopted were even less strict than the proposals. Revisions did include a small fine on members of illegal cartels (in the case of manufacturers, 2% of total sales during the period) and mandated that companies submit explanations for parallel price increases. Revisions also gave the Fair Trade Commission the ability to prevent industries from forming repeated cartels. Hence, the 1977 amendment did strengthen the Anti-Monopoly Law but not to a very large degree. Still, it did represent recognition that the government's promotion of industry co-ordination and increased firm size was not always beneficial.

[24] Although the sharp rise in the prosecution of illegal cartels provides evidence of this point, it can also be argued that the benefits accruing from the Law Concerning Emergency Measures for the Stabilization of the People's Livelihood far outweighed this rise in prices. The psychological impact of this law might have been so great that it stopped speculative demand that would otherwise have caused even greater inflation. That is, by providing an official guarantee of the availability of necessary items, this law may have halted the consumer hoarding that had led to the toilet paper shortage and ensuing panic in Nov. 1973.

[25] Not only depreciation per unit of output but also labour per unit of output would rise since the latter tends to be fixed in the short run especially in Japan.

would not have expected to be able to pass on these higher costs, and hence their forecasts of future profitability would have declined. This deterioration in expected profitability probably exacerbated the four-year decline in capital expenditure, deepening the economic recession and delaying recovery.

The extent of direct government intervention in the economy was greatly reduced during the second oil crisis. Although both the Law Concerning Emergency Measures for the Stabilization of the People's Livelihood and the Petroleum Supply and Demand Normalization Law remained on the books, the government did not attempt to set prices or ration oil after the second oil shock of 1979. Speculative demand did not increase, since consumers and producers had suffered no real shortages during the previous oil shock and official oil reserves had been doubled. Without hoarding, price increases did not get out of control, and hence the government was not tempted to activate price controls. This restraint undoubtedly contributed to Japan's rapid adjustment to the second oil shock, since industries were not motivated to raise prices ahead of the imposition of government controls.

If government policy towards pricing differed between the two oil shocks, at least one common characteristic links policy response—the growing emphasis on declining rather than emerging industries. After the first oil crisis, the focus of industrial policy shifted away from fostering the development of new industries towards managing the decline of troubled industries. Pro-growth policy became less concerned with fostering entirely new industries, restricting itself more to the promotion of new technologies and instances of market externalities such as optimal investment in anti-pollution equipment. At the same time, efforts to promote the orderly decline of the growing number of industries whose competitiveness had been undermined by higher energy costs increased. Because these efforts often entailed exempting select industries from competition, they embodied elements of anti-growth policy. However, such policy was expected to exempt troubled industries from market forces for only a short period of time while it facilitated adjustment to a changed environment. This adjustment policy was thus a short-term anti-growth policy.

Initially, adjustment policy consisted of familiar measures, such as government subsidies to scrap capacity. However, since the negative impact of the first oil crisis was far too large to be rapidly solved, the government quickly moved to expand both the range of adjustment policy and also the tools available to smooth the decline of select industries. In 1974 the government adopted the Employment Insurance Law (*Koyō Hoken Hō*), which provided government subsidies to both large and small firms in designated industries that laid off workers with pay. This was supplemented with further legislation in 1978, including the Law Concerning

Emergency Measures for Laid-off Workers in Specially Designated Depressed Industries (*Tokutei Fukyō Gyōshu Rishokusha Rinji Sochi Hō*) and the Law Concerning Emergency Measures for Laid-off Workers in Specially Designated Depressed Regions (*Tokutei Fukyō Chiiki Rishokusha Rinji Sochi Hō*), both of which provided government subsidies to designated firms which hired workers, extended unemployment benefits, and provided public funds for worker training. 1978 also saw the passage of the Law Concerning Emergency Measures for the Stabilization of Specially Designated Depressed Industries (*Tokutei Fukyō Sangyō Antei Rinji Sochi Hō*) as well as the Law Concerning Emergency Measures for Small and Medium Enterprises in Specially Designated Depressed Regions (*Tokutei Fukyō Chiiki Chūshō Kigyō Taisaku Rinji Sochi Hō*).

The 1978 legislation expanded and made more systematic the government's approach to declining industries. The Law Concerning Emergency Measures for the Stabilization of Specially Designated Depressed Industries formed the centre of government policy, not only providing funds to help scrap capacity in designated industries but also calling for the government to draft a timetable for capacity reductions in those industries.[26] Furthermore, in instances where the government did not expect firms voluntarily to co-operate with these plans, this law allowed the government to form industry cartels after discussions with the Fair Trade Commission. The application of other 1978 legislation, including employment support measures and aid to smaller enterprises, reinforced efforts towards industries selected under the law.[27] This emphasis on efforts to facilitate adjustment, one of the most striking characteristics of industrial policy in the 1970s, would dominate policy concerns in the 1980s.

7.2 Administrative Reform, Export-Led Growth, and Trade Friction—the Search for Balanced Development (1981–1990)

Although the second oil crisis had a comparatively mild impact on the Japanese economy, the economic expansion finally did turn down from February 1980, nine months after the second oil shock hit. Monetary tightening caused residential investment to decline, the adoption of less

---

[26] Designated industries included steel (blast furnace and electric arc furnace steel), aluminium refining, long nylon fibres, short acrylic fibres, long and short polyester fibres, ammonia, urea, phosphoric acid, cotton spinning, worsted yarn spinning, ferrosilicon, cardboard, and shipbuilding.

[27] Sekiguchi Sueo and Horiuchi Toshihiro, 'Bōeki to Chōsei Enjo', *Nihon no Sangyō Seisaku*, 327–44.

generous fiscal policy constrained domestic demand, and growth in con-sumer outlays dropped as labour unions moderated wage demands. Despite the sharp growth in exports accompanying the yen depreciation, the economy would not enter another expansionary phase, with growth accelerating, for three years. This downturn in the business cycle of thirty-six months would be the longest in post-war history, even though it was not particularly deep. In real terms, the economy grew at an average annual rate of 3.4 per cent between 1980 and 1983, less than the 4.7 per cent average for the previous decade (1971 to 1979), but quite favourable compared to the actual decline in GNP that occurred after the first oil crisis.

That economic activity in Japan remained somewhat sluggish for the first three years of the 1980s was the result of several factors. First, the government was growing increasingly reluctant to use expansionary fiscal policy because of the sharp rise in public sector debt. Deficit spending by the government had soared in the 1970s, initially under Tanaka's grandiose scheme to rebuild the Japanese islands, next in attempts to off-set the deflation of the first oil crisis, and finally in response to foreign pressure to act as an economic locomotive to the rest of the world. As a result, outstanding government debt as a percentage of GNP rose from 3.7 per cent in 1970 to 28.8 per cent by 1980, and debt service costs increased from 2.3 to 10.4 per cent.[28] Faced with this growing burden of debt, the government decided against expansionary fiscal policy as a means to accelerate economic growth.

Secondly, worries over public sector debt not only slowed government outlays, but also stimulated efforts to increase tax revenues. These efforts manifested themselves as the government abandoned its principle of rais-ing one-third of its revenues equally between individual income taxes, corporate income taxes, and indirect taxes. The government generally kept whatever revenues came in, which, because of the progressive nature of personal and corporate taxes, meant that the ratio of direct tax rev-enues to total revenues rose from 68.5 per cent in the 1976–80 period to 70.7 per cent in the 1981–4 period.[29] Individuals were squeezed as the ratio of taxes paid to total income rose from 8.7 per cent in 1975 to 16 per cent in 1985.[30] Hence, government policy contributed to stagnant growth in consumption and to a protracted time of sluggish economic activity.

---

[28] Debt service costs are defined here as interest payments on outstanding bonds. See Ōkurashō, *Zaisei Kinyū Tōkei Geppō*, 457 (May 1990) (Tokyo, Ōkurashō Insatsu Kyoku), 2–3.

[29] Ibid. 38.

[30] Sōmu Chō Tōkei Kyoku, *Kakei Chōsa Nenpō* (Tokyo, Nihon Tōkei Kyōkai, various years).

Probably the biggest culprits behind stagnant consumption were Japanese labour unions. By accepting nominal wage gains below both the inflation rate and the rise in labour productivity in 1980, unions may have helped to mitigate the inflationary impact of the second oil shock. However, the decline in real income for many workers in 1980 and only moderate wage gains thereafter contributed to weak growth in consumer expenditure. Moreover, this shift in union behaviour continued through the decade. As shown by Fig. 7.3, the gap between productivity gains and wage increases widened after 1975, proof of this moderation of union demands. Unions did not attempt to recapture or even maintain the share of total output going to workers. In effect, unions agreed that the majority of the gains from growth should accrue to corporations, and growth in consumer outlays has been constrained by only modest advances in wage income.

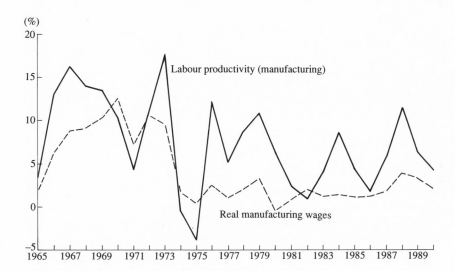

Fig. 7.3. Trends in Wages and Labour Productivity
Source: Nihon Seisansei Honbu, *Katsuyō Rōdō Tōkei.*

The lengthy economic downturn finally ended in February 1983, as exports accelerated and capital expenditure surged. Easier monetary policy and rising profits acted as catalysts to corporate investment; an expanding US economy and a weak yen drove exports. The government and the consumer had only minor roles in this recovery, hardly surprising in view of small wage gains, a rising individual tax burden, and continued fiscal prudence. Concern over the rising burden of public debt had caused the government to adopt in August 1983 a long-term plan to restructure government finances. While noting that the principal goals of government policy were full employment and price stability, the plan placed priority on fiscal reform, leading the Ministry of Finance to restrict government outlays even more. In fact, in real terms, total government expenditure grew only 0.6 per cent in 1983 and real government investment that year fell 2.2 per cent.

Not surprisingly, this fiscal conservatism was matched by a shift in perceptions about the role of government in the economy. Following a series of reports from a special review committee in the early 1980s, the Japanese government became committed to administrative reform, cutting back inefficient public management and privatizing government monopolies such as Japan Railway, Nippon Telephone and Telegraph, and the Japan Salt and Tobacco Corporation.[31] Since administrative reform was essentially an attempt to improve the functioning of government and the economy without using any further resources, it meshed extremely well with Japanese budget limitations. Nakasone, who accepted these reports as head of the Administrative Management Agency, made administrative reform the centre of his policies during his five-year term as Prime Minister from 1982.

The economic upturn that began in early 1983 would last for more than two years, but like the downturn that preceded it, the expansion was characterized by an increasingly skewed pattern of growth. Restrictions on government expenditure and consumption curtailed domestic demand; what growth did occur was thus often driven by exports. In fact, more than half of the expansion in real GNP in 1980, 1981, and 1984 was generated directly by export increases, whereas in the 25-year period prior to 1980, exports never contributed more than half to growth in GNP.[32] Not surprisingly, this export-led growth was accompanied by an increasing trade surplus—between 1981 and 1985, the Japanese trade surplus rose more than nine times, reaching a record 61 billion US dollars.

As Japan's dependence on exports as a source of growth rose, so too did trade friction. 1981 marked the beginning of the third major wave of trade friction to break over Japan in the post-war period. Like its predecessors, it would bring dramatic change, but would prove far more difficult to solve, lasting as it has to the present. The first period of trade friction, 1971–3, brought the US import surcharge, the end of fixed exchange rates, and the appreciation of the yen. The second wave from

[31] The Second Special Committee Investigating Administration (*Dainiji Rinji Gyōsei Chōsa Kai*), chaired by Dokō Toshio, made these recommendations in a series of reports given to Nakasone Yasuhiro, who was heading the Administrative Management Agency (*Gyōsei Kanri Chō*).

[32] However, in 1974, exports in real terms rose 23% over the previous year, and would have been the major contributor to GNP growth had the economy not contracted. As it was, export expansion that year certainly lessened the downturn.

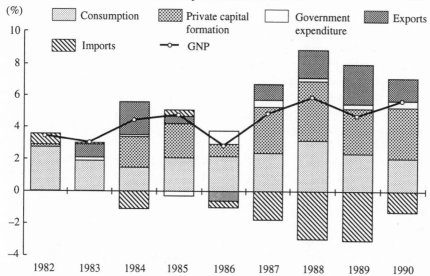

Fig. 7.4. GNP Growth and Contribution by Principal Component, 1982–1990
Source: Keizai Kikaku Chō, *Kokumin Keizai Kessan Nenpō*, 1991.

1976 to 1978 saw a major increase in Japanese government debt, but expansionary fiscal policy failed to prevent the trade surplus from rising to 20.5 billion US dollars in 1978. Like the first wave, this second period of trade friction was essentially 'solved' by an oil shock which pushed Japan's trade surplus into the red.

Initial government attempts to alleviate trade friction in the early 1980s failed. Voluntary export restraints on such major export items as cars did not stop the trade surplus from rising: with the volume of exports limited, Japanese producers shipped only the most expensive products, thus increasing the value of exports. Nor did Japan's liberalization of imports help. After reductions following the conclusion of the Tokyo Round of GATT in 1979, average Japanese tariff rates were well below those in the US and the UK,[33] and Japan also lowered non-tariff trade barriers in 1982.[34] Nevertheless, imports failed to show much growth because of sluggish domestic demand and because of the depreciation of the yen from 204.8 against the US dollar in 1980 to 252.05 in 1984.

Global trade friction, intensified by expanding trade surpluses in Japan and Europe, led to dramatic exchange rate movements: intervention

---

[33] See Komiya Ryūtarō, *The Japanese Economy: Trade, Industry, and Government* (Tokyo, University of Tokyo Press, 1990), 21–9.

[34] Following foreign complaints over Japanese non-tariff trade barriers, the Japanese government reviewed over 100 cases of import procedures, product standards, and product testing regulations, changing three-quarters of them.

following the G-5 meeting in January 1985 halted the depreciation of the yen and the mark, and, with the G-7 nations in September 1985 agreeing on the need for a weaker dollar, the appreciation of the yen accelerated. The yen gained more than 50 per cent against the US dollar,[35] and the Japanese economy turned down as exports collapsed. This downturn would last through most of 1986,[36] but was surprisingly shallow. With exports totalling more than 16 per cent of GNP and increases in exports accounting for most of economic growth, the sharp strengthening of the yen could have easily resulted in a contraction in total output. As it was, the yen appreciation did cause some exports to lose market share but it merely ate into profit margins for other products, steady shipments of which helped to put a floor under the decline in exports.

That the economy managed to expand 2.6 per cent in 1986 was also the result of an aggressive easing of monetary policy. The Bank of Japan cut interest rates four times in 1986, reducing the Official Discount Rate from 5 per cent at the beginning of the year to 3 per cent by year end. Government expenditure also contributed to growth, as the government increased outlays 4.5 per cent in real terms in 1986. However, monetary policy was forced to carry most of the burden, and the Bank of Japan reduced the ODR to an historic low of 2.5 per cent in February 1987, a level that was maintained for more than two years. Easier monetary policy both mitigated the severity of the downturn and sparked the second longest post-war expansion, although it also contributed to massive asset inflation. After bottoming in November 1986, growth accelerated, reaching 4.3 per cent in real terms in 1987, 6.2 per cent in 1988, 4.8 per cent in 1989, and 5.2 per cent in 1990.

The driving force behind this phenomenal economic expansion was capital expenditure, driven to record levels relative to GNP by at least four factors. First, interest rates helped to stimulate corporate investment by reducing the cost of funds.[37] More important was the sharp appreciation of the yen. With foreign products suddenly 50 per cent less expensive, Japanese corporations had to invest massively in new plant and equipment in order to raise productivity and survive. To this motivation was added the need to invest in labour-saving machinery because of a growing shortage of workers. Finally, capital expenditure was stimulated

[35] From its Feb. 1985 low of 263.65 against the US dollar, the yen strengthened to a high of 121.85 in Dec. 1987, an appreciation of 53.9%.

[36] Officially, the economy was in a decelerating growth period from June 1985 until Nov. 1986. Growth peaked three months before the Sept. 1985 accord, in part because the yen had begun appreciating against the US dollar from Feb. However, had the dramatic currency movements not occurred later in the year, the economy might well have recovered, lengthening the officially defined expansionary period.

[37] Not only did low interest rates reduce the cost of borrowing from banks, but they also lowered the cost of equity financing by stimulating advances in the stock market.

by the need to overcome the challenge of deregulation in select industries. In order to survive or gain market share as restrictions in such industries as distribution and communications were eased, firms increased outlays on new plant and equipment. As a result, capital expenditure growth exceeded 10 per cent from 1988 to 1990.[38] As a percentage of total output, capital expenditure in real terms rose to more than 20 per cent, unprecedented in post-war history.

The promotion of deregulation was at the centre of Japan's five-year economic plan for the period 1988–92.[39] To facilitate growth in the Japanese economy, the plan recommended liberalization and deregulation of such industries as agriculture, financial services, retailing, communications, warehousing, wholesaling, and transport and thus the further disengagement of traditional anti-growth policy. The concept of deregulation is quite similar to administrative reform: both hope to promote growth through eliminating inefficiencies without using government funds. However, deregulation is far broader and more ambitious in scope. Apart from stimulating capital expenditure, deregulation was also expected to support real consumer spending through the price declines it generated. The plan also called for a reduction in hours worked as another means to stimulate consumer outlays and specifically advocated the elimination of trade barriers. In short, the five-year plan, through deregulation and other measures, attempted to restore balance to Japan's growth pattern, promoting increased domestic demand and imports.

Government efforts to attain balanced growth are also apparent in the tax reform measures passed at the end of 1988. In order to return to equality between revenue sources, the government sharply cut personal taxes, moderately reduced corporate taxes, and raised indirect taxes.[40] With direct personal taxes reduced far more than indirect taxes were increased, tax reform hoped to stimulate consumer outlays by eliminating the constraint that had been imposed by a rising tax burden.

These attempts to address the problems of the early 1980s were partially successful. Strong growth in domestic demand from 1986 to 1990, together with the appreciation of the yen, has had a profound effect on imports. Japanese imports of manufactured goods more than doubled, even though this trend was obscured by the reduced value of

---

[38] These massive increases have proved unsustainable, and capital expenditure fell in 1992.

[39] Keizai Kikaku Chō, *Sekai to Tomo ni Ikiru Nihon (Economic Management in a Global Context)* (Tokyo, Keizai Kikaku Chō, 1988). While much of the plan focused on deregulation, it also called for greater government outlays on Japan's transportation network, improved land use, reduced working hours, and the elimination of trade barriers.

[40] Taxes directly paid by individuals (income, residential, inheritance, and capital gains taxes) were slashed by 3.7 trillion yen. Taxes directly paid by corporations were reduced by 0.9 trillion yen. Indirect taxes, primarily through the introduction of a Japanese VAT, were increased by 2 trillion yen.

raw material imports. That is, since raw material imports are not very sensitive to price changes, the sharp drop in yen-based raw material prices brought about by the appreciation of the yen tended to deflate the total value of Japan's import bill, a deflation that does not occur when measuring trade in constant prices. Although Japan showed a current account surplus in nominal US dollars of 35.8 billion in 1990, only somewhat lower than the 49.2 billion recorded in 1985, in real terms, the current account was in the red in both 1989 and 1990.

The recent economic downturn has undermined what progress was made towards achieving more balanced growth. The easing of monetary policy from 1986 to the spring of 1989 was excessive, contributing to massive asset inflation. As the Bank of Japan burst the asset bubble with tighter monetary policy from May 1989, the expansion faltered, and from the autumn of 1991 the economy fell into recession. By most measures, this recession has proved to be the second worst in modern history, and imports have fallen sharply as domestic demand stagnated. As a result, the trade surplus has expanded to new record highs, and the imbalance between domestic savings and investment in the Japanese economy has again fuelled trade friction.

Although the Japanese economy is far from equilibrium, much of the enormous structural change necessitated by the sharp appreciation of the yen was accomplished with surprising speed and agility. Whether or not Japan can adjust to asset deflation more readily than have other industrialized nations is not yet known, but Japan has shown remarkable flexibility in coping with the stronger yen and the second oil crisis. Interestingly, industrial policy played little role in effecting structural change in the 1980s. Measures to aid declining industries were not used any more extensively after the second oil crisis than the first. Moreover, industrial policy was not used specifically to help export industries adjust to change following the yen appreciation,[41] although the government did try to promote imports. Industrial policy continued to attempt to correct market externalities (i.e. investment to reduce pollution or the development of new technology), but it made far fewer efforts to promote winners and smooth adjustment for losers, a trend which continues to this day.

The second oil shock necessitated no new measures to help declining industries adjust. In fact, no new troubled industries really emerged. Industries that had been identified as the most adversely affected by the first oil shock were generally those hurt by the second, and the government did not extend its list of industries selected in 1978 to receive support under the Law Concerning Emergency Measures for the

---

[41] Policy was used to help small enterprises adjust, and it continued to be used to help industries that had been battered by the oil shocks. However, the government did not design new measures to aid the major exporters.

Stabilization of Specially Designated Depressed Industries. Industrial policy continued to subsidize capacity reductions for such energy-intensive industries as aluminium and steel, as well as providing wage subsidies and worker assistance for depressed industries and depressed regions.

Policy towards declining industries, unaffected by the second oil shock, did shift as 1978 legislation expired and was replaced with a series of new laws in 1983.[42] The government, no longer content with simply managing cut-backs, also began to encourage depressed industries to diversify and/or specialize in order to regain competitiveness. For instance, the Law Concerning Emergency Measures to Improve the Structure of Designated Industries called for government reorganization plans for industries to include not only an outline of capacity to be eliminated but also an outline of R&D investment, possible mergers, and production specialization plans. To realize these goals, the law called for a variety of new subsidies and special tax breaks in addition to government funding for the scrapping of capacity.[43] What was not new about this legislation was its coverage: of the seven industries specifically listed, only the petrochemical industry was a new addition to the list of depressed industries, replacing shipbuilding which had had some success in restructuring.[44]

[42] The Law Concerning Emergency Measures for Laid-off Workers in Specially Designated Depressed Industries (*Tokutei Fukyō Gyōshu Rishokusha Rinji Sochi Hō*) and the Law Concerning Emergency Measures for Laid-off Workers in Specially Designated Depressed Regions (*Tokutei Fukyō Chiiki Rishokusha Rinji Sochi Hō*) were replaced with the Law Concerning Special Measures for the Stabilization of Employment in Depressed Areas and Depressed Industries (*Tokutei Fukyō Gyōshu/Tokutei Fukyō Chiiki Kankei Rōdōsha no Koyō no Antei ni Kansuru Tokubetsu Sochi Hō*). The Law Concerning Emergency Measures to Improve the Structure of Designated Industries (*Tokutei Sangyō Kōzō Kaizen Rinji Sochi Hō*) replaced the Law Concerning Emergency Measures for the Stabilization of Designated Depressed Industries (*Tokutei Fukyō Sangyō Antei Rinji Sochi Hō*). Much of the legislation passed in 1983 either expired in 1988 and was replaced or was extended. For example, the Law Concerning Emergency Measures to Improve the Structure of Designated Industries was replaced with the Law Concerning Emergency Measures to Facilitate the Adjustment of the Industrial Structure (*Sangyō Kōzō Tenkan Enkatsuka Rinji Sochi Hō*) in 1987. However, the positive focus remained, with the government not only supporting the scrapping of capacity but also the standardization and/or diversification of a troubled industry.The Law Concerning Emergency Measures to Facilitate the Adjustment of the Industrial Structure was meant to be implemented in a way consistent with the Maekawa Report, an outline of various measures to stimulate domestic demand and reduce trade barriers in order to eliminate trade friction. Even so, industries actually designated under the law as needing government assistance to contract were largely those that had been designated under previous adjustment laws. These included steel, cotton fibre, various synthetic fibres, and cement in addition to such newly designated industries as mining equipment, compression equipment, copper smelting, and zinc smelting. (Tsūshō Sangyō Shō Sangyō Seisaku Kyoku, *Kōzō Tenkan Enkatsu Hō no Kaisetsu* (Tokyo, Tsūshō Sangyō Chōsa Kai, 1988), 3–36.

[43] Tax breaks included accelerated depreciation of newly purchased equipment and the carrying over of losses to set against corporate taxes. Subsidies were granted for the development of new industrial technologies as well as the development of new energy sources and funds to convert to coal-generated electricity.

[44] The Law Concerning Emergency Measures to Improve the Structure of Designated Industries listed steel (electric furnace produced and half-finished products), aluminium

The government's more positive approach to adjustment was also apparent in other legislation. Employment measures focused on providing subsidies to retrain workers before they were laid off. This pre-emptive measure, applicable to select industries in select areas, was designed to minimize unemployment by providing workers in industries that were likely to shed jobs with new skills to gain employment elsewhere. Legislation for smaller enterprises granted subsidies to companies in select regions to promote diversification into new products, new technologies, and new markets. Here again, the government was not concerned simply with smoothing the decline of certain industrial areas but also with promoting new industries in such regions.

That industrial policy towards declining industries became somewhat more positive from 1983 was the result of several factors. First, industrial policy had been constrained by the need to promote free trade and competition, thus limiting Japan's ability to aggressively promote new industries. Although support of free trade and competition remained necessary, international rules concerning appropriate policy response towards declining industries were clarified by the OECD in 1983.[45] These rules recognized the need for government policy to stimulate the transfer of resources from declining industries to other fields, thus providing a justification for Japan's more positive approach. Secondly, such a positive approach was more in character with Japanese industrial policy. Policymakers, battered by enormous external economic shocks as well as plunging popularity, were reduced in the latter half of the 1970s to simply reacting to events. As these shocks faded, policy somewhat reasserted itself, attempting to facilitate change rather than trying to only slow it down. To some extent, this represented the synthesis of traditional anti-growth and pro-growth policies. The government no longer only orchestrated decline, but it also supported diversification into new areas.

Despite this more positive approach towards declining industries, the general role of industrial policy has continued to wane. The government devotes few resources towards the promotion of new growth industries, not only because of worries of foreign criticism but also because of very real budget constraints. Those pro-growth measures that are used are largely limited to support for the development of new technology. Since technology development is often very risky and difficult to appropriate, public subsidies may be the only practical way to achieve the optimal level of investment in R&D. Similar problems also occur in cases of anti-

refining, chemical fibre manufacturing, fertilizers, paper, and petrochemicals as specific designated industries, but contained a provision that made the law easily extendable to other industries. *Roppō Zensho*, 1988, 3150–3.

[45] *Positive Adjustment Policy: Managing Structural Changes* (Paris, Organisation for Economic Co-operation and Development, 1983).

pollution investment and investment for energy conservation, both of which have been targeted by industrial policy. In short, pro-growth industrial policy has come to be restricted to the usual instances of market failures and externalities which face all industrialized nations. This more limited approach contrasts sharply with the three decades following the war when policy actively directed resources towards numerous infant industries.

This major disengagement in pro-growth industrial policy was set against both a further disengagement of traditional anti-growth policy and the appearance of a new type of adjustment policy synthesizing anti-growth and pro-growth policy measures. Some measures that had blocked competition solely to ensure full employment were eased, most notably in the area of distribution as the government reversed its policy stance of the 1970s. Policy actively advocated the deregulation and liberalization of retailing, wholesaling, warehousing, and transport in the latter half of the 1980s, and as restrictions on store openings and new entrants were eased, competition increased, fostering a streamlining of the industry. The major exception to this was significant: policy towards agriculture continued to be highly protectionist, supporting the continued employment of farmers at the cost of sharply higher food prices. At the same time, policy towards declining industries expanded in scope, and efforts to slow the rise in unemployment in such industries offset to some extent the disengagement of policy to block competition in distribution.

The generally diminished role for industrial policy occurred despite potentially destabilizing shocks. The second oil crisis was as large in magnitude as the first, yet the Japanese economy easily transcended it. The 50 per cent appreciation of the yen after 1985 presented a more difficult challenge to the economy, affecting as it did all tradable goods, but this proved to be a relatively easy hurdle to overcome. As Chapter 8 will show, what flexibility and success the Japanese economy showed in the 1980s had less to do with an active industrial policy than with its absence.

8

Evaluating Recent Industrial Policy
(1973–1990)

The conditions of policy rationality and policy impact remain crucial to assessing the impact industrial policy has had on Japanese economic performance in the 1970s and 1980s. For policy to have improved economic performance, it must be capable of serving an economic purpose which in the absence of policy would be unfulfilled. If industrial policy does not fulfil this condition of rationality, then, by using up resources to no avail, it can only impede the performance of the economy. The second necessary condition for policy effectiveness is an impact on resource allocation. Unless industrial policy affects economic activity, then, no matter how rational, it cannot affect performance. These necessary conditions must also be supplemented by flexibility, to enable policy-makers to correct inevitable mistakes.

Although standards for evaluating industrial policy remain unchanged, the range of economic purposes that industrial policy is needed to fulfil has narrowed as Japan has become increasingly developed. For an advanced country, the promotion of infant industries becomes more difficult to justify: cases where another country has an advantage in an industry simply by having produced first become increasingly rare. Similarly, as development proceeds, worries about worker survival ease, and hence the need to guarantee employment by blocking competition in inefficient industries disappears. Traditional anti-growth policy thus becomes unnecessary. Despite this narrowed range, the need for policy intervention arguably still exists in a developed country. While market failures or externalities associated with infant industries, such as capital market imperfections, imperfect foresight, or the inability to appropriate returns on investment, may decrease with development, they do not disappear. In particular, imperfect foresight and appropriability problems accompany the development of a new technology, for an advanced as well as a developing country. This can imply the need for government intervention to support at least the development of technology. If these technological advances lead to the creation of new industries, then infant industry arguments may also apply in cases where other nations have a lead. Similarly, rigidities in the movement of labour and capital from one industry or region to another can create a role for policy to facilitate such movement, a role that could be of particular importance to a declining industry.

Other market externalities, such as those associated with pollution control or energy security, also necessitate government intervention.

This chapter will evaluate the efficacy of industrial policy in the 1970s and the 1980s, examining both the rationality of such policy and its impact. It seems probable that industrial policy acted as a drag on economic performance during much of the 1970s. Certainly, measures designed to ease inflation after the first oil crisis probably exacerbated it, and difficulties in adjusting to this external shock may have been compounded by past policy measures. However, by the 1980s policy rationality returned. With the notable exception of agriculture, policy has fostered even greater competition in distribution and amongst smaller companies, disengaging traditional anti-growth policy. Pro-growth policy has been reduced in scope and is associated increasingly with the development of new technologies. Finally, temporary adjustment measures have now combined elements of pro-growth policy with anti-growth policy, an appropriate response to declining industries.

8.1   Reaction to the Oil Crises: Policy Rationality and Policy Impact in the 1970s

Loans of the Japan Development Bank in the 1970s reveal that industrial policy focused increasingly on energy-related industries. As a percentage of new loans granted, those related to energy rose from 14 per cent of the total in 1973 to more than 30 per cent by the end of the decade. Policy also emphasized investment in social capital: loans for railway investment, urban redevelopment, and regional development accounted for approximately one-third of JDB loans throughout the decade.[1] JDB loans also focused on the development of new technologies, with slightly more than one-tenth of JDB lending going for this purpose. Loans for investment in anti-pollution equipment declined as a percentage of the total, falling to 9 per cent by the end of the decade after peaking at 27 per cent in 1975, and the marine transport industry saw its percentage of loans halve from 17.8 per cent of the total in 1973 to 8.6 per cent in 1979. Loans to modernize the distribution system also fell in importance.

Industrial policy, as revealed by these lending patterns, probably passes standards for rationality. Many of the loans may be linked to market failures or market externalities. Because the electric power and gas industries tend to be natural monopolies, government intervention is needed to assure optimal investment and pricing. In addition, the enormous risks to

---

[1] Such loans reached almost 40% of JDB lending in 1977, but fell back to slightly more than 30% by the end of the decade.

Table 8.1. Breakdown of Loans of the Japan Development Bank in the 1970s (%)

	1971	1973	1975	1977	1979
Energy related	10.50	14.29	12.08	21.42	31.55
Electric power/nuclear	6.08	7.38	4.98	9.95	10.35
Energy diversification	0.00	0.00	1.60	5.12	12.92
Gas	0.66	2.24	2.22	4.45	1.69
Conversion of oil generators	0.00	0.00	0.00	0.00	0.00
Promoting energy substitutes	0.00	0.00	0.00	0.00	0.00
Oil	3.76	4.64	2.55	0.31	4.35
Energy-saving investment	0.00	0.02	0.74	1.59	2.23
Technology promotion	14.89	10.50	12.00	10.57	11.43
Marine transport	27.11	17.78	9.86	2.98	8.64
Urban investment	15.24	18.55	18.14	20.19	18.74
Private railway	0.00	8.46	6.40	8.02	7.16
Urban redevelopment	0.00	7.73	8.92	10.76	9.89
Modernization of distribution	2.62	2.36	2.82	1.42	1.68
Regional development	15.64	14.90	14.63	20.20	13.21
Life-style improvement	7.02	15.70	28.52	18.32	10.91
Anti-pollution	5.75	13.99	26.82	15.17	9.04
Safety equipment	0.00	0.00	1.27	2.14	1.01
Food related	1.27	1.71	0.43	1.02	0.86
Other	9.59	8.28	4.77	6.32	5.52
TOTAL	100.00	100.00	100.00	100.00	100.00

Note: Classifications for 1971 are not strictly comparable with those for 1973–9 because of changes in the definitions of the categories. However, the classifications used for 1973–9 are comparable to those used in Table 8.4 for the 1980s.

Source: Nihon Kaihatsu Ginkō, *Nihon Kaihatsu Ginkō Nijūgonen Shi*; *Tōkei Yōran*.

society posed by nuclear power generation make necessary government control over the construction and operation of nuclear reactors. To the extent that the first oil crisis made energy an issue of national security, government promotion of energy conservation, energy diversification, and the development of alternative energy sources also is necessary. The goal of energy independence is a clear example of a market externality: because this issue has no relation to market prices, government subsidies are needed to achieve it.[2]

Pollution is another example of an externality: in the absence of government intervention, firms can freely dispose of toxic materials. As a

[2] Government promotion of energy conservation and diversification may also have been necessitated by a market failure, the divergence between social and market discount rates. Markets may worry little about the potential exhaustion of petroleum resources, since such an event lies in the distant future. However, if petroleum resources are to be exhausted within the next few centuries, society may place a higher emphasis on this depletion now, implying the need for government subsidies to generate socially optimal levels of investment in energy conservation and diversification.

result, only through government policy can firms be given incentives to invest in anti-pollution equipment. Japan chose to provide incentives through subsidizing such investment, a policy solution that is not theoretically first-best. Optimal policy would entail forcing firms that pollute to pay for the pollution, thus providing a direct, market-based incentive to reduce pollution. Subsidies for anti-pollution equipment are a second-best solution. Although they do promote a reduction in pollution, subsidies do not reduce the profitability of investment in new capacity by polluting industries and can lead to greater capacity than is socially optimal. Despite these drawbacks, the theoretical first-best solution may not have been feasible for Japan in the 1970s. That is, those industries which were the largest polluters (steel, electric power, chemicals) also tended to be those industries most hurt by first the yen appreciation in the early 1970s and then the first oil shock. Had the government made these industries pay for the cost of polluting, this additional burden on firms in an already weakened state may have increased bankruptcies, raising unemployment and reducing industry capacity below its socially optimal level.[3]

Loans for the development of social capital accounted for roughly one-third of JDB activities in the 1970s, with policy emphasizing urban redevelopment, regional development, and railway investment. Because the benefits of a strong infrastructure spill over into the rest of the economy, social capital provides another example of a market externality. For example, a good transportation network promotes efficiency gains in other industries, making possible lower inventories and reduced costs. To guarantee optimal investment levels, government control could well be necessary.[4] Similarly, government promotion of regional development could be needed to help alleviate such a market externality as urban overcrowding.[5]

Government policy in support of the development of new technology can also be rational. The magnitude of expenditure for some development projects can be so large that firms cannot individually undertake the risk. For development to take place, government funding or guidance is

[3] First-best policy response is even more complicated in reality, especially if pollution is a global rather than a local problem. A country would not only want to charge its own industries for pollution, but it would need to place tariffs on related imports from countries that did not charge polluters. Without such tariffs, importers would have an advantage which might lead to the disappearance of the domestic industry and an increase in world pollution levels.

[4] Alternatively, government intervention might be necessitated by a market failure, the divergence between social and private information. Users of a transport system might not be willing to pay for improvements because of an inability to anticipate how this advance will improve inventory investment and adjustment. The government, which has a broader view than single industries, might be better able to anticipate the possible synergy between investment in transportation and efficiency gains in the rest of the economy.

[5] A market failure, such as the inability of labour to move easily from rural to urban areas, might also lie behind government support of regional development.

needed. Additionally, it is often difficult for a firm developing a technology to appropriate all the returns from that technology. Since technologies can be copied or can be associated with spill-over effects,
government promotion of new technology is needed to ensure that optimal levels of investment actually do take place.

Finally, the drop in government lending for marine transport, as well
as modest outlays for the modernization of distribution, also have elements of rationality. Chapter 3 argued for the rationality of anti-growth
policy, measures designed to block competition and maintain employment, but primarily in an environment where the survival of the work-
force was an issue. Certainly by 1960, survival concerns had dissipated,
suggesting the need for a disengagement of anti-growth policy, the speed
of which depended upon the cost of relocating workers and the ability of
the protected industry to show some technological advances.[6] Industrial
policy, which had blocked the rationalization of distribution to maintain
employment, switched in the early 1960s to promoting liberalization and
competition, a trend which continued in the 1970s. Support of the marine
transport industry, which had never been a first-best policy solution, also
waned in the 1970s. This retreat from a mistaken policy is also evidence
of policy rationality.

In general, JDB lending in the 1970s reveals that industrial policy could
well have been beneficial, serving functions that would not have occurred
in its absence. In most instances, loans can be associated with market
externalities or market failures, an indication of possible policy rationality.
Pro-growth policy was more focused, concentrating on new technologies
rather than new industries. Since Japan at this point was an industrialized
nation, it was increasingly improbable that infant industry arguments
could apply—by 1970, few industries in Japan were likely to be at a disadvantage simply because competitors in other nations had a head-start in
production. Equally important, because Japan had caught up with the rest
of the world, it no longer had historical examples of how development
would proceed and what industries were most likely to grow. Hence, this
shift from promoting entire industries towards promoting only new technologies is another very positive indication for policy rationality.

If JDB loans meet most of the conditions for policy rationality, they
also serve as proof that policy had an impact on economic activity. The
size of JDB loans relative to all loans for industrial investment fell from
roughly 5 per cent in the 1960s to about 4 per cent in the 1970s, but this
amount was certainly enough to affect investment activities at the margin.
Government loans through the Smaller Business Finance Corporation
and other government financial institutions including the Hokkaido and

[6] For more details, see the discussion on pp. 66–8.

Tōhoku Development Corporation, the People's Finance Corporation, and the Agriculture, Forestry, and Fisheries Finance Corporation also were substantial in the 1970s, totalling two to three times the size of JDB loans. Furthermore, special tax breaks, including accelerated depreciation and special reserve accounts, also affected economic activity.

Unfortunately, it is premature to conclude here that the necessary conditions for policy efficacy, namely policy rationality and policy impact, were both fulfilled in the 1970s. The problem lies in the rationality of industrial policy and the ability of JDB loans to serve as a summary of policy intent. That ability eroded as direct government support for industries became more contentious internationally and less popular domestically. As a consequence, the government moved away from loans and subsidies and relied more on administrative guidance, cartels, and legislation for particular policy goals, a trend that was reinforced by a genuine disengagement of industrial policy in Japan. Hence, consideration of these other measures is necessary to assess policy rationality in recent decades, and a more careful consideration of these issues undermines the contention of rationality in the 1970s.

First, in response to the hyper-inflation that accompanied the first oil crisis, the Japanese government quickly implemented price and production controls. The economic rationale for these controls is far from clear: without massive market failure on a very wide scale, government control over pricing and production cannot allocate resources more efficiently than markets. The first oil shock itself is not evidence of such market failure. The 4.5 times increase in oil prices, because it was the result of monopolistic behaviour by suppliers, arguably did require government policy to cushion the blow. However, optimal policy should have consisted of subsidies and tax incentives to promote adjustment rather than attempts to restrain prices of final goods.[7] In this case, price and production controls do not serve a purpose that would otherwise be unfulfilled.

It is possible that such government intervention could have been rational if the oil shock, combined with inflationary trends already present in Japan, so undermined confidence that consumers expected economic collapse, hyper-inflation, and acute shortages. If so, and the toilet paper panic of late 1973 does support this contention, the market mechanism would have jammed with mounting speculative demand, and government intervention would have been necessary to reassure markets. While price and production controls may have helped to calm market fears, they were

---

[7] Appropriate policy response to the oil crisis depended to a large extent on expectations about future oil prices. Under expectations that OPEC would fail and oil prices would fall, the rational policy response is to subsidize oil consumption. Under expectations that the price increase is permanent, government encouragement of adjustment is necessary if labour and capital do not move freely and immediately between industries.

also extremely costly, so much so that they are unlikely to have been a first-best solution even here. Although price controls under the Law Concerning Emergency Measures for the Stabilization of the People's Livelihood were applied to only a limited number of products, concern in other industries that their prices might become subject to control caused many industries to raise prices ahead of government intervention. In other words, government controls to check inflation led to price rises in many industries. That this was the case can be seen from the dramatic rise in the number of illegal cartels successfully prosecuted by the Fair Trade Commission. Government controls over production had a similar impact on inflation. Possible government rationing of energy reduced corporate expectations about levels of capacity utilization, thus decreasing the expected profitability of investment. This drag on investment in turn limited future supply and raised pressure on future prices.

Hence, not only is the rationality of price and production controls questionable, but even if they did help to halt speculative demand, they were probably not a first-best policy. A better solution to consumer fears might have been a reasoned publicity campaign by the government. By detailing the impact of higher oil costs on the Japanese economy, the government could have lessened the insecurity that accompanied the first oil crisis; announcing government support to help offset the impact of higher oil prices would have raised confidence. A well-run campaign could perhaps have halted speculative demand, and at much lower cost to the economy than price and production controls entailed.

In order to help mitigate the first oil shock, industrial policy empha-sized cartels, encouraging firms in select industries to collaborate to regu-late prices, output, and/or investment. This was not a new policy tool, having been in use since 1953. Nevertheless, cartels became an increas-ingly important policy measure, particularly as a means to facilitate adjustment. The need to support employment by blocking competition in industries on a regular basis had faded. This declining need to implement long-term anti-growth policy measures was met by a declining ability: for-eign pressure on Japan to liberalize and the growing strength of private industries tied government hands. However, as long-term policy decreased in importance, the relative role of short-term adjustment policy soared as external shocks and rising wage costs undermined the competitive posi-tion of many Japanese industries.

In 1971 and 1972, cartels were used to help industries adjust to the shock of the yen appreciation. Industries allowed to form recession car-tels during those years included steel, chemicals, paper, and glass fibres while rationalization cartels covered textile fibres and dyes.[8] All of these

---

[8] Revisions to the Anti-Monopoly Law in 1953 allowed the formation of recession cartels to hasten industry adjustment to downturns; rationalization cartels were established under

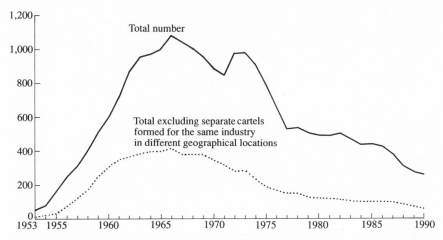

Fig. 8.1.   Trends in Legally Recognized Cartels
Source: Kōsei Torihiki Iinkai, *Kōsei Torihiki Iinkai Nenji Hōkoku*.

particular cartels had been disbanded by 1974, but many reappeared in different guises shortly thereafter. The textile fibre industry was permitted to establish a recession cartel from December 1974 until May 1975; the recession cartel for glass fibre was reformed from November 1975 until January 1976, and paper reappeared as a recession cartel from September 1977 to March 1978. Other designated recession cartels between 1973 and 1978 included aluminium sheet, steel tube, asbestos slate, and cement.[9] Many of these industries, such as paper, aluminium, and cement, were energy-intensive, and thus were particularly hard hit by the first oil crisis. To other industries, such as textiles, higher energy costs were just one of a number of problems facing the industry.[10]

The government systematized policy towards declining industries with 1978 legislation, of which the Law Concerning Emergency Measures for the Stabilization of Specially Designated Depressed Industries (*Tokutei Fukyō Sangyō Antei Rinji Sochi Hō*) formed the core. Cartels formed under the auspices of this law included synthetic fibres, wool spinning, ammonia, urea, and cardboard. A recession cartel was set up for

the Law to Promote the Rationalization of Enterprises (*Kigyō Gōrika Sokushin Hō*) in order to help companies in designated industries modernize their production facilities. Textile fibres and dyes had been designated for rationalization since the mid-1950s or early 1960s, depending on the product produced. The yen appreciation was thus not the sole reason behind the desire to rationalize these industries.

[9] Kōsei Torihiki Iinkai, *Kōsei Torihiki Iinkai Nenji Hōkoku*, various years.
[10] Other problems include the growing competitiveness of rival firms in low-wage countries and the appreciation of the yen.

Table 8.2. Trends in Cartels for Selected Industries

Industry	Recession cartels (1953–present)	Rationalization cartels (1953–present)	Machinery promotion cartels (1957–71)	General and electronic machinery (1972–8)	Machinery and information industry (1979–85)	Stabilization cartels (1978–83)	Structural improvement cartels (1983–8)
Stainless steel	1971–3						
Steel scrap	1955–74						
Synthetic dyes	1960–1, 1980–2	1961–72					
Spun rayon thread	1974–8, 1981	1961–72					
Bearings	1972, 1982–3	1955–66	1966–71	1972–8	1979–83		
Ethylene							1983–8
Cardboard						1979–83	1984–8
Textile machinery			1962–71	1972–8	1980–1, 1984–5		
Artificial grindstones			1965–71	1972–8			
Cement	1975–6, 1983						1985–8
Civil engineering equipment			1969–71	1976–8			

Source: Kōsei Torihiki Iinkai, *Kōsei Torihiki Iinkai Nenji Hokoku.*

shipbuilding in the August 1979–March 1982 period, while synthetic textile dye manufacturers formed a rationalization cartel.

Industrial policy attempted to ease the adjustment process for these industries battered by the fluctuation of the yen and sharp increases in oil prices. To that end, the government subsidized the scrapping of capacity, co-ordinated investment plans, and subsidized wage costs and worker retraining. These measures certainly affected resource allocation. The government provided more than 20 billion yen to scrap capacity, funds that definitely had an impact on recipient industries. Moreover, these measures initially pass the test of rationality: because labour and capital do not move freely and costlessly between regions and industries, government policy to facilitate mobility serves a purpose that would otherwise be unfulfilled. Not only were measures rational, but industries shrank more or less according to plan. As can be seen from Table 8.5, targets of capacity to be scrapped under the 1978–83 Law Concerning Emergency Measures for the Stabilization of Specially Designated Depressed Industries were generally achieved.

Despite potential rationality and impact, it is not clear that measures helped industries adjust any more quickly than would have been the case in the absence of policy. Cartels to promote the orderly shrinking of an industry have one notable drawback: they tended to reappear time and again for the same industries. As a result, Japanese industries could well have expected such cartels to be a permanent or regular measure rather than a one-time occurrence. In such a case, cartels may appear to help smooth adjustment in periods of economic decline, but the reassurance that the cartel crutch would be available again in the future would accelerate investment outlays during economic booms. That is, cartel policy can create a vicious circle, with government guarantees of support in a recession promoting so much investment in an economic expansion that needed government support in the next downturn increases. Table 8.2 summarizes select industries for which recession, rationalization, stabilization, and adjustment cartels have been permitted since 1955. That the same industries appear repeatedly suggests that cartels may indeed be self-perpetuating rather than helping to ease adjustment in an industry.

The overall impact of cartel policy was thus probably negative. The costs of these policy mistakes may have been somewhat offset by measures more appropriately designed to facilitate adjustment, such as subsidies to retrain workers and funds granted to firms to scrap capacity or retain employees. Even so, adjustment policy was not an unqualified success. Evidence for traditional anti-growth policy—impediments to competition designed to support employment—is more clearly negative. First, policy continued to protect and support agriculture throughout the 1970s. With little need to subsidize employment, measures to support agriculture only acted as a drag on economic performance, lowering the purchasing power of consumers and negatively affecting resource allocation by maintaining agricultural output. Secondly, efforts to liberalize distribution were substantially slowed with the enactment in March 1974 of the Large-Scale Retail Store Law (*Daikibo Kouri Tenpo ni Okeru Kourigyō no Jigyō Katsudō no Chōsei ni Kansuru Hōritsu*). This law replaced the 1956 Department Store Law, and covered not just department stores but also supermarkets and other large chain stores. By necessitating government approval for the expansion of existing large stores and the establishment of new ones, this law helped to maintain employment in inefficient small establishments, probably at a cost to total economic efficiency.[11] Just as in the case of agriculture, this policy mistake arose because of the political power of a minority group, the small distributors.

Pro-growth industrial policy in the 1970s more successfully fulfils the condition of rationality. First, by the 1970s, cartels were no longer being extensively used to foster new industries, thus avoiding the potential 'cartel begets cartel' problem. Rationalization cartels had been used in such industries as steel scrap in the 1950s in order to promote the development of what were thought to be infant industries; cartels were also designated under such laws as the Law Concerning Emergency Measures to Promote Designated Machinery Industries (*Tokutei Kikai Kōgyō Shinkō Rinji Sochi Hō*) (1956–71) and the Law Concerning Emergency Measures to Promote Designated Electronic Industries (*Tokutei Denshi Kōgyō Shinkō Rinji Sochi Hō*)(1957–71). Although the cartels formed under these laws did help to promote such infant industries as computer peripherals (1969–71), as time passed there was a decreasing emphasis on promoting the development of infant industries and an increased emphasis on using these laws to maintain the status quo or to assist in adjustment. Hence, these laws were used to form cartels in industries such as textile machinery, bearings, and woodworking machinery whose further survival was questionable.

After these laws expired in 1971, they were replaced with a single measure, the Law Concerning Emergency Measures to Promote Designated Machinery Industries and Designated Electronics Industries (*Tokutei Denshi Kōgyō Oyobi Tokutei Kikai Kōgyō Shinkō Rinji Sochi Hō*), in force until 1978. Industries designated under this law were all mature

[11] Growth in the number of new wholesale and retail establishments accelerated in the 1972–82 period compared to the previous decade and the number of workers per wholesale establishment fell to 9.5 in 1982 after rising to 11.6 in 1972 from 9.5 in 1962. The rise in workers per establishment in the retail sector also slowed in the 1972–82 period: after rising from 2.8 in 1962 to 3.4 in 1972, that ratio had advanced only to 3.7 by 1982. (Itō Takatoshi, *The Japanese Economy*, 388–9.)

industries using relatively low levels of technology.[12] Hence, despite its name, the Law Concerning Emergency Measures to Promote Designated Machinery Industries and Designated Electronics Industries was in fact used to help industries adjust, not grow, and as such fits into the previous discussion of the rationality of cartels under anti-growth rather than pro-growth policy. More recently, this trend still continues. Under the Law for the Promotion of Designated Machinery and Information Industries (1978–85) (*Tokutei Kikai Jōhō Sangyō Shinkō Rinji Sochi Hō*), the successor to the Law Concerning Emergency Measures to Promote Designated Machinery Industries and Designated Electronics Industries, cartels were formed for bearings and synthetic grindstones in order to facilitate adjustment (Table 8.2).

That cartels, government loans, and subsidies were not generally used to promote the development of new infant industries reflects the disengagement of pro-growth policy. This disengagement was eminently rational: Japan in the 1970s was a major industrialized nation, and Japanese industries that were at a disadvantage simply because foreign competitors had developed first were few in number. Industrial policy did not totally abandon its interest in growth, but this interest was narrowed. Policy emphasized the development of new technology rather than the growth of an entire industry. In some instances, however, this promotion of new technology was closely linked to support for new industries, particularly those related to information processing.

To assist in developing new technologies, the government employed its usual collection of policy tools. First, it provided subsidies in the form of low-interest loans through the Japan Development Bank. The government also granted subsidies through funds administered across most ministries though the Science and Technology Agency and MITI had the most important role in dispensing these funds.[13] Thirdly, the government directly funded specific projects. Finally, tax policy was also used to promote R&D: measures included tax credits for increased amounts of R&D expenditure, tax credits for technology exports, accelerated depreciation for R&D equipment, and 100 per cent tax deductions for corporate R&D

---

[12] Between Apr. 1971 and Mar. 1978 when this law was in force, industries designated to form cartels were textile machinery, agricultural machinery, industrial instruments, bearings (ball and roller), synthetic grindstones, plastic moulding equipment, transport equipment (conveyor belts, equipment to automate warehousing), civil engineering equipment (tractors, power shovels), and tools made from speciality steel.

[13] Of government funds specifically used to promote science and technology, 52% were administered directly by the Science and Technology Agency in 1975, while the next most important agency was MITI with 18%. Figures for 1979 were 55% and 16%. In its own programmes, the Science and Technology Agency emphasized the development of energy technology and space technology. MITI, despite its smaller budget, had more flexibility in granting subsidies across projects and companies. MITI also was able to augment its smaller budget with discretionary funds received from bicycle racing and energy taxes.

Evaluating Recent Industrial Policy

expenditure under the auspices of government-sponsored joint R&D projects.

Table 8.3 summarizes MITI's large-scale research projects in the 1970s in addition to expenditure on energy technologies. Large-scale projects were specifically designed to develop needed new technologies that because of risk, high cost, and a lengthy development period would have been shunned by the private sector. These needed technologies were defined as those that upgrade the industrial structure, prevent pollution, efficiently utilize resources, and positively influence manufacturing. MITI supplemented these projects directly funded by the government through its own discretionary funds, emphasizing information technologies in particular. Of the projects associated with MITI's discretionary funds, the

Table 8.3. Principal MITI-Sponsored R&D Projects in the 1970s

Project breakdown	Period	Total funding (yen bn.)
I. *Large-Scale Projects*		
Pattern information processing systems	1971–81	22.1
High-temperature reduction process		
for manufacturing steel	1973–81	14.0
Electric car development	1971–7	5.7
Motor vehicle traffic control technology	1973–9	7.4
Manufacture of olefin from heavy oil	1975–83	14.2
Jet engines for aircraft	1971–82	19.7
Resource recycling systems	1972–87	13.0
Desalination technology	1969–77	7.0
Deep-water oil extraction technology	1970–4	4.5
II. *Energy Development**		
Solar power	1974–	8.4
Thermal energy	1974–	8.4
Coal liquification/gassification	1974–	4.1
Hydrogen manufacture, storage		
transportation technology	1974–	3.2
III. *Labour-Saving/Energy-Saving Technology*		
Heat-recycling technology	1976–81	2.1
Magnetohydrodynamic generation (stage II)	1976–83	5.0
Total MITI expenditure related to R&D†	1970–80	676.0
MITI expenditure as a percentage of total		
government outlays on R&D	1970–80	9.0%

* Energy projects have been ongoing since 1974. Outlay totals are for the period 1974–80.
† In addition to funds to promote the development of technologies, this includes grants to government laboratories and other related outlays. Outlays directly concerned with promoting the development of technologies are less than 30% of MITI's R&D budget.

Source: Kagaku Gijutsu Chō, *Kagaku Gijutsu Hakusho*; Kōgyō Gijutsu In, *Ōgata Purojekuto 20 Nen no Ayumi: Waga Kuni Sangyō Gijutsu no Shi o Kizuku*.

most well-known was the VLSI (Very Large-Scale Integrated Circuit) project of the late 1970s.[14]

The VLSI project advanced Japan's semiconductor industry substantially, particularly in regard to process technology.[15] By providing a forum in which semiconductor device and equipment makers worked together, the project enabled both groups to better understand the other's needs, contributing to the development of superior products and the growth of both groups of companies.[16] Additionally, the project undoubtedly helped to diffuse technologies across companies within these two groups, thus increasing competition and improving performance.

This project in itself does not show that industrial policy was attempting to support the 'infant' semiconductor industry. The goal of the project was technology development: that this stimulated the growth of the semiconductor industry was a secondary benefit. However, the semiconductor industry was also subject to tariffs, a tool that the government had used in the past to promote 'infant' industries, suggesting that policy may have also been somewhat concerned with the development of the industry. This use of tariffs was probably not rational, since they entailed a cost on users of semiconductors that could have been avoided had the government used direct subsidies instead.

Tariff policy towards semiconductors may also be interpreted as a strategic trade policy, an attempt to capture economies of scale by closing the domestic market to foreign competitors. In the case of 16K DRAMs, this interpretation may hold some validity. However, evidence also suggests that Japan would have been better off not using tariffs to establish the 16K DRAM industry. Furthermore, had protection triggered a trade war with the US, then Japan would have been even worse off.[17]

Despite the occasional use of tariffs, pro-growth policy in the 1970s had as its primary goal the development of new technologies rather than the support of infant industries. This government support for technology could well have been rational. Given problems in appropriating returns, project risk, and the magnitude of investment required, sub-optimal investment in technology development would have resulted in the absence of government measures. Policy certainly had an impact on resource allocation: government funding accounted for 27 per cent of total R&D

[14] Details on MITI involvement in information technologies, such as the VLSI project and computer development, can be found in Daniel Okimoto, *Between MITI and the Market: Japanese Industrial Policy for High Technology*, 55–111.

[15] However, there were few breakthroughs regarding frontier technologies (ibid. 71).

[16] Jay S. Stowsky, 'Weak Links, Strong Bonds: US–Japanese Competition in Semiconductor Production Equipment', in Chalmers Johnson, Laura D'Andrea Tyson, and John Zysman (eds.), *Politics and Productivity: How Japan's Development Strategy Works* (New York, HarperBusiness, 1989), 252–6.

[17] Elhanan Helpman and Paul Krugman, *Trade Policy and Market Structure*, 169–74.

expenditure in the 1975–9 period. Whether or not government promotion of R&D actually helped to improve overall performance of the economy in the 1970s is a more difficult issue. Because the development of a new technology is uncertain, successful development does not necessarily increase substantially with increased expenditure. Hence, government support may have had little favourable impact on technology. Moreover, by diverting resources to government-selected projects, policy may have undermined the development of other technologies or policy may have used resources that firms could have put to better use in the form of new equipment. Despite these qualifications, technology policy probably did not lower growth. Since the selection of technologies to be promoted was based on the best information of both corporations and the government, a misallocation of resources is unlikely to have occurred.[18] Moreover, policy not only attempted to promote the development of new technologies; it also encouraged the diffusion of new technologies through joint R&D projects. This latter function almost certainly had a positive impact on economic performance,[19] even if policy did not in fact do much to speed up technology development.

Although this assessment favours a generally positive role for pro-growth policy in the 1970s, the analysis also points to a negative contribution on the part of traditional anti-growth policy and short-term adjustment policy. By continuing to protect agriculture and increasing restraints on competition in distribution, traditional anti-growth policy certainly worsened economic performance. Moreover, attempts to smooth the adjustment process of troubled industries may have largely backfired. Instead of promoting capacity reductions, policy increased the need for future reductions by over-stimulating investment. Finally, and perhaps most seriously, industrial policy probably delayed recovery from the first oil crisis. Price controls and production controls increased inflation and slowed investment, exacerbating the price spiral and blocking recovery. Despite many positive features, industrial policy on balance in the 1970s may well have worsened Japan's economic performance.

[18] If policy directed resources to the appropriate projects, misallocation of resources could have occurred only if policy measures caused over-investment in technology. Since Japanese R&D spending as a percentage of GNP was less than 1.8% in the 1970s, a level substantially lower than that for the US and West Germany, this is unlikely to have been a problem. Interestingly, governments in these other countries funded far more of total R&D outlays than did the Japanese government. (The US government provided roughly half of the total, while the West German government provided more than 40%.)

[19] Daniel Okimoto and Gary Saxonhouse, 'Technology and the Future of the Economy', in Kozo Yamamura and Yasuba Yasukichi (eds.), *The Political Economy of Japan*, 1 (Stanford, Calif., Stanford University Press, 1987), 385–419.

8.2 Policy Rationality and Policy Impact in the 1980s

Some of the problems associated with industrial policy in the 1970s were absent in the 1980s, while others abated. As a result, not only was industrial policy more rational in the 1980s but it may also be the case that policy actually helped to improve overall economic performance. Such improvement, however, could at most be marginal. Policy rationality dictated a decreasing role for industrial policy, since market imperfections and externalities were reduced by Japan's successful development. Not surprisingly, this decreasing role for policy was accompanied by a decline in potential policy gains. Smaller benefits were also at least partially offset by the cost of several economically irrational policies, such as those arising from the continued protection of agriculture. Hence, industrial

Table 8.4. Breakdown of Loans of the Japan Development Bank in the 1980s

	1981	1983	1985	1987	1989
Energy related	38.69	45.72	42.54	30.90	28.28
Electric power/nuclear	13.46	18.62	19.78	13.38	13.17
Energy diversification	13.09	11.61	11.44	9.74	7.94
Gas	1.48	1.47	1.45	0.87	0.91
Conversion of oil generators	1.48	3.34	0.24	0.00	0.00
Promoting energy substitutes	1.67	1.17	1.76	1.28	0.00
Oil	4.63	5.40	5.86	3.42	2.96
Energy-saving investment*	2.88	4.09	2.01	2.21	3.31
Technology promotion	8.92	11.11	14.79	15.25	14.81
Marine transport	11.91	8.68	7.28	1.86	2.57
Air transport	0.00	0.00	0.00	3.75	4.68
Urban investment	13.37	11.36	13.69	18.78	18.92
Private railway	5.57	6.54	7.72	7.30	7.68
Urban redevelopment	6.43	4.02	4.41	9.49	9.82
Modernization of distribution	1.37	0.80	1.56	1.99	1.42
Regional development	14.48	10.41	9.84	11.90	10.66
Life-style improvement	9.44	9.14	7.93	4.87	4.73
Anti-pollution	7.96	8.16	7.50	4.26	4.43
Social welfare	0.64	0.29	0.09	0.10	0.00
Food related†	0.84	0.68	0.34	0.52	0.29
Basic railway equipment	0.00	0.00	0.00	6.61	8.41
Adjusting industrial structure	0.00	0.00	0.00	2.34	3.85
Other	3.19	3.58	3.93	3.73	3.09
TOTAL	100.00	100.00	100.00	100.00	100.00

* From 1989, energy-saving investment is combined with the promotion of energy substitutes.
† Also from 1989, loans for social welfare are combined with those for food.
Source: Nihon Kaihatsu Ginkō, *Tōkei Yōran*.

policy could have had at most a small positive effect on economic performance in the 1980s.

Industrial policy in the 1980s concentrated increasingly on the development of new technologies. Loans from the Japan Development Bank show that the promotion of technology accounted for 9 per cent of new funds handed out in 1981, but that that amount had risen to 15 per cent in 1987. Energy-related loans were also quite important, accounting for more than one-third of Japan Development Bank funds dispersed in the first half of the decade. Industrial policy continued to target social capital: railway-related loans rose from 5.6 per cent of JDB lending in 1981 to 13.9 per cent in 1987, and loans for urban redevelopment, despite fluctuations, grew from 6.4 per cent to 9.5 per cent. Similarly, loans to modernize distribution also increased slightly from 1.4 per cent to 2.0 per cent. Regional development remained a policy priority, accounting for about 10 per cent of JDB lending in the 1980s, even though this was down from the 15 per cent figures of the 1970s. Japan Development Bank loans also show an emphasis on helping the industrial structure adjust to the shock of the yen appreciation after 1985.

Lending patterns also reveal a declining emphasis on marine transport, with loans to this industry falling from more than 10 per cent in 1981 to less than 2 per cent by 1987. Policy placed less emphasis on anti-pollution investment: loans from the JDB had decreased to 4 per cent in 1987 from approximately 20 per cent ten years prior to this. Finally, although energy-related loans accounted for more JDB funding than any other category, they nevertheless fell as a percentage of total loans after 1985, as policy emphasized rail transport and urban redevelopment.

Just as was the case for the 1970s, industrial policy as reflected in lending behaviour by the Japan Development Bank can be viewed as rational. The previous arguments all apply—government guidance of the energy industry is necessary given safety risks, the monopolistic nature of the industry, dynamic investment complementarities with other industries, and the national goal of energy independence. Government support of technology is needed because of the difficulties that private sector firms may have in appropriating returns from the technologies that they develop as well as the large risks that can be associated with technology development. Government support for investment in social capital is needed, since such investment also affects the profitability of other industries. To the extent that labour and capital do not move freely from one area to another, regional development is also a rational policy. This same reason can help explain the emphasis on facilitating adjustment in industries faced with the sharp appreciation of the yen.

The declining importance of support for anti-pollution investment could also have been rational. As air quality improved dramatically, the need to further stimulate such investment decreased. Moreover, anti-pollution loans had not been a first-best policy: this approach did not charge polluting firms for their pollution, and thus did not affect decisions to increase output and capacity by polluting industries. Decreased support for marine transport also reflected rationality since loans here had also never been a first-best policy. Designed to support shipbuilding, they had generated excess capacity in the marine transport industry. Finally, a renewed commitment to the disengagement of anti-growth policy, as shown by further support to modernize distribution in the second half of the decade, was probably rational. Because the survival of the work-force was no longer an issue, policy correctly disengaged measures designed to maintain the status quo by blocking competition in such industries as distribution.

While this assessment of policy rationality based on JDB lending is the same as that of the previous decade, a broader analysis shows that industrial policy in the 1980s avoided some of the pitfalls of the 1970s. First, and most important, policy did not attempt to regulate directly economic activity. Even in the face of the second oil crisis, the government did not try to control prices or production, although the legal basis from which to do so was still in place.[20] Not only was the rationality of these controls questionable when they were implemented, but it is likely that the controls had actually exacerbated inflation by limiting investment and by motivating industries to increase prices ahead of possible controls. Policy response to the second oil crisis avoided this mistake, focusing instead on the promotion of energy-saving investment and energy diversification, rational if energy independence is a goal of national security.

Secondly, the government used cartels less frequently as a policy tool as the decade progressed. Fig. 8.1 shows that the absolute number of cartels recognized fell from about 1,000 in the early 1970s to about half that by the early 1980s. The number then further halved to 261 by 1990. In terms of industries covered by cartels, those numbers showed the same dramatic decline from approximately 300 in the early 1970s to 61 in 1990. Cartels were not used specifically to respond to the second oil crisis: industries negatively affected by higher oil costs had been identified after the first oil shock and designated throughout the 1970s. Additionally, by the end of the decade, some of the laws commonly used to promote the cartelization of industries expired and were not replaced. For example, special laws to promote machinery and electronics expired in 1978 after having been in existence in one form or another since 1956. Furthermore,

---

[20] The Law Concerning Emergency Measures for the Stabilization of the People's Livelihood (*Kokumin Seikatsu Antei Kinkyū Sochi Hō*) and the Petroleum Supply and Demand Normalization Law (*Sekiyu Jukyū Tekiseika Hō*) which provided the legal basis for intervention after the first oil crisis both remain in force today.

recession cartels under the 1953 revision of the Anti-Monopoly Law only totalled 13 in the first half of the 1980s compared to more than 25 in the 1970s, and disappeared totally after 1985. Rationalization cartels have also not been recognized since 1981. This reduction in the use of cartels lessened the probability that designated industries would over-invest in economic booms, helping to avoid the problem of cartels creating the need to form additional cartels in the future.

While less reliance on cartels and direct economic controls reduced the potential negative impact of government attempts to facilitate the shrinking of an industry, the rationality of policy measures actually used also rose from 1983. At that time, the government enacted the Law Concerning Emergency Measures to Improve the Structure of Designated Industries (*Tokutei Sangyō Kōzō Kaizen Rinji Sochi Hō*) to replace the Law Concerning Emergency Measures for the Stabilization of Designated Depressed Industries (*Tokutei Fukyō Sangyō Antei Rinji Sochi Hō*). With this, the focus of industrial policy switched from simply promoting the decline of an industry to also encouraging its diversification. To that end, the government continued to provide subsidies for wages, worker retraining, and the scrapping of capacity, but it also provided tax breaks for new equipment and R&D, as well as providing diversification plans and outlines of possible mergers. In theory at least, these new measures were rational: they not only encouraged a declining industry to promote the mobility of its labour and capital, but they also encouraged the industry itself to make use of these resources in producing other products. In addition to rationality,[21] these measures were also consistent with OECD guidelines.[22]

In a sense, this represented a synthesis of pro-growth policy with anti-growth policy. The focus of anti-growth policy had already changed in the 1970s with more emphasis on facilitating the decline of troubled industries rather than on blocking competition to maintain employment and the status quo. The 1980s witnessed this focus combine with positive efforts to promote survival through diversification, specialization, or mergers. Policy no longer protected certain industries, nor did it simply attempt to shrink these industries. Rather, while facilitating reduced production of traditional products, policy now promoted diversification into new products and new industries.

Although this new approach fulfilled conditions of rationality, the final impact of these measures is difficult to assess. Some evidence exists of a favourable contribution to economic performance, particularly in the

---

[21] If labour is totally immobile between regions, or if it is not socially desirable to promote labour movement because of such reasons as urban overcrowding, policy measures should help provide employment opportunities in regions where jobs are lost.
[22] OECD, *Positive Adjustment Policy: Managing Structural Changes* (1983).

Table 8.5. Government Plans for Scrapping Capacity in Designated Industries, 1978–1988

Industry	Under Law Concerning Emergency Measures to Improve the Structure of Designated Industries (1978–83)			Under Law Concerning Emergency Measures to Facilitate the Adjustment of the Industrial Structure (1983–88)	
	Total ('000 tons)	% of industry capacity	Reduction achieved (%)	Total ('000 tons)	% of industry capacity
Steel	2,850.0	14.0	14.0	3,800.0	14.0
Aluminium	530.0	32.0	NA	930.0	57.0
Continuous nylon fibre	71.5	20.0	20.0	Capacity reductions completed; Only new investment is restricted	
Short acryl fibre	73.2	17.0	20.0		
Continuous polyester fibre	36.8	11.0	10.0		
Short polyester fibre	67.6	17.0	18.0		
Cardboard	1,147.0	15.0	14.0		
Urea	1,790.0	45.0	42.0	830.0	36.0
Ammonia	1,190.0	26.0	26.0	660.0	20.0
Phosphoric acid (wet process)	190.0	20.0	18.0	130.0	17.0
Ferrosilicon	100.0	21.0	21.0	50.0	14.0
Shipbuilding	3,420.0	35.0		Capacity reductions achieved and not re-designated	
Cotton spinning	67.1	6.0			
Wool spinning	18.3	10.0			
Short viscose fibre	Only designated in the 1983-88 period			47.7	15.0
Phosphate fertilizer (fused)				240.0	32.0
Chemical fertilizer				810.0	13.0
Paper				950.0	11.0
Ethylene				2,290.0	36.0
Polyolephene				900.0	22.0
Polyvinyl chloride				490.0	24.0
Ethylene oxide				210.0	27.0
Hard PVC pipes				116.0	18.0
Sugar				1,000.0	26.0

Source: Tsūshō Sangyō Shō, *Sankō Hō no Kaisetsu*; *Kōzō Fukyō Hō no Kaisetsu*; Sekiguchi Sueo and Horiuchi Toshihiro, *Nihon no Sangyō Seisaku*.

210 *Evaluating Recent Industrial Policy*

1978–83 period. Specifically, government plans to reduce capacity in select industries were largely achieved, many with the help of cartels and government subsidies. Figures, summarized in Table 8.5, are not in themselves enough to prove policy efficacy: industries might have more rapidly reduced capacity without government support. Another problem lies in the validity of the numbers themselves. Capacity scrapped often means just the mothballing of plants. Because this capacity can often be brought back on line if wanted, adjustment may not be as complete as the numbers suggest. However, that government targets for shrinking an industry were met in some way or another does preclude dismissing out of hand a positive or neutral evaluation of policy.[23]

Despite this difficulty in assessing impact, by insisting on diversification and change, new measures to assist adjustment could well have undermined beliefs that the government would always help a troubled industry. As a result, these measures probably had a more favourable impact than did adjustment measures which centred on the formation of cartels. New measures may also have encouraged some diversification. For example, government attempts to encourage steel producers to move into electronics met with some success.[24] Of course, whether diversification would have occurred in the absence of government support, and whether it would have occurred more quickly, are questions that cannot be answered. What can be concluded is that the potential of anti-growth policy to have damaged economic performance in the 1980s is less than that in the 1970s, not only because of this change in policy focus but also because of the decreased use of cartels as an adjustment mechanism.

If adjustment policy showed greater rationality in the 1980s, so too did traditional anti-growth policy. Agricultural policy was the sole exception to this, since measures continued to block change through protectionism and government control. Agricultural policy had become increasingly politicized after 1960; because of unequal representation and the power of the rural voter, government policy has exempted agriculture from compe-

[23] At least one example against policy efficacy is provided by recent developments in the ethylene industry. Despite 'scrapping' more than one-third of its capacity under government supervision, when demand recovered late in the decade, the industry brought mothballed plants back into production. Not only did it raise output this way, but the industry also began the construction of new ethylene facilities against government guidance and despite clear indications that global over-supply would again be a problem within a decade. At present, companies are in the process of delaying original construction plans: Tōsō, for example, has announced that it will delay opening its new ethylene centre in Mie Prefecture until 1995 because of perceived over-supply (*Nihon Keizai Shinbun*, 4 Sept. 1991). In other words, not only did government support to 'scrap' capacity in the ethylene industry not really result in a permanent reduction in capacity, but this support and expectations of future government aid may have contributed to the industry's subsequent overly aggressive expansion plans.
[24] Diversification did take place, implying that measures might have been somewhat successful. However, the profitability of diversification is still open to question.

tition, ensuring the survival of inefficient farmers at the expense of the overall economy.[25] Some justification for this stance may be provided on the grounds that self-sufficiency in food is an issue of national security, thus divorcing the issue from purely economic considerations. However, protection of agriculture in Japan has entailed enormous costs, borne largely by the Japanese consumer, who faced higher food prices. From strictly an economic view, protection of agriculture cannot be rational since the survival of workers is no longer an issue and whatever technological gains were to be obtained have long since been exhausted.[26]

Anti-growth policy towards distribution and towards smaller enterprises in the 1980s presents a favourable counter-example to the irrationality of agricultural policy. After halting rationalization in the 1970s and tightening the implementation of the Large–Scale Retail Law in the early 1980s, the government in the latter half of the decade renewed attempts to dismantle measures that had blocked competition or supported the status quo, relaxing restrictions on new store openings, store hours, and transport licences. Policy towards smaller companies also supported technological innovation and change. This drive towards the modernization and liberalization of these sectors was rational: not only did Japan no longer need to worry about worker survival, but in the latter half of the decade, there was an acute shortage of labour. The ending of policies to support employment would thus not only improve efficiency in protected industries but it would also contribute to easing the shortage of workers elsewhere in the economy. Although it is of course far from clear that these measures were dismantled at an optimal rate, partial liberalization was at least better than none at all.

Moreover, the government is firmly committed to ending all traditional anti-growth measures by promoting competition, as is readily apparent from the 1988 five-year economic plan 'Economic Management in a Global Context' (*Sekai to tomo ni Ikiru Nihon*). This plan calls for a two-pronged approach to stimulate growth—to increase spending on the infrastructure, on the one side, and on the other, to liberalize and rationalize distribution, real estate, financial markets, communications, and even agriculture. With the exception of agriculture, the rhetoric of the

---

[25] Unequal representation is such a problem that the Japanese Supreme Court has ruled election results since the 1970s unconstitutional because of this. (The Court has nevertheless refrained from overturning any of these results.) The politicization of agricultural policy is apparent in the yearly negotiations about the price at which the government buys rice from producers. Bureaucratic agreements forged by the Ministry of Finance have been regularly overturned by the ruling Liberal Democratic Party in blatant attempts to keep rural voter support.

[26] The government should gradually reduce support and protectionism in agriculture if it wants policy to be rational. The immediate and total liberalization of this sector is probably not the correct solution, given costs involved in relocating workers.

plan has been consistent with government action.[27] In other words, this plan has helped to provide and disseminate information about the direction of economic policy. This function of government plans has been a long-standing characteristic: its immediate predecessor, the 'Outlook and Guide to the Economy and Society in the 1980s' (*80 Nendai Keizai Shakai no Tenbō to Shishin*), accurately reflected emphasis on administrative reform, while the 'Seven-Year Plan for a New Economic Society' (*Shin Keizai Shakai no 7 kanen Keikaku*) focused on achieving stable growth, improving the quality of life, and contributing to the world economy. Economic plans are generally consistent with later policy because they are extremely general and non-controversial. Moreover, input is provided not only by the government, but also by academics and the private sector. Whatever the reason, information supplied by economic plans in the 1980s as well as before has helped to reduce corporate uncertainty about the future. Even though this information has been quite general, it has probably acted to improve the dynamic allocation of resources, ensuring that industries do not invest according to incorrect expectations about the future direction of the economy.

The heightened rationality of adjustment policy and traditional anti-growth policy (excepting agriculture) in the 1980s was matched with rationality for pro-growth policy. Measures focused on supporting new technologies, necessary given the uncertainty of developing and appropriating new technologies. Measures used were the same as those of the previous decade—tax breaks, subsidies, and government loans. Table 8.6 summarizes not only MITI involvement in large-scale projects and energy technologies in the 1980s but also efforts to promote the development of next-generation technologies. Subsidies for the development of next-generation technologies, started in 1981, were designed to promote technologies that required long-lead times and large funding requirements. Projects were not only risky but were also selected on the grounds that other nations were pursuing comparable research.

Moreover, there was also a further reduction in trade barriers, which, together with government lending practices, suggests that pro-growth policy was not directly concerned with promoting the development of entire industries. By 1982, the average tariff level on mining and manufacturing products in Japan was lower than those for the US and members of the EEC; more importantly, after signing the Multilateral Trade Negotiations in 1979, Japan eliminated special tariff protection on high-technology

[27] Although actual policy and rhetoric towards agriculture did not match in the 1980s, it is quite probable that the government is serious about wanting to liberalize the sector. Demographic trends will ensure the continued erosion of the rural power base of the ruling Liberal Democratic Party (the agricultural population is ageing twice as rapidly as the rest). The LDP must eventually broaden its base of support, and the most effective way for it to do so is to liberalize agriculture, reversing a policy that has long irritated urban voters.

Table 8.6. Principal MITI R&D Projects Funded in the 1980s

Project breakdown	Period	Total funding* (yen bn.)
I. *Large-Scale Projects*		
Machine production systems using high-performance lasers	1977–85	13.5
Optical measurement control systems	1979–86	15.8
Chemical manufacturing using carbon monoxide	1980–7	10.6
Deep-water manganese extraction	1981–91	6.4
Deep-water oil extraction technology	1978–84	18.1
Super-computers	1981–9	13.5
Automated garment production	1982–90	5.3
Robots which function under extreme conditions (deep-sea/high-radiation environments)	1983–90	7.5
Water-recycling technology	1985–90	3.2
Data-base systems	1985–91	1.9
High-tech assembly systems	1986–93	1.1
Satellite sensing for resource deposits	1984–90	9.6
II. *Energy Development†*		
Solar power	1980–	10.7
Thermal energy	1980–	9.6
Coal liquification/gassification	1980–	5.3
Hydrogen manufacture, storage, transportation technology	1980–	2.7
III. *Labour-Saving/Energy-Saving Technology*		
High efficiency gas turbines	1978–87	4.0
New battery technology (such as batteries for solar power)	1980–5	1.4
Batteries using new fuels (hydrogen, methanol, etc.)	1981–90	1.5
Sterling engines	1982–7	0.8
Super heat pump/energy accumulation systems	1984–91	0.5
IV. *Basic Technologies for Next-Generation Industries‡*		
New materials — Fine ceramics, materials for efficient membrane filtration, conductive macro-molecular materials, crystalline macro-molecular materials, composite materials, etc.	1981–	15.9
Biotechnology — Bio-reactors, cell-cultivation technology, technology using recombinant DNA	1981–	7.6

cont.

Table 8.6. *cont.*

Project breakdown	Period	Total funding* (yen bn.)
Others Developing materials using technologies that control at the atomic level, third-generation circuit materials, materials unaffected by light, bio-materials, etc.	1981–	9.3
Total MITI expenditure related to R&D§	1981–7	1347.2
MITI expenditure as a percentage of total government outlays on R&D	1981–7	12.7%

* Where projects finished before 1988, figures represent the entire amount spent for the project. In other cases, figures represent the total amount spent since the beginning of the project until 1987.

† Energy projects have been ongoing since 1974. Outlay totals are for the period 1981–7.

‡ Detailed information about the funding and time span of separate projects under the Next-Generation Technologies Programme is only readily available for the years 1983–7. Lack of detailed information about 1981 and 1982 necessitated the aggregation of spending on individual projects, which in turn eliminated any meaning that individual project time periods may have had. Expenditure totals are for the period 1981–7.

§ In addition to funds to promote the development of technologies, this includes grants to government laboratories and other related outlays. Outlays directly concerned with promoting the development of technologies are less than 30% of MITI's R&D budget.

Source: Kagaku Gijutsu Chō, *Kagaku Gijutsu Hakusho*; Kōgyō Gijutsu In, *Ōgata Purojekuto 20 Nen no Ayumi: Waga Kuni Sangyō Gijutsu no Shi o Kizuku.*

products.[28] Hence, Japan in the 1980s showed little inclination to foster the growth of infant industries, rational since Japan had caught up with competitors in almost all areas.[29] Nor did Japan use trade controls as a strategic policy in an attempt to capture economies of scale, probably rational given potential retaliation and insufficient information about the behaviour of firms.

While pro-growth policy in the 1980s fulfilled both necessary conditions of rationality and resource impact, whether or not it positively stimulated economic growth is a question which cannot be answered conclusively. Evidence on the success of government research projects is mixed, and the successes that did occur might have happened in the absence of government policy. Even so, policy measures almost certainly did not hamper

---

[28] Gary Saxonhouse, 'Industrial Policy and Factor Markets: Biotechnology in Japan and the United States', in Hugh Patrick and Larry Meissner (eds.), *Japan's High Technology Industries* (Seattle, University of Washington Press, 1986), 101–2.

[29] Of course, the promotion of new technologies can stimulate the development of new industries. However, policy goals focused on the former rather than the latter.

the development of new technologies. More importantly, the use of joint venture projects helped to diffuse new technologies throughout the economy, thus heightening competition and increasing economic efficiency. Hence, measures to promote new technologies most probably had a positive, if small, impact on economic performance.

8.3   Lessons for Industrialized Nations

Industrial policy in the 1970s differed from that in the 1980s. After the first oil crisis, policy interfered directly with the market mechanism, introducing price and production controls. These probably had an adverse effect on growth by fuelling inflation. Policy towards declining industries may also not have had a desirable outcome, since cartels tended to be self-perpetuating. Moreover, there were also continued costs associated with irrational agricultural policy, and new restraints on distribution may well have lowered efficiency in that sector. Pro-growth policy in support of new technologies may have helped to stimulate the economy, but benefits in some cases may have been offset by the inappropriate use of tariffs. In general, industrial policy in the 1970s hindered rather than helped economic performance.

The case for policy in the 1980s is better. Industrial policy did not attempt to use price and production controls. Although adjustment measures still utilized cartels, cartels were used less frequently and policy also promoted the diversification and specialization of troubled industries. This switch may have generated a belief that government-sponsored cartels would not always be available to a troubled industry, thus breaking the cycle of cartels generating more cartels. Agricultural policy continued to be irrational, but the government made further commitments to eliminating the vestiges of traditional anti-growth policy in other industries. Finally, pro-growth policy eschewed trade controls and continued to support the development of new technologies through measures that were rational and possibly effective. On balance, industrial policy in the 1980s was certainly better than that in the previous decade, and it may have contributed to Japan's favourable economic performance.

These conclusions must necessarily remain tentative. Constraints on Japanese economic growth over the last two decades have probably been threefold. First were the numerous shocks which battered the economy, shocks which industrial policy did little to overcome. Policy probably delayed recovery from the first oil crisis, and recovery from the second oil crisis as well as the appreciation of the yen is better correlated with the absence of industrial policy than its presence. A second constraint on growth has probably been the excess of domestic savings over investment.[30] Macroeconomic policy, particularly in the 1980s, may have helped to narrow this gap by eliminating savings incentives[31] as well as by stimulating investment. Not only did the government raise outlays on social capital, but economic plans continued to reduce uncertainty about the future, thus stimulating investment by the private sector. A third constraint on growth, one that faces all industrialized countries, has been the development of new technologies. Industrial policy may have helped to foster such development, but the relation between government support and technology development is far from clear.[32]

If industrial policy did play a positive role in supporting Japanese economic performance in the 1980s, it did so because it had changed beyond recognition. Unlike earlier policy, the government refrained from interfering with the market mechanism. Policy had become much more passive: it no longer attempted to direct resources to growth industries; nor did it attempt to block competition in whole sectors of the economy. These policy functions, which were rational at the beginning of post-war development, were no longer needed as development succeeded and markets matured. Industrial policy, which had always used competition as a tool, was increasingly able to 'use' it simply by introducing competition and then leaving industries alone.

As the scope of market failures and externalities narrowed, an event that always accompanies successful development, the scope of industrial policy also shrank. Infant industry support was replaced by measures to promote new technology, and efforts to maintain the status quo in some sectors gave way first to an emphasis on helping industries to contract and then on smoothing such contraction while promoting diversification and specialization. As the need for separate pro-growth and anti-growth measures faded, these two types of industrial policy were merged into one. Thus, while facilitating the decline of the steel industry, the government also provided it with subsidies to develop not just new steel-making technology but also to diversify into new materials and electronics.

This disengagement of industrial policy, this dramatic narrowing of its scope, certainly helped to ensure that policy did not harm economic performance in recent years as it might have otherwise. This disengagement,

---

[30] It is not absolutely clear that over time this is a real constraint on economic performance. Since domestic savings can be used to invest overseas, future economic performance is not necessarily hindered by a surplus of domestic savings over domestic investment.

[31] Tax exemptions for designated savings accounts were eliminated in 1988.

[32] To the extent that the government encourages private sector companies to direct resources to projects that prove unsuccessful, policy could undermine growth. However, despite this risk, it seems more probable that since the government increases total funds spent on R&D, total technological development will improve even if some projects are unsuccessful.

however, may owe more to external factors than it does to a conscious decision on the part of policy-makers. It was certainly facilitated by economic and institutional checks and balances. A firm commitment to free trade, necessary because of the importance of exports to growth (and thus related to past policies promoting exports), reduced Japan's ability to support and protect infant industries. It was this, possibly more than the advanced status of most Japanese industries, that caused policy-makers to back away from pro-growth measures. Similarly, traditional anti-growth policy, blocking competition in designated sectors to support employment, was undermined more by budget constraints than it was by recognition of the decreased necessity of such policy. Rising government deficits limited the ability of the government to use fiscal policy to stimulate growth; in its place, the government turned first to administrative reform and then to the liberalization and rationalization of protected sectors as a means to boost economic performance. Fiscal realities undoubtedly hastened the demise of measures which had blocked competition and the achievement of efficiency.

Industrial policy in Japan today probably plays much the same role it fulfils in other countries. It helps to cover market externalities and failures in regard to the development of new technologies. It also attempts to overcome rigidities in the mobility of labour and capital, providing government funds to retrain and relocate workers, to reduce capacity in troubled industries, and to encourage the diversification of such industries into new product areas. Such types of measures are common, and as such hold few lessons for other industrialized nations. One difference which may be of importance is Japan's greater emphasis on joint development projects between private sector companies and the government. By encouraging companies to create technologies together, new technology may spread more rapidly across the economy than would otherwise be the case, increasing economic efficiency.[33] Another important difference may be Japan's emphasis on promoting applications for new technologies rather than only basic research, hence enhancing the ability of corporations to successfully utilize new technologies.

Japanese economic performance in the 1980s owed more to the reduced role of industrial policy than the benefits that may have accrued from it. Even so, industrial policy embodied two characteristics which probably resulted in it having a positive impact on economic activity. First, the reduced use of industrial policy, while undoubtedly the result of a complex

---

[33] Since the government underwrites the development of the technology, the problem of a private company being unable to appropriate sufficient gains is absent. Moreover, the spread of technology amongst competing firms occurs immediately, resulting in a more efficient outcome than would be the case if a single firm were a monopoly supplier of the technology.

system of checks and balances, also reflected policy flexibility. Policy avoided becoming locked in a single direction (excepting measures for agriculture). Flexibility arguably arose because of the lack of a firm ideology behind policy, plurality in policy formulation, and the divorcing of policy from politics, but whatever the case, it certainly contributed to success.

If industrial policy was flexible, at the same time it exhibited continuity. When policy direction shifted, it was only after a thorough consideration which limited the likelihood of a subsequent reversal of policy to its original course. In other words, policy did not often contradict itself. Economic plans provide an excellent example of this continuity in policy: goals and directions do shift, but they are consistent over long periods of time and change is gradual. That economic plans can be characterized thus indicates just how general and non-controversial they are. Even so, this general information probably reduced uncertainty about the future. Thus, continuity, the second characteristic of industrial policy, helped to raise the efficiency of resource allocation over time. Without continuity and flexibility, even the modest gains that might have accrued from recent Japanese industrial policy would not have been attainable.

It does seem highly probable that the policy measures Japan has employed may have been more effective than those utilized in other industrialized nations. Certainly, Japan's technology policy may have effected a very efficient distribution of new technologies, and it may also have promoted their successful application. Policy measures to facilitate decline may also have been more successful, particularly since their implementation was of limited duration. But whatever lessons these measures may contain, the scope of Japanese policy is now no broader than it is elsewhere. It is this narrow focus of industrial policy that has contributed to its rationality, and this may be the most important lesson for others wishing to emulate Japan.

Other lessons are likely to be less transferable. Consistency, continuity, and flexibility in Japanese policy are primarily the result of her historical and institutional legacies. That other developed nations may have met with less success than Japan in promoting technologies and facilitating the decline of sunset industries could well reflect important institutional and cultural differences. It may be feasible for some countries to expand input into policy across groups and to increase the government's role in diffusing information about the composition and direction of economic growth, but the ability of others to do so may be limited by their own existing practices and institutions.

9

Japanese Industrial Policy, Past and Future

Over the last four and a half decades, industrial policy has changed enormously. Instrumental in determining the allocation of resources in the first ten years after World War II, the power and scope of policy has gradually waned. Government measures to support employment by blocking competition have, despite fluctuations, been gradually decreased from about 1960, and policies to support new industries have also been used with less frequency as time passed. With the external shocks of the 1970s, industrial policy focused increasingly on facilitating adjustment. Short-term goals replaced longer-term ambitions, and the government attempted to help shrink depressed industries by encouraging diversification and mergers, thus effectively combining anti-growth policy with pro-growth policy. Industrial policy in Japan today is hardly more ambitious than policy in the US: both support the development of new technologies and both provide special measures for depressed industries.

If the scope of industrial policy in Japan now is generally no broader than that of other industrialized nations, Japanese industrial policy is perhaps differentiated by its consistency. Some effort is made to assess individual policies in a general framework, one that is provided by the five-year economic plans of the government. Because an economic plan contains nothing controversial, being merely the aggregated consensus view of bureaucrats, businessmen, and academics, that framework is very loosely constructed. Even so, it provides a perspective for formulating policy, lending it some degree of consistency. Equally important, plans have also contributed to the continuity of industrial policy, since policy design has taken account of general economic trends.

The continuity and the consistency of industrial policy in Japan are closely linked to the way in which policy is formulated.[1] Although not totally divorced from politics, economic policy in Japan has been entrusted largely to professional bureaucrats. Thus, it avoids being unduly influenced by special interest groups. Moreover, measures adopted generally reflect the views not only of bureaucrats but also of businessmen and academics. Because policy measures incorporate such a broad

[1] For more on policy formulation see, for example, Daniel Okimoto, *Between MITI and the Market: Japanese Industrial Policy for High Technology* (Stanford, Calif., Stanford University Press, 1990).

base of information and experience, instances where policy needs to be reversed or cut off are rare. Put differently, the formulation of industrial policy in Japan is biased against controversial or radical measures, and the continuity and consistency shown by Japanese industrial policy to a large extent may derive from the government adopting conservative, middle-of-the-road policy prescriptions.[2]

Throughout much of its post-war history, Japanese industrial policy has been economically rational. It has not only served purposes which in the absence of policy would have been unfulfilled, but it has also had an impact on resource allocation. Although it has come to resemble policy in other industrialized nations, the breadth of industrial policy in the early post-war years was enormous. This demonstrably large impact on economic activity, together with the rationality of policy, lends credence to the view that post-war policy in its first two decades contributed to Japan's phenomenally rapid growth, with a particularly large contribution in the 1950s. Because of mistakes, policy in the first half of the 1970s probably worsened Japan's economic performance. However, policy rationality had largely been regained by the end of that decade as the scope of policy shrank. Although this more limited scope suggests a smaller potential impact on economic performance, it is probable that industrial policy has favourably contributed to Japan's recent better-than-average economic performance and may have some positive part to play in Japan's economic future.

9.1   Industrial Policy as an Explanation for Growth

Japanese industrial policy in the first two decades after World War II had two goals, maintaining employment and promoting growth in select industries. These goals were to some extent contradictory. Resources that the government had at its disposal were quite limited, and industries selected for growth were capital-intensive. Measures to promote these industries therefore did not lead immediately to the creation of new jobs. Thus, the government balanced these measures with others designed to support employment in inefficient or less efficient sectors of the economy. Specifically, the government first blocked competition in the distribution sector and exempted small companies from the rigours of competition to

---

[2] Policy does not always respond quickly to public need in Japan, as can be seen from bureaucratic response to pollution and turmoil in the coal industry. However, even when response is necessitated by pressures approaching crisis proportion, it occurs within the system rather than leading to a change of the system, reflecting the conservative nature of policy-making in Japan. (Kent Calder, *Crisis and Compensation: Public Policy and Political Stability in Japan*, 39–42.)

ensure that jobs were not lost. Later, coal mining and agriculture were subject to these anti-growth measures.

These two types of policy are at least theoretically rational. To the extent that the growth industries selected were associated with market failures and externalities, then government support was necessary to ensure that optimal investment took place. It seems probable that capital market imperfections existed on a wide scale at least until 1960, that dynamic production externalities existed for the energy sector *vis-à-vis* the rest of the economy, and that learning by doing effects could have been important for a wide variety of industries, particularly those importing new technologies. Anti-growth policy, which consists of measures that block competition to support employment, could also have been rational given surplus labour, the potential for limited technological innovation, and the costs associated with transferring labour and capital from less efficient industries to more efficient ones.

In addition to often fulfilling the necessary conditions of rationality and impact, industrial policy may also have stimulated aggregate savings and investment, providing further evidence that policy stimulated economic growth. Both savings and investment increased beyond historical trends after 1945, and industrial policy could well have been one factor behind these rises. Accelerated depreciation directly raised corporate savings; other tax breaks could well have stimulated personal savings.[3] Corporate investment in select industries was certainly increased by the subsidies and tax breaks provided through industrial policy. Additionally, total corporate investment may have been raised since industrial policy reduced risk by providing information about the future direction of the economy through five-year economic plans.

The evaluation of industrial policy from the 1960s is not as favourable. Policy rationality probably failed from the late 1960s, with cartels for steel, paper, and chemicals helping to ignite inflation, thus worsening the downturn following the first oil shock. Policy arguably reached a nadir in reacting to this shock: direct economic controls probably lengthened the recession and increased inflation. However, policy was in the process of being transformed. Significant progress was made in disengaging policy in the 1960s, as the government dismantled barriers to competition in some areas and switched from promoting growth in heavy industries to fostering electronics and other high value-added sectors. After the temporary intensification of intervention after the first oil shock, industrial policy in the 1980s was characterized by even further disengagement. Pro-growth policy came to focus on promoting new technologies rather than new

---

[3] Tax exemptions for interest income from savings accounts (the *Maruyū* system) probably contributed to a higher savings rate. Strictly speaking, however, these exemptions were a tool of macroeconomic policy rather than of industrial policy.

industries; anti-growth policy was replaced by a hybrid that attempts to help an industry to contract while promoting its expansion into other areas. As policy was transformed, it again became rational. A reduced scope for policy was needed since market imperfections and externalities decreased with Japan's successful development. Even so, externalities and market failures continued in areas such as the development of new technologies and the mobility of labour and capital between areas and industries. Industrial policy in Japan today does little more than address these issues, and as such does not differ substantially from industrial policy in most other industrialized nations.

Excepting the late 1960s and much of the 1970s, available evidence favours the contention that industrial policy has stimulated economic growth. This impact cannot be quantified, but it has clearly lessened as the scope of policy has shrunk. With policy today concerned mainly with supporting the development of new technologies or facilitating the shrinking and diversification of depressed industries, its impact on the economy is marginal, especially when compared with the role it played in the past in helping to determine investment levels for most manufacturing industries. Yet even in its heyday of the 1950s, industrial policy was not the most important factor behind Japanese growth. The Korean War arguably stimulated economic recovery more than did efforts to promote the rationalization of heavy industries. Rapid growth in world trade also contributed to Japan's remarkable 10 per cent average yearly growth between 1955 and 1972. Imports of new technology may account more for rapid development than any other single factor.[4] Beside supporting more efficient production, the introduction of new technologies generated if not economies of scale in many industries then at least substantial declines in costs over the long term.[5]

Appropriate macroeconomic policy also overshadows the contribution of industrial policy to growth. That this is so is apparent from policy hierarchy: the goals of industrial policy came second to macroeconomic

---

[4] Neoclassical growth accounting breaks down the sources of growth into contributions from factor inputs such as labour, capital, and skilled labour. The unexplained portion of growth is then generally interpreted as arising from technological change. This approach is somewhat unsatisfactory, since the unexplained portion could well be caused by factors other than technology, such as industrial policy. Still, a sizeable amount of this unexplained portion probably does arise from technological change. Evidence of this is provided by the strong correlation between technology imports and the unexplained residual of neoclassical growth accounting. (James E. Vestal, 'Evidence on the Determinants and Factor Content Characteristics of Japanese Technology Trade, 1977–1981', *Review of Economics and Statistics*, 61.4 (1989) (Cambridge, Mass., Harvard University Press), 565–71.

[5] Many Japanese industries such as steel and shipbuilding witnessed a substantial decline in costs as output rose. This could have been caused simply by scale economies, or it could also have been the result of the introduction of ever newer technologies, whose introduction lowered the cost of production. Whatever the case, government intervention in the industry would probably have been necessary to prevent the creation of a monopoly.

policy when conflicts between the two arose. Government loans and subsidies were slashed when the economy over-heated, even though this ran counter to industry interests. Similarly, government funding was increased in downturns. Although this volatility in funding may have been less preferable from an industry point of view, it did contribute to a better performance of the overall economy. In turn, improved economic performance then reinforced the government's ability to utilize industrial policy. In other words, the leeway to implement industrial policy arose from adequate management of the macroeconomy.

Subservience to macroeconomic policy helps partially to explain the disengagement of industrial policy. MITI's inability to control the size of its own budget necessitated abandoning measures in support of some industries when it desired to target others. While this check over MITI's power promoted policy retreat in select industries, fiscal constraints and worries over government debt have contributed to the general disengagement of policy in recent years. With less money to spend, the government has been far less generous with subsidies, tax breaks, and government loans.

This check provided by macroeconomic policy concerns is only one of many that contributed to policy disengagement in recent decades. The growing strength of Japanese companies reduced the power of the government to implement industrial policy; corporate success in overseas markets also increased foreign pressure, limiting the government's ability to protect and promote select industries; and the diversification of national interests that accompanied successful development undermined public support for industrial policy. By accomplishing what it set out to do, industrial policy eliminated the need for its continued use. In short, industrial policy contained if not the seeds of its own destruction at least the motivation for a major disengagement.

Although it was certainly not the only or even the most important factor behind rapid growth, Japan's post-war experience with industrial policy suggests that such policy can help to facilitate the development process of other nations. Most interesting is the explicit trade-off between promoting the growth of select industries and maintaining employment by blocking competition in other areas. This lesson may be of particular importance to the republics of the former Soviet Union and Eastern European countries, nations that can benefit greatly from imported technology but that will face intolerable levels of unemployment should all market forces be freed overnight. The use of competition as a policy tool is also important: Japanese industrial policy probably succeeded in promoting growth industries by fostering competition between them. Policy rewarded winners and punished losers,[6] thus helping to foster a high

[6] For instance, winners were rewarded through tax breaks based on increases in exports, through the granting of technology licences, and through the allocation of imported

degree of competition in the economy. This may be one of the principal benefits of industrial policy in Japan: it has acted to promote competition even amongst large companies which might otherwise have behaved in an oligopolistic fashion, leading to more competition and greater efficiency in Japan than elsewhere.[7] Finally, Japan's success in disengaging policy has lessons for developing countries today, providing a concrete example of the benefits of reducing government intervention as markets improve. Perhaps more importantly, however, policy disengagement highlights the need for checks and balances in policy formulation.[8] Without such checks and balances, it is unlikely that policy-makers would have reduced intervention as quickly as they did.

At the same time, Japan's experiences with industrial policy have few lessons for other industrialized nations. Industrial policy has been disengaged to such an extent that it now differs little in intent from policies implemented in other industrialized nations. The argument that other industrialized nations need a 'Japan-style' industrial policy in order to compete fails to appreciate this fact. Japanese policy no longer resembles that of the 1950s; that Japan today no longer uses a 'Japan-style' industrial policy is a telling argument against advocates elsewhere. The role that Japanese industrial policy still fulfils in disseminating information about future economic directions may be more transferable, as might lessons about the importance of continuity and consistency in policy.[9] The role that policy can play in stimulating competition by spreading technological advances and information across firms may also find application elsewhere. Japan's ability to decrease support for declining industries, possibly arising from its practical rather than ideological approach to government intervention, may also hold lessons for other industrialized nations. However, it is only these specific policy prescriptions which may

machinery and materials. The failure to compete or succeed was met with government guidance over business strategy if not government control through placing a bureaucrat in top management.

[7] Industrial policy ensured competition amongst large firms through widespread dissemination of technological advances, through tax breaks that rewarded sales increases, and through the spread of information. Industry cartels, set up to curtail investment or production, often had the reverse impact since cartels acquainted companies with the strategies of their competitors. Apart from industrial policy, competition was fostered by the very rapid growth of the economy (which made oligopolistic collusion less likely since market share and size was inherently volatile) and the decreasing long-run cost curve facing Japanese companies.

[8] The transferability of industrial policy also depends on the availability of a well-trained bureaucracy, the ability to forge consensus about policy goals (equivalent to the ability to shield policy from special interest groups), and the power to implement policy.

[9] This depends on institutional factors in other nations. Although industrial policy in Japan is not centralized and the continuity and consistency exhibited by policy is rather loose, these characteristics can be transferred to other countries so long as special interest groups do not have sufficient power to implement policy that runs counter to the outline of broad future economic trends.

be of value: Japan's attempts to promote technology or orchestrate the orderly decline of an industry are motivations for government intervention accepted everywhere.

9.2   The Future Role of Industrial Policy in Japan

Although Japanese industrial policy plays a much smaller role in influencing economic activity now than it has in the past, it nevertheless contributes to the development of new technologies, the diversification of declining industries, and the mobility of labour and capital between industries and geographical regions. Industrial policy also addresses pollution, setting emission standards, and subsidizing the development of alternative energy. In addition, it continues to disseminate basic information about future economic trends through government plans. Policy also promotes competition by disseminating new technologies in addition to general information. Finally, it supports competition by keeping the playing field level, acting to guarantee that no single firm dominates others and supporting weak firms in danger of bankruptcy. These functions will continue to be of importance, but it is also interesting to assess the role industrial policy might play in addressing the problems and changes the Japanese economy is likely to face in the future.

The single biggest problem in the Japanese economy today is unbalanced growth. Domestic savings continue to outstrip domestic investment, contributing to the persistent current account surplus. Unfair trading practices alone do not satisfactorily explain this current account surplus: Japanese tariff rates are lower than those in the US and EEC nations, and non-tariff trade barriers have been substantially reduced. Moreover, Japanese trade flows do respond normally to price changes. Following the 50 per cent appreciation of the yen in the second half of the 1980s, manufactured imports into Japan have more than doubled. Despite price changes and few trade barriers, the current account surplus has persisted, which suggests that the Japanese economy shows a fundamental inability to absorb its output through consumption, investment, and government spending. This inability to absorb output has become a chronic problem only in the last decade. Current account surpluses had occurred regularly between 1968 and 1973, but as a percentage of GNP peaked at 2.6 per cent in 1972. Surpluses also disappeared after the first and second oil shocks for two years. However, since 1981, the current account has shown a persistent surplus, rising as high as 4.3 per cent of GNP in 1986, before 'correcting' to 1.4 per cent in 1990.[10] That a

[10] However, the current account surplus has again expanded, rising to 2.5% of GNP in 1991 and 3.3% in 1992.

persistent surplus is a relatively recent phenomenon implies that its cause must also be recent; the dramatic decline in the bargaining power of labour unions and the consequent constraints on wage growth are the probable culprits. After the high wage settlement in 1974 exacerbated inflation and the economic downturn, the Ministry of Finance under Fukuda Takeo called in labour union leaders to point this out and to request moderation in wage increases in 1975. This administrative guidance by the government was perhaps overly successful: not only did unions refrain from demanding wage increases equal to productivity gains, but they also broke the link between inflation and wage negotiations. World assessment that labour unions contributed to stagflation further undermined the power of unions in Japan. After accepting declines in real wages following the second oil shock, labour unions have kept wage increases throughout the 1980s well below productivity gains.

The spending power of Japanese consumers was also eroded from the mid-1970s by a rising tax burden. The government, worried about its rising deficit, abandoned its principle of raising one-third of its revenues equally from personal income taxes, corporate income taxes, and indirect taxes. The progressive nature of personal income taxes placed an increasing burden on the individual as the economy grew, with the result that taxes as a percentage of household income rose from 8.3 per cent in 1970 to 16 per cent by 1985.[11] In an attempt to broaden its tax base and increase its role in raising living standards, the government in 1979 proposed the introduction of a value-added tax, but this proposal was rejected by the public in the election of that year. Interestingly, labour unions were among the most adamantly opposed to this new tax. This was the second time that government efforts to take the lead in raising social welfare and improving living standards failed, the first attempt being the ill-fated increases in government outlays in the early 1970s.

As economic growth rewarded the consumer with less and less frequency from the late 1970s, domestic absorption fell and the current account surplus soared. This skewed growth pattern, the biggest problem facing Japan at present, can be restated as a lack of pluralism. Workers and consumers have placed their own immediate interests second to those of businesses. They have also voted strongly against a role for government in improving social welfare. Of the triad of powers in the 1950s and 1960s, namely business, government, and the general public, business interests have come to dominate. This trend has naturally buoyed corporate earnings and corporate investment, but even the rise in corporate investment to more than 20 per cent of GNP was not enough to drive the current account surplus to zero. In fact, corporations to some extent have

---

[11] Sōmu Chō Tōkei Kyoku, *Kakei Chōsa Nenpō, 1970 and 1985*. Taxes here also include social security contributions.

generated their own vicious circle. As investment increased, so too did exports. Rising exports put pressure on the yen, and the appreciation of the yen acted as a catalyst for further investment since without capital expenditure, competitiveness would have been eroded. Investment then increased exports, leading to further yen appreciation. This growth pattern, the result of placing corporate interests above all others, is not sustainable. Not only is it inherently unstable, but the trade friction it has generated has led to attempts to change it.

The government has already made some efforts to achieve a more balanced growth path. It more aggressively increased government outlays in the second half of the 1980s compared to those in the first half, thus raising domestic absorption.[12] More importantly, the government has attempted to ease the tax burden of the individual, reducing personal taxes by more than revenues were raised with the introduction at long last of a VAT in 1989. However, efforts have not gone far enough and the problem of too much of the rewards from growth accruing to corporate interests remains unsolved. Even if corporations are being squeezed in the 1991–3 downturn, there are few signs that they will not benefit excessively in the next upturn.

It seems unlikely that industrial policy can do much to address this issue. The problem is partly institutional in nature,[13] partly the result of past government guidance, and partly the choice of the Japanese people themselves. The government could attempt to undo the damage that its restraint of labour unions in the 1970s wrought, possibly by educating them as to the problems of excessively low wage demands. However, such education would not really be an example of industrial policy, since it would not influence the allocation of resources to selected industries but would rather raise the cost of labour for all industries. The government can also do little through industrial policy to reduce the current account surplus.[14] Policy has called for tax breaks for increased imports in select industries and has also called upon major companies to raise direct imports. However, these policy measures may be misguided since they undermine the price mechanism. To the extent that imports rise, reduced trade friction would possibly keep pressure off the yen. In other words, these attempts to raise imports can serve to subsidize exports by keeping the yen undervalued.

[12] Despite increasingly spending more than originally planned, greater than expected growth in the economy raised government revenues. As a result, the government actually showed a growing surplus in the latter half of the 1980s.

[13] Because post-war labour unions have generally been organized at the individual company level rather than the industry level, Japanese labour unions have been weaker than their Western counterparts.

[14] This statement implicitly assumes that the Japanese do not have an innate bias against purchasing foreign goods. If the grouping of Japanese firms into *keiretsu* has acted to exclude competitive imports as some assert, then policy can perhaps be used to overcome this.

Industrial policy has little role to play in alleviating Japan's skewed growth path, but government education of labour unions is important. Should this fail, then trade friction will persist, implying future shocks to the Japanese economy either in the form of another major appreciation of its currency and/or sanctions introduced by trading partners. However, within the next two decades, this problem will naturally disappear, as its successor, the ageing population, 'solves' the imbalance between domestic savings and investment. Japan has one of the most rapidly ageing populations in the world: by 2010, 18.8 per cent of Japan's population will be over the age of 64 compared to 11.5 per cent for the US and 15.6 per cent for the UK.[15] This sharp rise in the proportion of the elderly in Japan, up from about 12 per cent at present, will constrain domestic savings, since it is the middle-aged households that tend to save the most. However, as demographic trends help to ease the excess of domestic savings over investment, Japan will be faced with the problem of caring for its elderly and at the same time overcoming a possible shortage of labour.

Once again, it seems probable that industrial policy will have little role to play in helping the economy to adjust to these demographic shifts. In a sense, policy has already fulfilled this function. It has made these trends well known, and diffusion of this information should give all industries an equal chance to adjust. As such, there is no need to subsidize labour-saving investment, since industries will not be shocked by the labour shortage in the future. Industrial policy will undoubtedly be used to help those industries which have failed to adjust, promoting diversification and mergers, the scrapping of capacity, and even the retraining of workers, but industrial policy will not need to change from its current form to address this issue.

Nor will major changes in industrial policy be required to deal with the problem of pollution. Policy will undoubtedly continue to subsidize the development of new anti-pollution technologies and non-polluting energy sources. It will also continue to set emission standards. Japanese policy towards pollution should become increasingly market-orientated, placing the burden on polluting industries but perhaps allowing, as the US has proposed, companies to trade pollution quotas amongst themselves. Anti-pollution policy in Japan will also have to address pollution in neighbouring countries such as China, the major cause behind acid rain in Japan. Probable measures will be government aid for investment in anti-pollution equipment in these countries, perhaps not a first-best policy solution but probably the only feasible one.[16]

---

[15] Keizai Kikaku Chō Sōgō Keikaku Kyoku, *Nisennen no Nihon: Kakuron*, 2 (Tokyo, Ōkurashō Insatsu Kyoku, 1982), 87.

[16] If Japan merely subsidizes anti-pollution investment, then polluters in foreign countries have no incentive to reduce production and investment. A first-best solution might be

The use of industrial policy in identifying potential growth industries will certainly not increase in the future. Japan no longer has any model to follow; it is one of the most advanced economies in the world. There are no longer any historical lessons as to which industries might experience substantial learning by doing effects over time, nor are there many industries, if any at all, where Japan is at a disadvantage simply because foreign competitors have been producing longer. Japan has already recognized that markets are as effective as the government in identifying potential new winners, and it is for this reason that measures to support new industries have been largely abandoned. Instead, the government promotes the development of new technologies, a pattern that will persist in the future. Market externalities and failures associated with developing technologies are unlikely to change with time, so that government support will remain necessary to achieve optimal investment levels.[17]

The Japanese government has not totally abandoned support for new industries in Japan, although such support emphasizes technology development. In some instances, these measures might be mistaken. For example, the government in 1991 proposed setting up a joint effort between the government and private sector companies to develop satellite technology. The project, begun in 1992, is scheduled to receive total funds of 12 billion yen, with one-third of this provided by the government and two-thirds by private companies.[18] Although concerned with technology development, this project is designed to produce independently in Japan technology that already exists in the US and Europe. Its goal is essentially reverse engineering, not the creation of an entirely new technology. This somewhat undermines the arguments presented previously regarding the need for government support in technology development, since the outcome of R&D efforts in cases of reverse engineering is known, risk is small, and appropriability may not be that large an issue. With the usual market externalities and failures less clear, funding for projects to copy old technologies must be primarily justified on infant industry grounds.

In the case of satellites, Japan might be able to claim that US and European makers have benefited from government support provided through defence and aerospace expenditure. Without this support, Japan might assert, its producers have been unable to enter the industry, necessitating government support now. However, this argument is extremely weak. Costs in the satellite industry are very high; world demand may not adequately support another major producer. More importantly,

one that couples aid with other funds to promote investment in non-polluting industries. Still, direct aid for anti-pollution equipment is at least a second-best solution.

[17] The magnitude of investment required to develop new products and technologies, such as those associated with new aircraft, may increase the number of multinational R&D projects. However, this will not eliminate the need for government support for such projects.

[18] *Nihon Keizai Shinbun*, 4 Sept. 1991.

Japanese electronics firms are among the most advanced in the world, and support received from defence expenditure by US satellite makers has probably not been that large. In short, should Japanese firms wish to enter the satellite market, they should be more than capable of doing it on their own. That they chose not to do so is probably a good indication that the venture will not prove profitable. Government support for satellite production in Japan, although it primarily promotes technology development, should probably be viewed as an example of a policy to promote a new industry: as such, it is probably a policy mistake.

Instances of government support for new industries will probably decrease even more in the future, as Japan eliminates potential sources of trade friction and opens its economy even further. The promotion of new technologies will, however, continue. Industrial policy will also continue to support declining industries, subsidizing the scrapping of capacity and promoting diversification, worker retraining, and mergers. Policy towards declining industry has not been a total success: industries probably still expect government support in downturns, leading them to over-invest in expansion periods. Although recent policy measures have helped to correct this problem, in order to totally eliminate it, the government must make clear that aid is temporary and will not be repeated in instances where the industry acts counter to government advice. To establish credibility, the government must make an example of some notable policy failures. For instance, the government might punish the ethylene industry by refusing to help reduce its capacity in downturns, since increased capacity was counter to government guidance.

The function of industrial policy in Japan's future will continue to be correcting market externalities and failures. Since these have decreased, so too has the role of industrial policy, a trend which is unlikely to be reversed. Industrial policy has also served another vital function in Japan's development process, effectively planning for change. Using as a blueprint the development experience of others, Japan was able to identify infant industries, direct resources to these, and at the same time maintain social stability through anti-growth policy. The ability of industrial policy to plan for change has greatly eroded, since no other nation provides Japan with an example of how its development should proceed from here. Even so, by collating opinions in government, business, and academia, industrial policy can help to identify broad trends which will affect economic growth and at the very least disseminate information about these trends, for instance demographic shifts or technological changes. Such efforts help reduce uncertainty about the future and lend consistency and continuity to government policy and private sector investment. Finally, policy has also helped foster competition amongst even large companies, by rewarding winners and punishing losers but at the same time ensuring that no single firm dominated an industry. Industrial policy will probably continue to generate not only competition but continuity and consistency as well, all characteristics which have benefited Japan in the past and will undoubtedly contribute at least modestly to Japan's economic performance in the future.

9.3 Some Qualifications

This study has attempted to lay the groundwork for an informed judgement about the efficacy of industrial policy in Japan. Conclusions are probable rather than definite; it is not feasible to quantify the impact that policy has had upon growth. Moreover, the criteria used to assess policy, namely rationality and impact on resource allocation, are not totally objective. This is especially true in evaluating policy rationality: it is relatively easy to identify instances where this is lacking, but it is impossible to prove that hypothetically rational policy measures were in fact so. Despite this, the emphasis on rationality does highlight important characteristics that policy measures must possess in order to be successful, particularly valuable in drawing lessons for policy-makers elsewhere.

By placing industrial policy primarily in an economic dimension, this study hopefully captures important factors behind its successes and failures. At the same time, this approach does not provide a framework which shows how policy was actually formulated and implemented. That is, the causality between actual policy decisions and the framework used in this analysis is quite weak. Japanese policy-makers were not super-rational economic agents, inclined to formulate policy solely on economic grounds. Policy formulation in practice arose from the complex interaction of institutional factors, political factors, culture, and history. This dynamic accounts for many of the successes of industrial policy, and other nations who wish to imitate Japan may find their ability to do so severely limited by their own cultures and experiences.

While numerous detailed studies of the Japanese institutional, historical, and political dynamic exist, the multi-layered system of checks and balances on industrial policy which arose from it were crucial to the rationality of policy response. Power over policy was vested across ministries, and representatives of business, academia, and the general public often sat on policy committees. The interaction between bureaucrats and businessmen was greatly deepened through industrial organizations, groups formed largely after the war. These organizations benefited both: they provided the government with access to the expertise of businessmen as well as detailed information about industry output and trends; they gave businesses information about policy and sometimes helped to lobby gave businesses information about policy and sometimes helped to lobby on their behalf. Plurality in policy response was further enhanced by the role played by public financial institutions, such as the Japan Development Bank, and the practice of *amakudari* created additional channels between the public and private sector. These institutional, historical, and cultural checks and balances were reinforced by those economic in nature. Not only were the interests of industrial policy subservient to those of macroeconomic policy, but wherever possible, policy utilized competition to meet its goals.

The Japanese system of checks and balances contributed to consistency, continuity, and flexibility, characteristics of a rational industrial policy. To a great extent, however, the particular dynamic of policy-making in Japan is not replicable elsewhere. For others to implement industrial policy successfully requires introducing different systems of checks and balances, ones consistent with their own histories and cultures. The difficulties of doing so cannot be understated: even Japan's elaborate checks and balances occasionally failed to prevent inappropriate policy response. For example, special interest groups sometimes derailed rational policy response, even though the domination of a single party, the LDP, over post-war Japanese politics enhanced the power of the bureaucrats in policy formulation. This issue of creating appropriate systems of checks and balances elsewhere lies beyond the scope of this book, but it is one that must be addressed by anyone attempting to utilize an industrial policy. Mere recognition of the validity of economic criteria in implementing policy does not suffice; it must be matched with guarantees that such criteria are actually followed.

BIBLIOGRAPHY

Amaya, Naohiro, 'Sangyō Seisaku no Hanshō to Tenkai no Tame ni', *Tsūsan Jaanaru*, 2.5 (1969) (Tokyo, Tsūshō Sangyō Shō).

Arisawa, Hiromi (ed.), *Shōwa Keizai Shi: Fukkō kara Sekiyu Shokku made*, 2 (Tokyo, Nihon Keizai Shinbun Sha, 1980).

Bain, Joseph, *Industrial Organization* (New York, John Wiley & Sons, 1963).

Baldwin, Robert E., 'Are Economists' Traditional Trade Policy Views Still Valid?', *Journal of Economic Literature*, 30 (June 1992) (Nashville, Tenn., American Economic Association).

Branson, William, Giersch, Herbert, and Peterson, Peter, 'Trends in the United States International Trade and Investment', in Martin Feldstein (ed.), *The American Economy in Transition* (Chicago, National Bureau of Economic Research, 1990).

Calder, Kent E., *Crisis and Compensation: Public Policy and Political Stability in Japan* (Princeton, NJ, Princeton University Press, 1988).

Chūshō Kigyō Chō, *Chūshō Kigyō Hakusho* (Tokyo, Ōkurashō Insatsu Kyoku, 1963).

Chūshō Kigyō Kinyū Kōko, *Chūshō Kigyō Kinyū Kōko Sanjūnen Shi* (Tokyo, Chūshō Kigyō Kinyū Kōko, 1984).

Corbett, Jenny, 'International Perspectives on Financing: Evidence from Japan', *Oxford Review of Economic Policy*, 3.4 (1990) (Oxford, Oxford University Press).

Corden, W.M., *Trade Policy and Economic Welfare* (Oxford, Clarendon Press, 1974).

Eads, George, and Kozo, Yamamura, 'The Future of Industrial Policy', in Kozo Yamamura and Yasuba Yasukichi (eds.), *The Political Economy of Japan*, 1, (Stanford, Calif., Stanford University Press, 1987).

Esposito, F., and Esposito, L., 'Excess Capacity and Market Structure', *Review of Economics and Statistics*, 56 (May 1974) (Cambridge, Mass., Harvard University Press).

Hadley, Eleanor M., *Antitrust in Japan* (Princeton, NJ, Princeton University Press, 1970).

Harris, John R., and Todaro, Michael P., 'Migration, Unemployment, and Development: A Two-Sector Analysis', *American Economic Review*, 60 (Mar. 1970) (Menasha, Wis., American Economic Association).

Hayami, Yūjirō and Yamada, Saburō, *The Agricultural Development of Japan* (Tokyo, University of Tokyo Press, 1991).

Hein, Laura, *Fueling Growth: The Energy Revolution and Economic Policy in Postwar Japan* (Cambridge, Mass., Harvard University Press, 1990).

Helpman, Elhanan, and Krugman, Paul R., *Trade Policy and Market Structure* (Cambridge, Mass., MIT Press, 1989).

Itō, Takatoshi, *The Japanese Economy* (Cambridge, Mass., MIT Press, 1992).

Johnson, Chalmers, *MITI and the Japanese Miracle: The Growth of Industrial Policy 1925–1975* (Stanford, Calif., Stanford University Press, 1982).

Kagaku Gijutsu Chō, *Kagaku Gijutsu Hakusho* (Tokyo, Ōkurashō Insatsu Kyoku, 1964).

Keizai Kikaku Chō, *Keizai Hakusho* (Tokyo, Ōkurashō Insatsu Kyoku, 1956).

—— *Keizai Hakusho* (Tokyo, Ōkurashō Insatsu Kyoku, 1960).

—— *Kokumin Keizai Kessan Hōkoku: Shōwa 30 Nen–Shōwa 44 Nen* (Tokyo, Ōkurashō Insatsu Kyoku, 1988).

—— *Kokumin Keizai Kessan Nenpō* (Tokyo, Ōkurashō Insatsu Kyoku, various years).

—— Se*kai to Tomo ni Ikiru Nihon (Economic Management in a Global Context)* (Tokyo, Keizai Kikaku Chō, 1988).

Keizai Kikaku Chō Chōsei Kyoku, 'Bōeki Kawase Jiyūka Keikaku Taikō', *Bōeki Kawase Jiyūka Keikaku* (Tokyo, Keizai Kikaku Chō Chōsei Kyoku, 1960).

Keizai Kikaku Chō Keizai Kenkyūsho Kokumin Shotoku Bu, *Minkan Kigyō Shihon Sutokku* (Tokyo, Ōkurashō Insatsu Kyoku, various years).

Keizai Kikaku Chō Keizai Shingi Kai, *Kokumin Shotoku Baizō Keikaku* (Tokyo, Ōkurashō Insatsu Kyoku, 1960).

Keizai Kikaku Chō Sōgō Keikaku Kyoku, *Nisennen no Nihon: Kakuron*, 2 (Tokyo, Ōkurashō Insatsu Kyoku, 1982).

Kōgyō Gijutsu In Kenkyū Kaihatsu Kanshitsu, *Ōgata Purojekuto 20 Nen no Ayumi: Waga Kuni Sangyō Gijutsu no Shi o Kizuku* (Tokyo, Tsūshō Sangyō Chōsa Kai, 1987).

Komiya, Ryūtarō, *The Japanese Economy: Trade, Industry, and Government* (Tokyo, University of Tokyo Press, 1990).

Kōsai Yutaka, *Kōdo Seichō no Jidai* (Tokyo, Nihon Hyōron Sha, 1981).

—— 'Fukkōki', in Komiya Ryūtarō, Okuno Masahiro, Suzumura Kōtarō (eds.), *Nihon no Sangyō Seisaku* (Tokyo, University of Tokyo Press, 1984).

Kōsei Torihiki Iinkai, *Kōsei Torihiki Iinkai Nenji Hōkoku* (Tokyo, Ōkurashō Insatsu Kyoku, 1971).

—— *Kōsei Torihiki Iinkai Nenji Hōkoku* (Tokyo, Ōkurashō Insatsu Kyoku, various years).

Kuroda, Masahiro, *Economic Growth and Structural Change in Japan*, 1 (Tokyo, Keio University, 1991).

—— 'Price and Goods Control in the Japanese Postwar Inflationary Period', in Teranishi Jurō and Kōsai Yutaka (eds.), *The Japanese Experience in Economic Reforms* (New York, Macmillan, forthcoming).

Nakamura, Takafusa, *The Postwar Japanese Economy: Its Development and Structure* (Tokyo, University of Tokyo Press, 1981).

Nawa, Shūichi, *Sangyō Gōrika ka Shitsugyō Gōrika* (Tokyo, Shunyōdō, 1930).

Nihon Ginkō Chōsa Tōkei Kyoku, *Honpō Keizai Nenpō* (Tokyo, Nihon Ginkō, various years).

—— *Keizai Tōkei Nenpō* (Tokyo, Nihon Ginkō, various years).

—— *Kokusai Hikaku Tōkei* (Tokyo, Nihon Ginkō, various years).

Nihon Ginkō Hyakunen Shi Hensan Iinkai, *Nihon Ginkō Hyakunen Shi*, 5 (Tokyo, Nihon Ginkō, 1986).

Nihon Kaihatsu Ginkō Jūnen Shi Hensan Iinkai, *Nihon Kaihatsu Ginkō Jūnen Shi*

(Tokyo, Nihon Kaihatsu Ginkō, 1963).

Nihon Kaihatsu Ginkō, *Nihon Kaihatsu Ginkō Nijūgonen Shi* (Tokyo, Nihon Kaihatsu Ginkō, 1976).

Nihon Kaihatsu Ginkō Chōsa Bu, *Tōkei Yōran* (Tokyo, Nihon Kaihatsu Ginkō Chōsa Bu, various years).

Nihon Seisansei Honbu Katsuyō Rōdō Tōkei Iinkai, *Katsuyō Rōdō Tōkei* (Tokyo, Nihon Seisansei Honbu, 1990).

Nihon Tekkō Renmei Tekkō Tōkei Iinkai, *Tekkō Tōkei Yōran* (Tokyo, Nihon Tekkō Renmei, 1991).

Nihon Tekkō Renmei, *Tekkō Jūnen Shi, Shōwa 33 Nen–Shōwa 42 Nen* (Tokyo, Nihon Tekkō Renmei, 1969).

OECD, *Positive Adjustment Policy: Managing Structural Changes* (Paris, Organisation for Economic Co-operation and Development, 1983).

Okimoto, Daniel, *Between MITI and the Market: Japanese Industrial Policy for High Technology* (Stanford, Calif., Stanford University Press, 1990).

—— and Saxonhouse, Gary, 'Technology and the Future of the Economy', in Kozo Yamamura and Yasuba Yasukichi (eds.), *The Political Economy of Japan*, 1 (Stanford, Calif., Stanford University Press, 1987).

Ōkurashō, *Zaisei Kinyū Tōkei Geppō*, 457 (May 1990) (Tokyo, Ōkurashō Insatsu Kyoku).

Ōkurashō Zaisei Shi Shitsu, *Shōwa Zaisei Shi: Shūsen kara Kōwa made*, 5 (Tokyo, Tōyō Keizai Shinpō Sha, 1982).

—— *Shōwa Zaisei Shi: Shūsen kara Kōwa made*, 10 (Tokyo, Tōyō Keizai Shinpō Sha, 1978).

—— *Shōwa Zaisei Shi: Shūsen kara Kōwa made*, 19 (Tokyo, Tōyō Keizai Shinpō Sha, 1978).

—— *Shōwa Zaisei Shi: Shūsen kara Kōwa made*, 20 (Tokyo, Tōyō Keizai Shinpō Sha, 1982).

Ozaki, Iwao, 'The Effects of Technological Change on the Economic Growth of Japan, 1955–1970', in Karen Polenske and Jiri Skolka (eds.), *Advances in Input-Output Analysis* (Cambridge, Mass., Ballinger Publishing Company, 1976).

Ozawa, Terutomo, *Japan's Technological Challenge to the West, 1950-1974: Motivation and Accomplishment* (Cambridge, Mass., MIT Press, 1974).

Patrick, Hugh, and Hideo, Satō, 'The Political Economy of United States–Japan Trade in Steel', in Kozo Yamamura (ed.), *Policy and Trade Issues of the Japanese Economy* (Seattle, University of Washington Press, 1982).

Pechman, Joseph, and Kaizuka, Keimei, 'Taxation', in Hugh Patrick and Henry Rosovsky (eds.), *Asia's New Giant: How the Japanese Economy Works* (Washington, DC, The Brookings Institute, 1976).

Peck, Merton, and Shūji, Tamura, 'Technology', in Hugh Patrick and Henry Rosovsky (eds.), *Asia's New Giant: How the Japanese Economy Works* (Washington, DC, The Brookings Institute, 1976).

Roppō Zensho, 2 (Tokyo, Yūhikaku, 1990).

Sangyō Kōzō Shingikai, '70 Nendai no Tsūshō Sangyō Seisaku', *Tsūsan Jaanaru*, 4.3 (1971) (Tokyo, Tsūshō Sangyō Shō).

Saxonhouse, Gary, 'Industrial Policy and Factor Markets: Biotechnology in Japan and the United States', in Hugh Patrick and Larry Meissner (eds.),

Japan's High Technology Industries (Seattle, University of Washington Press, 1986).

Scitovsky, Tibor, *Welfare and Competition* (Chicago, Richard D. Irwin, 1951 and 1971).

Seifu Kankei Tokubetsu Hōjin Rōdō Kumiai Kyōgikai, *Seirōkyō Amakudari Hakusho* (Tokyo, Seifu Kankei Tokubetsu Hōjin Rōdō Kumiai Kyōgikai, 1986).

Sekiguchi, Sueo and Horiuchi, Toshihiro, 'Bōeki to Chōsei Enjo', in Komiya Ryūtarō, Okuno Masahiro, Suzumura Kōtarō (eds.), *Nihon no Sangyō Seisaku* (Tokyo, University of Tokyo Press, 1984).

Shinjō, Kōji, 'Konpyūtā Sangyō', in Komiya Ryūtarō, Okuno Masahiro, Suzumura Kōtarō (eds.), *Nihon no Sangyō Seisaku* (Tokyo, University of Tokyo Press, 1984).

Shinkai, Yoichi, 'Oil Crises and Stagflation in Japan', in Kozo Yamamura (ed.), *Policy and Trade Issues of the Japanese Economy* (Seattle, University of Washington Press, 1982).

Sōmu Chō Tōkei Kyoku, *Kakei Chōsa Nenpō* (Tokyo, Nihon Tōkei Kyōkai, various years).

—— *Nihon Chōki Tōkei Sōran*, 2 (Tokyo, Nihon Tōkei Kyōkai, 1988).

—— *Nihon Chōki Tōkei Sōran*, 3 (Tokyo, Nihon Tōkei Kyōkai, 1988).

—— *Nihon Chōki Tōkei Sōran*, 4 (Tokyo, Nihon Tōkei Kyōkai, 1988).

Stowsky, Jay S., 'Weak Links, Strong Bonds: US–Japanese Competition in Semiconductor Production Equipment', in Chalmers Johnson, Laura D'Andrea Tyson, and John Zysman (eds.), *Politics and Productivity: How Japan's Development Strategy Works* (New York, HarperBusiness, 1989).

Suzuki, Yoshio, *The Japanese Financial System* (Oxford, Oxford University Press, 1987).

Tsujimura, Kōtarō, Kuroda, Masahiro, and Shimada, Haruo, *Economic Policy and General Interdependence* (Tokyo, Kogakusha, 1981).

Tsuruta, Toshimasa, *Sengo Nihon no Sangyō Seisaku* (Tokyo, Nihon Keizai Shinbun Sha, 1982).

Tsūsanshō Kigyō Kyoku, *Kigyō Gōrika no Shomondai* (Tokyo, Daini Dōkō Sha, 1952).

—— *Sangyō Gōrika Hakusho* (Tokyo, Nikkan Kōgyō Shinbun Sha, 1957).

Tsūshō Sangyō Daijin Kanbō Chōsa Bu, *Kōgyō Tōkei Hyō: Sangyō Hen* (Tokyo, Ōkurashō Insatsu Kyoku, 1973 and 1975).

Tsūshō Sangyō Shō Kigyō Kyoku, *Gaishi Dōnyū: Sono Seido to Jittai* (Tokyo, Tsūshō Sangyō Chōsa Kai, 1960).

Tsūshō Sangyō Shō Kigyō Gijutsuin, *Gijutsu Kakushin to Nihon no Kogyō* (Tokyo, Nikkan Kōgyō Shinbun Sha, 1964).

Tsūshō Sangyō Shō Kigyō Seisaku Kyoku, *Kōzō Tenkan Enkatsu Hō no Kaisetsu* (Tokyo, Tsūshō Sangyō Chōsa Kai, 1988).

Tsūshō Sangyō Shō Tsūshō Sangyō Seisaku Kyoku, *Kōzō Fukyō Hō no Kaisetsu: Tokutei Fukyō Sangyō Antei Rinji Soch Hō* (Tokyo, Tsūshō Sangyō Chōsa Kai, 1978).

—— *Sankō Hō no Kaisetsu: Arata na Sangyō Chōsei e Mukete* (Tokyo, Tsūshō Sangyō Chōsa Kai, 1983).

Tsūshō Sangyō Shō Tsūshō Sangyō Seisaku Shi Hensan Iinkai, *Tsūshō Sangyō Shi*, 2 (Tokyo, Tsūshō Sangyō Chōsa Kai, 1991).
—— *Tsūshō Sangyō Seisaku Shi*, 5 (Tokyo, Tsūshō Sangyō Chōsa Kai, 1991).
—— *Tsūshō Sangyō Seisaku Shi*, 6 (Tokyo, Tsūshō Sangyō Chōsa Kai, 1990).
—— *Tsūshō Sangyō Seisaku Shi*, 16 (Tokyo, Tsūshō Sangyō Chōsa Kai, 1992).
Uchino, Tatsurō, *Japan's Postwar Economy: An Insider's View of its History and its Future* (Tokyo, Kodansha International, 1983).
Vestal, James E., 'Evidence on the Determinants and Factor Content Characteristics of Japanese Technology Trade, 1977–1981', *Review of Economics and Statistics*, 61 (Nov. 1989) (Cambridge, Mass., Harvard University Press).
Yamamura, Kozo, 'Success that Soured: Administrative Guidance and Cartels in Japan', in Yamamura (ed.), *Policy and Trade Issues in the Japanese Economy* (Seattle, University of Seattle Press, 1982).
Yamawaki, Hideki, 'Market Structure, Capacity Expansion and Pricing: A Model Applied to the Japanese Steel Industry', *International Journal of Industrial Organization*, 2 (Amsterdam, North Holland Publishing Co., 1984).
—— 'Tekkō Sangyō', in Komiya Ryūtarō, Okuno Masahiro, Suzumura Kōtarō (eds.), *Nihon no Sangyō Seisaku* (Tokyo, University of Tokyo Press, 1984).
Yamazawa, Ippei, 'Seni Sangyō', in Komiya Ryūtarō, Okuno Masahiro, Suzumura Kōtarō (eds.), *Nihon no Sangyō Seisaku* (Tokyo, University of Tokyo Press, 1984).
Yonekura, Seiichirō, 'The Postwar Japanese Iron & Steel Industry: Continuity and Discontinuity', in Abe Tetsuo and Suzuki Yoshitake (eds.), *Changing Patterns of International Rivalry* (Tokyo, University of Tokyo Press, 1991).
Yoshioka, Kanji, *Nihon no Seizōgyō/Kinyūgyō no Seisansei Bunseki: Kibo no Keizaisei/Gijutsu Henka No Jisshō Kenkyū* (Tokyo, Tōyō Keizai Shinpō Sha, 1989).
Yoshitomi, Masaru, *Nihon Keizai: Sekai Keizai no Arata na Kiki to Nihon* (Tokyo, Tōyō Keizai Shinpō Sha, 1981).
Zysman, John, *Governments, Markets, and Growth* (Ithaca, NY, Cornell University Press, 1983).

INDEX

paper industry 195–7, 221
People's Finance Corporation 195
petrochemical industry 37, 93, 98, 187
petroleum refiners 177
Plan for the Restructuring of the Japanese Archipelago (1972) 59
plans 21–2, 36–8, 44–5, 50, 59, 86, 126, 212, 219, 221, 225
plurality of policy 7, 157, 161–2, 164–5, 232
pollution 54–6, 98, 111–12, 115, 126, 175, 189, 192, 225, 228–9
anti-equipment 47, 52, 93, 98, 191–3, 206
power of government 3, 16, 47, 61, 77, 109–11, 114, 129, 141, 156, 164, 176, 223, 232
price:
controls 18, 20, 22, 27, 169, 182, 195–6, 204, 207, 215
fixing 75, 96, 176–7
mechanism 77–9
monitoring system 129
Prince/Nissan Motors merger 52
priority production systems (keisha seisan hoshiki) 17–18, 20, 25, 34, 116–17
privatization 23, 182
protectionism 7, 9, 42, 46, 49, 53–4, 62–3, 71–2, 75, 77–8, 93, 96, 99, 105, 138, 145, 147, 153, 160, 163, 165, 167, 189, 205, 208, 210–11, 223

rationality of policy 66, 68, 81–98, 143, 145, 152–3, 157, 165, 220–2, 231–2
in 70s 190–1, 194–6, 199–201, 203
in 80s 204–14, 216
rationalization (gorika) 24–5, 30–1, 34, 36–8, 42–3, 48, 53, 99, 101, 107–8, 114, 118–25
Reconstruction Finance Bank 18, 21, 25
Reconstruction Finance Corporation 17–18, 20–3, 26, 75, 117, 148
reparations policy 14–15
research and development 57, 135, 138, 143, 188, 201–4, 208, 213–14, 229
resources, allocation of 1–2, 5–8, 10–11, 41–2, 62, 66–9, 75–7, 79, 81, 88, 90, 98–102, 107, 116, 138, 145, 151–3, 158, 160, 166, 188, 190, 195, 199–200, 203–4, 212, 216, 218–20, 227, 230–1
restructuring of industry 30, 48, 187
retailing industry 185, 189
retraining 97, 199, 208, 217, 228, 230

San Francisco Peace Treaty (1951) 26
Sanyō Special Steel 50
satellite industry 229–30
Satō Eisaku 59
savings 24, 27, 102–8, 114, 145, 147, 149, 167, 186, 215, 221

domestic 225, 228
scale, economies of 53, 64–5, 71, 88, 95, 141, 203, 214, 222
Science and Technology Agency 201
'Seven-Year Plan for a New Economic Society' 212
shipbuilding industry 14, 35, 37, 43, 47, 49, 52, 82–3, 85, 87–90, 95, 121, 140, 150–1, 153, 158, 162, 187, 199, 206
Shoup, Carl 25
Showa Denko 27
size of firm 30–1, 38, 46, 48, 51–4, 77, 88, 98, 132
Smaller Business Finance Corporation 35, 48, 53, 82, 194
Smithsonian Agreement (1971) 58, 60
social capital 59, 191–3, 205–6, 216
social welfare 44, 54, 56–7, 59, 111, 146–7, 179, 226
South Korea 161
Soviet Union, former republics of 5, 11, 146, 167, 223
Spring Labour Offensive (1974) 171
Spring Labour Offensive (1980) 175
steel industry 14, 17–18, 20, 25, 34–5, 37, 40, 47, 52, 58, 65, 79, 82–3, 85–9, 94–5, 98–9, 109, 112, 145, 149, 151–3, 156, 158, 187, 193, 196, 200, 210, 216, 221
evaluation of industrial policy 136–44
First Rationalization Plan 118–20, 122, 125
Second Rationalization Plan 121–5
Third Rationalization Plan 125–8
priority production system (1945–9) 116–17
rationalization and modernization (1950–60) 118–25
trade liberalization, mergers, and excess capacity (1961–73) 125–33
policy towards a declining industry (1971–90) 133–6
Steel Subcommittee of the Industrial Structure Council 128
stock market 24, 48
subsidies 62–4, 66–7, 69–70, 73–4, 84–5
to agriculture 53, 78, 96
cuts in 22, 24
exports 16, 72, 150–1, 153
government 18–21, 25, 77, 89–91, 100–1, 103, 107, 146, 149–50, 155, 159–60, 178–9, 187–8, 192–3, 195, 199, 201, 203, 208, 212, 221–3, 225, 230
to steel industry 117–19, 136, 138, 140–1, 143, 216
subsidized loans 46, 82, 99, 147
Sun Wave 50